Imaginal
Memory
and the
Place of
Hiroshima

Imaginal Memory and the Place of Hiroshima

MICHAEL
PERLMAN

STATE UNIVERSITY OF NEW YORK PRESS

Published by
State University of New York Press, Albany
© 1988 State University of New York
All rights reserved
Printed in the United States of America
No part of this book may be used or reproduced
in any manner whatsoever without written permission
except in the case of brief quotations embodied in
critical articles and reviews.
For information, address State University of New York
Press, State University Plaza, Albany, N.Y., 12246
Library of Congress Cataloging-in-Publication Data

Perlman, Michael, 1957–
   Imaginal memory and the place of Hiroshima / Michael Perlman.
      p.   cm.
   Bibliography: p.
   ISBN 0-88706-746-8.   ISBN 0-88706-747-6 (pbk.)
   1. Memory. 2. Imagery (Psychology) 3. Hiroshima-shi (Japan)—
Bombardment, 1945. 4. Nuclear warfare—Psychological aspects.
   5. Peace—Psychological aspects. 6. Archetype (Psychology)
   I. Title.
   BF371.P383   1988
   153.1'2--dc19   87-22322
                                                              CIP

10 9 8 7 6 5 4 3 2 1

Contents

PART IV
APPENDIXES

Preface

"Hiroshima," the placename, evokes—together with images of the first atomic bombing—the largest dilemmas of the nuclear age and humankind's capacity for massive violence. It also evokes the theme of memory. Images arising from the place of Hiroshima speak to us: Remember Hiroshima. Hiroshima never again. We "hear" this rhetoric of memory whenever Hiroshima comes to mind. Yet, as Robert Jay Lifton observes, "The great majority of people no longer experience—increasingly few remember—the original impact of the totality of nuclear killing" (*BC*, pp. 386–7). This first place of nuclear violence, together with its "original impact," claims a crucial yet neglected place in the psychic terrain of our individual and collective memories. How can this claim be acknowledged and given its proper place?

In her book, *The Art of Memory*, Frances Yates describes a method of imagining used by classical rhetoricians and their predecessors, the tellers of myth and story, to remember essential information as they spoke. The art of memory involves the formation of remembered places in the imagination, such as the distinct features and rooms of a house. In these places mnemonic images are deposited that remind one of associated information through their "striking and unusual, . . . beautiful or hideous, comic or obscene" character (*AM*, p. 10). In this tradition of memory, as in its mythic parentage, the power of precisely defined and strange images to move, to "strike" the soul, is displayed. There are affinities, as James Hillman has observed, between this art of memory and contemporary archetypal psychology,[1] which likewise seeks to cultivate a precise awareness of "places" and images of the psyche, and emphasizes the moving power of unusual, disturbing or "unnatural" shapes of imagination.

This book begins with two premises. The first is that while present movements toward disarmament are encouraging, much more is needed. These movements must deepen into a sustained cultural commitment to peace if the

vii

world is to finally avoid being blasted into "striking and unusual" shapes of death, and if we are to witness instead the "death" of mass violence itself. The second premise is that images associated with the place of Hiroshima embody unsuspected psychological values beyond their role as reminders of the concrete horror of nuclear war. The remembering of these values is crucial to a deeper-going commitment to peace and to contemporary psychological life in general.

The traditional art of memory and imagination, archetypal psychology's attention to psychic images, and the call to remember and honor the claim that the place of Hiroshima has upon us all, are interwoven in the present work. We shall work out a psychological mode or practice of remembering nuclear images, "housing" them in memory, so that their psychic depths are revealed and engaged. This moves us toward a deeper apprehension of memory and the soul that simultaneously deepens our commitment to a worldwide movement toward peace. The place of Hiroshima will be given place in individual and collective or cultural imaginings, and the images of nuclear memory will be heard speaking to the world's present and future as they evoke a past that—like the art of memory itself—is at once history, and an echoing of the telling of myth.

This work requires a close psychological engagement, at once critical and evocative, with traditional images of memory as well as remembered images associated with Hiroshima and the nuclear world. It is not enough to say that we must remember; we need to explore cultural images and metaphors that guide the work of memory and illuminate its largely-forgotten possibilities, and its possible weaknesses, blind spots and deceptions as well. Then, in developing the practice of remembering nuclear images, we can pay closer attention to the precise ways in which these reveal psychic qualities of the nuclear world, embodying "memories" of the collective psyche that transcend the history of the nuclear age as they make this reality immediately present.

Let us outline the course of our engagement. Part I (chapters 1 and 2) is an anticipatory exploration of certain aspects of memory particularly relevant in the context of the nuclear age, and key psychological themes revealed by the historical unfolding of the nuclear dilemma. Chapter 1 considers some pitfalls of memory that appear particularly in certain forms of nationalistic consciousness, and also deeper possibilities of memory that open into transnational and transhistorical, essentially religious, concerns of the soul. Chapter 2 looks at cultural images that have fueled the development of nuclear and other literalized "defense" systems. It will become apparent that these constitute a defense against a full acknowledgement of the place of death in the life of the soul, which place is remembered by images associated with the place of Hiroshima.

Part II is an exploration of primary images, or imaginal phenomena, found in the "house" of memory. Chapter 3 focuses on certain source-images of memory, with particular reference to Greek myth and thought. This provides a basis for the exploration of the art of memory, together with its pertinent psychological features, in chapter 4. The traditions of ancient Greece and the art of memory in its various transformations engage the vitality of soul in the latter's movement toward death.

Part III, "Remembering the Place of Hiroshima," explores and engages with basic images of the nuclear age. Chapter 5 first focuses on major motifs and themes associated with remembered images of Hiroshima and Nagasaki, and the general place of these in contemporary context. Then the more specific practice of remembering these images is laid out. While chapter 5 aims at circumscribing the frame of this practice, and its place vis-a-vis, the place of Hiroshima, chapter 6 opens more broadly toward a variety of images associated with the nuclear dilemma. Through explorations of these images, it will become apparent that they show, with stark exactitude, what has gone on and is now present in the psychic underworld of our situation. A number of ways in which one may engage such images will be proposed in the course of our exploration.

Chapter 7 shows that the work of imaginal memory in the nuclear world speaks quite precisely to certain psychological dilemmas of our culture that must be addressed in the development of the enduring commitment to peace cited above. In this way, Hiroshima, the "blasting" at the foundation of our dwelling in the nuclear world, will become effectively present in memory.

Finally, there are two appendixes containing more involved discussions of certain aspects of memory that the reader may find interesting, but are not essential to understanding the book and its arguments as a whole. The first of these discusses the interplay of memory and forgetfulness as evident in religious developments of classical and postclassical Greece. The second appendix takes up the theme with which we began: the close relationship between memory and rhetorical perspective.

It will be helpful to indicate here, in a provisional way, the particular sense in which I use certain terms, though their fuller connotations can only become evident as our exploration develops.

First there is *imaginal memory* itself. The term "imaginal" refers to that which is shaped by realities and powers of imagination.[2] Imaginal memory refers both to that aspect of memory that involves some kind of imagining, and to a specific practice of remembering images elaborated in this book. Memory and imagination most often occur simultaneously: when I remember something, some kind of image (not necessarily a visual or even conscious one) is called forth. Imagination, conversely, most often embodies some form of memory. In various ways, Freud, Jung and subsequent depth psychologists have disclosed the elements of memory inherent in images. "Imaginal memory" can be defined first as that phenomenon of imagination that presents the awareness of what-has-been. The use of the word "presents" is deliberate: as will become evident

in a number of ways throughout this book, the imagination of what-has-been reveals or presents what-is-present in imagination, and also opens into the imagining and remembering of future possibilities.

The practitioners of the art of memory draw upon this copresence of memory and imagination in the psyche, engaging and making present whatever images most deeply stir and "impress" the memory. Imaginal memory, in its second sense, refers to the "practice of remembering images" as envisioned in the
art of memory and, most specifically, Part III of this book. The practice of imaginal memory as envisioned here is a method of psychological exploration of
powerful images (this possibility is developed in varying degrees and less
explicitly by the previous practitioners of the art of memory). While this book
elaborates imaginal memory with specific regard to the nuclear dilemma, the
reader is invited to explore and further develop its practice with regard to other
dilemmas and psychological exploration in general. For an underlying premise
of this book is that there is much the world can gain from a deeper engagement
with psyche, memory and imagination than is usually encouraged by our
culture.

Memory as imagined here is a phenomenon of *soul*—a term whose multiple connotations elude any single and inclusive definition, but which gives the
primary focus of this work.[3] Various significances of soul will become evident
through the text and practice of this work, but it will be helpful to cite a few of
these here. Soul, following Freud and Jung, is used here interchangeably with
"psyche" to evoke those qualities of human existence, and the world itself,
which are felt as most profound and essential. Though soul connotes, in part,
the unique qualities of the individual, it also pertains to the collective or cultural
and transhuman dimensions of the world. We are mainly, though not exclusively, concerned with soul in its collective aspect; more, soul is envisioned
here as inherent in the world, not something pertaining exclusively to the sphere
of human subjectivity.

A guiding image of soul is examined by Hillman with reference to the work
of R. B. Onians: the ancient Greek *psyche* as used to describe the images or
shades of the underworld.[4] Soul is revealed in images of death and memory: in
images disclosing what is of abiding essence in persons and the world. The images revealing essential psychic significances appear in the "death" of the
densely literal perspective with which life is usually viewed. To give an example
from the present context: images associated with the place of Hiroshima will be
seen not only as literal representations of actual and potential events, but as
basic images of the soul, freighted with psychological significance for the contemporary world.

The *interplay between literal and metaphoric perspectives* is an important
part of our psychological engagement. The nuclear dilemma, together with all
the forms that mass violence may take, is a literal and actual reality of the world.

It is also a metaphoric expression of the most fundamental psychological realities of human being, and the very being of the world. In Part III, we will glimpse some of the wealth of metaphor embodied in images associated with the place of Hiroshima. The world, in its beauty, violence, pain and passion, must be taken literally *and* metaphorically. The nuclear dilemma is real on both levels. The experience of the psychological involves a movement between, and a simultaneous presence of, the literal and metaphoric. For example, I apply the "rules" of the art of memory quite—but not only—literally with regard to nuclear images. The literal placing of such images in memory is at the same time a metaphor for our acknowledgement of the place these images claim in our psychic lives. The literal is itself seen in metaphoric perspective. And literal applications must be sharply distinguished from literal*ized* perspectives, which insist that an image or experience has only one meaning and exclude all ambiguities and doubts.

We have evoked the underworld of *myth* in relation to memory and the mnemonic art, and it is worth stressing that myth is taken here as an expression of above mentioned fundamental *realities* of imagination, a revelation in motif and story (*muthos*) of archetypal powers of the soul which, as C. G. Jung emphasized, can "over"-power human persons and history. Myth takes place when one is seized, knowing or not, by "divine" powers of images, or imaginal patterns, which embody the ultimate and fateful factors of individual and collective life and death. Here we seek to remember nuclear reality as we remember ways in which we may be "seized" by myth.

The exhortation to "remember Hiroshima" is clearly prudential in character; memory and prudence are traditionally imagined in close association. *Prudence* in this book is understood in its common, pragmatically cautionary and moral sense. But there is, as our citing of myth suggests, another significance of prudence. It is also a religious activity—religion in the sense of *relegere*, meaning to pay heed to the divine or most powerful factors of existence. This religious aspect of prudence will be present as we take account of these factors through remembering nuclear images, considering what necessities of the soul they reveal.

In general terms, one such psychic activity is that of what Hillman calls "pathologizing." By this he understands "the psyche's autonomous ability to create illness, morbidity, disorder, abnormality, and suffering in any aspect of its behavior and experience and imagine life through this deformed and afflicted perspective" (*RP*, p. 57). Pathologizing images disclose how an individual or culture is seized by myth, revealing a power beyond, and countering, our desires for health, strength and wholeness. "Nobody wants a nuclear war," it is claimed; yet the nuclear danger remains. Remembering the place of Hiroshima, we remember fateful powers of the soul's sufferings and seek to allow them a place in imagination.

Throughout this work there are references to the place of *the imagination of place itself* in soul and memory. Images of place are themselves archetypal powers. These will be considered at various points in the course of our exploration. A place is delimited by its particularities: its situating, orienting, differentiating and habitating qualities that distinguish it from other places. (Remember, for instance, significant ["powerful"] places you have been or lived in [or otherwise encounter in imagination, e.g., in dream, literature, painting]: these places are *structuring powers* both constituting and transcending personal and biographical life.) Imaginal memory gives careful heed to the powers of particular places in which soul dwells.

Two more general comments will help define the scope of this work. First, its exploration of images of memory remains within the boundaries, the imaginal places, of Western and particularly Greek, cultural imaginations. Our focus gains precision by sticking to these cultural images, though there will be some references to memorial perspectives of other cultures, and the motif of memory as that which leads one back to original, truest or divine realities is apparent worldwide.

Second, there is the psychological frame of this work. It is clear that it draws heavily from the perspectives of C. G. Jung, and upon the elaborations of this by Hillman and other archetypal psychologists. Of crucial importance too is the work of Robert Jay Lifton. Lifton focuses upon the psychic implications of our actual mortality, and of historical episodes of mass violence; Hillman elaborates more precisely on imaginal and metaphoric realms of death in the soul, or the *myth* of death. Both psychological perspectives are crucial to this study. Archetypal perspective, when brought to bear on processes of victimization and mass violence, can help deliteralize their destructiveness so that this is given metaphoric place and not acted out against humans, other beings, and finally, the being of the world itself.

Acknowledgements

My deep gratitude goes to my friends and colleagues who took time to read some or all of this text, and to offer their support, reflections, questions and criticisms. I am particularly grateful to Herbert Mason, whose enthusiasm, encouragement and challenges were indispensable to the development of the book; to Merlin Swartz, whose concern and philosophical acumen helped me to better understand my own methods; and to Margaret Gorman, whose grasp of the relation between psychology and the moral imagination proved a vital contribution to the book's reflections on that subject. Special thanks are due Edward Casey, whose support of my project and numerous writings on the place of memory in our world are at the core of this work. Marie Cantlon gave the manuscript a close reading and offered suggestions for revisions that greatly strengthened the book. Long discussions with Tom Quinn resulted in important refinements, both in the style of the book and in its theoretical framework. Others to whom I am indebted for their encouragement and thoughtful questions regarding my text include: Lester Arond, Rodolfo Cardona, Andrew Geller, Ethne Gray, Petra Hesse, Gene Hower, Greg Lum, Monty Montgomery, and, not least, my father, Donald Perlman.

Carola Sautter, my editor, provided vital support, careful guidance and helpful suggestions as I worked at rendering the initial manuscript into book form. I am deeply appreciative of her efforts.

Abbreviations

The following frequently cited works will be referenced in the text using the abbreviations given below.

AM *The Art of Memory*, by Frances Yates (Chicago: University of Chicago Press, 1966).

BC *The Broken Connection*, by Robert Jay Lifton (New York: Simon & Schuster, 1979).

CW *Collected Works*, by C. G. Jung, trans. R. R. C. Hull, vols. 1–20 (Princeton: Princeton University Press, Bollingen Series XX, 1953ff); indicated in text by volume and paragraph nos.

DL *Death in Life: Survivors of Hiroshima*, by Robert Jay Lifton (New York: Random House, 1967).

DU *The Dream and the Underworld*, by James Hillman (New York: Harper & Row, 1979).

MA *The Myth of Analysis*, by James Hillman (New York: Harper & Row, 1978 [1972]).

MDR *Memories, Dreams, Reflections*, by C. G. Jung, trans. Richard and Clara Winston (New York: Vintage Books, 1965).

"ML" "Mnemosyne—Lesmosyne: On the 'Springs' of Memory and Forgetting," by Carl Kerenyi, trans. Jay Stoner in *Spring 1977*.

PS *The Poetics of Space*, by Gaston Bachelard, trans. Etienne Gilson (Boston: Beacon Press, 1966).

R *Remembering: A Phonomenological Study*, by Edward S. Casey (Bloomington, IN: University of Indiana Press, 1987).

RP *Re-Visioning Psychology*, by James Hillman (New York: Harper & Row, 1975).

Part I

Opening Reflections

1

Possibilities of Memory

A thirteenth century writer on rhetoric and memory, Boncompagno da Signa, said that "We must assiduously remember the invisible joys of Paradise and the eternal torments of Hell."[1] Placed in contemporary context, da Signa's words echo a chorus or warnings sounded since the opening of the nuclear era: Let us remember the joyful possibilities of a world at peace and the torments of nuclear hell revealed at Hiroshima and Nagasaki. In both contexts—that of Medieval piety and that of the present—remembering evokes future possibilities. Conversely, imagining the future inevitably involves a look into the past; future possibilities are linked and laden with memory. This is evident in one recent religious document on the threat of nuclear holocaust by the U.S. Catholic Bishops, the 1983 pastoral letter on *The Challenge of Peace*. The bishops assert that in order to truly repudiate the use of nuclear weapons, it will be necessary "for our country to express profound sorrow over the atomic bombing in 1945."[2] The challenge of peace, of the future, is simultaneously a challenge to our capabilities of memory. The echoes of memory in contemporary nuclear images suggest that the medieval world-picture, with its stress on remembering Paradise and Hell, is relevant to the present.

The difference between the divinely revealed hell of the medieval world and the man-made hells of Hiroshima and Nagasaki is evident. In the former, the souls of sinners undergo punishments which, if described with sadistic relish, are within the medieval worldview well-deserved, corresponding precisely to sins committed. In the latter hells we find hapless victims of what Robert Jay Lifton names "unlimited technological violence and absurd death" (*DL*, p. 541). The medieval damned were more often than not remembered with scorn and moralistic condemnation, and with fear that one might, if imprudent, meet a similar fate. When past, present and potential victims of nuclear hell are remembered, we sense the "profound sorrow" spoken of by the bishops, together with discomfort that may include elements of guilt and of fear that we may be next, regardless of how moral our lives. Still, much as our utopian visions of peace (never absent, even when rendered unconscious by fashionable cynicism) recall their older religious counterparts, so do our visions and memories of nuclear hell.

For there is a common psychological context to the remembering of the medieval and nuclear worlds, a fascination inherent in the visioning of hell together with overtly pleasurable realms. Having passed the gate of hell and sighted the River Acheron, the Virgil of Dante's *Inferno* tells us that "here/Divine Justice transforms and spurs [the damned] so/their dread turns wish: they yearn for what they fear" (III. 122–3).[3] At this threshold, as later in Freud, wish and fear meet. Foreshadowed too is an episode deeper in the *Inferno* that Dante remembers:

> I turned like one who cannot wait to see
> the thing he dreads, and who, in sudden fright,
> runs while he looks, his curiosity
>
> competing with his terror—and at my back
> I saw a figure that came running toward us
> across the ridge, a Demon huge and black.
>
> (XXI. 25–30)

Were it not for Virgil's reasoned restraint, reflects Dante, the latter might have gone over the brink, lured by the demon at the back.

As Alfred Ziegler, in an essay "On Pain and Punishment" that reflects on psychological dimensions of physical pain and disease says: "Mankind possesses a deep longing for the Kingdom of God" with its "divine wholeness and health."[4] Yet

> Just as a longing creates a Kingdom of God, so a Hell is created with an equal degree of necessity. It seems as if there were some imbedded urge attracting us, a bottomless fascination emitted by those hells of ours. . . . Human pride and self-esteem seem to require a primeval

mistrust as well, a hate of creation; they seem to require the cultivating of an annihilating "No" and the desire to be suffering and sick.

Witnessing the varieties of suffering, sickness and death in history, myth, art, literature, religion and politics, we indeed remember profound powers of soul: powers as various as the portrayals of demons and sufferers of hells. These powers work their ill effects in spite of conscious desires and efforts to the contrary. A decisive and sustained movement toward the elimination of the nuclear threat would be an occasion for great joy; yet this joy would lack depth unless a "profound sorrow," in the bishops' words, were also given a place. For in one shape and another, the spectre of that which is incurable will be with us always.

The presence of the Incurable suggests a necessity to find some place wherein the soul's ill effects can dwell, to house in imagination what Paul Ricoeur calls "the pain of being," to build in memory a house of death. Remembering hell is more than a literal moral affair; it can become an imaginal and metaphoric realization of the "imbedded urges" whose fascination is bottomless. Then deeper values of moral concern and prudence will be realized too. By remembering hell, giving it a psychological place, we are more likely to sustain efforts to lessen its compulsive acting-out on the historical stage. We are remembering to save (also, *in order* to save) hell, and the fascinated demons within.

In insisting upon the value of keeping the memory of historical and psychological realities alive, we tacitly assert the value of keeping *memory itself* alive. To explore and develop a practice of "imaginal memory" goes against a long trend in Western culture toward a general devaluation of memory and imagination themselves, culminating in an increasing reliance on external media and computers to store "memories." Thus, James Hillman speaks of "psychology's loss of 'memory'" (*MA*, pp. 169–82) to describe how the acute sense of the power of psychic images gets lost in the development of Enlightenment and post-Enlightenment thought. Edward Casey traces the diminishing prestige of memory since an earlier "time when [it] was deeply revered and rigorously trained, as it was in ancient Greece" (*R*, p. 11). Memory itself has been largely forgotten, observes Casey. "It is only in unusual circumstances that remembering remains an item of central concern on contemporary agendas" (*R*, p. 2). This forgetting of the place of memory, as subsequent chapters will indicate, has had a quite specific, but largely-unnoticed effect on the unfolding of the nuclear dilemma.

Memory is once again remembered, says Casey, in the "unusual circumstances" obtaining in the procedures of psychoanalysis, Oriental meditation and cognitive psychological experiments on memory. Recall too the "striking and unusual" images envisioned in the practice of the art of memory. What is unusual serves to deepen and revivify the impressions of memory in our lives, to remind us of the place of memory in human existence.

There remains an inherent fascination with what is memorable, and with memory itself. A countervailing interest in and respect for memory is discernible in a variety of works on the subject appearing over the past decade. Cognitive and neuropsychological researchers excitedly discover and speculate over a multiplicity of discrete facets of memory and the location of these in different areas of the brain. There is a resurgence of concern with historical memory and the need to keep alive the dark images of this century's horrors lest we, in forgetfulness, allow their continuation on a yet greater scale. In recent years the film *Shoah* has provided poignant, anguished remembrances of the Nazi Holocaust; while in the Soviet Union, the novel and film *Repentance* have reflected a struggle for a more open and critical remembering of the horrors of the Stalin era. On a smaller scale, Casey notices a continuing respect accorded memory in everyday affairs (the increasing awareness of Alzheimer's disease is significant in this regard), our amazement over unusual feats of memory,[5] and "a haunting sense that something abidingly important has been lost in the near-elimination of memorization from education" (*R*, p. 10) . . .

This book's exploration of "places" of memory and imagination is in accordance with this countervailing trend. The remembering of destruction in the service of preventing future holocaust is envisioned here as a way of serving the powers of memory and imagination themselves. We remember destruction in order that we may *go on remembering*. This is not a new assertion. It is found in the *Odyssey* when Alkinoos, one of Odysseus's hosts, responds to the former's grieving during a remembering in song of the Trojan War. The Gods, says Alkinoos, ordained this war and its destruction (*olethros*) for men in order that it might become a song for those to come (*Od.* VIII. 577–80). Images of war, destruction, pain and grief serve to remind us of memory's intrinsic value as they deepen our awareness of the hell of what has been. In these images we can hear a song.

Imaginal memory as explored and elaborated in this book becomes a primary value of the psyche in its own right: we work in order that memory may be kept alive. Part II, which assays what might be called the "history of imaginal memory," is intended to invite the reader to explore a vividness of memory and imagination that in our time has been largely forgotten, left without a place in our awareness. In Part III, this invitation is further extended, addressing a more practical and specific form of imaginal memory engaging images associated with the place of Hiroshima. The art of memory, from its earliest days, combines an intense involvement with psychic images with a strong practical orientation. We know that to remember often requires much practice, time, repetition. This holds true for any deep-going exploration of imaginal realms and powers. If this book inspires the reader to practice imaginal memory (in whatever manner seems most appropriate to the individual), or even to seriously entertain the possibilities of such a practice, it will have served one of its main purposes.

The nuclear threat is approached here in indirect as well as direct ways. By valuing imaginal memory in its own right, prior to exploring its potential to address this threat, we become more immediately aware of precisely this potential. The development of a deepened psychological sensitivity to the power of remembered images points toward a deepening sensitivity to the nuclear threat and other global dilemmas that often appear remote, abstract and removed from daily concerns.

Some further initial reflections on traditional ways of imagining memory against the backdrop of nuclear threat will suggest the broader relevance of imaginal memory for present history. More possibilities of memory are revealed through a consideration of the relation of memory and *prudence, forgetfulness,* and the *imagination of the archaic.*

Da Signa's insistence upon remembering Paradise and Hell, reflecting the virtue of prudence, evokes a tradition which goes back at least to Plato's time. In the *Republic* (621A) Socrates declares that souls about to be reincarnated must drink a measure of the water of the River Un-Care (*Ameles*) at the edge of the Plain of Forgetfulness. (*Lethe*; those not saved by *phronesis*—"wisdom" or "prudence"—drink more than their measure.) In the context of Plato's valuation of memory and recollection the implicit connection between memory and prudent wisdom becomes apparent: prudent souls, having drunk less of the draught of heedless forgetfulness, will best be able to remember the real world of Being.

The connection between memory and prudence is made more explicit by Cicero, who observes that knowledge of the past and prudent concern for the present and future are closely linked.[6] Da Signa's prudential exhortation expresses the religious concerns of the Scholastics, who stressed the moral and ethical aspects of memory (its connection with Prudence, now a cardinal virtue, having been given by the authority of Cicero).

It is immediately evident that the current insistence upon remembering this century's mass violence continues this traditional relation of memory and prudence. Without memory there can be neither appreciation of what has happened or is now taking place, nor a foundation for intelligent and foresightful action aimed at the prevention of future—in this case, nuclear—catastrophe. The appeal to memory gains power because its relation with prudence is not only practical but (as Plato implies) primordially or archetypally given. Still, it is questionable how great a role the prudential power of memory has played in history. The proliferation of nuclear bombs since Hiroshima is not reassuring. The undercurrent of desire to evade the anxiety associated with care, and the unwisdom and imprudence of certain types of forgetfulness, are at least as strong now as in classical Greece, and more dangerous than ever given the numbers and types of nuclear weapons and international conflicts.

I speak of the imprudence of *certain* types of forgetfulness, because I do not want to imply that forgetfulness *per se* equals imprudence and a lack of moral and psychological concern, or even that memory and forgetfulness are always polar opposites (although an oppositional conception was tacitly assumed above in my discussion of the forgetting of memory).[7] The relation between the two is far more complex and ambiguous than that. Consider one type of prudential memory that is at once a form of imprudent forgetfulness. This sort of memory is captured in the chauvinistic slogans of groups and nations, which evoke the past wrongs done them by others to justify self-righteous militarism and aggression. Remember the Maine! Or Pearl Harbor, Munich, Napoleon, Hitler (the latter figure having been used by each superpower to characterize the other and justify its own weapons-buildup). Such slogans, together with idealized memories of one's own group's behavior in war, tell of a way of memory, which is a way of forgetting, of repression—a screen memory in Freud's sense, by which the actual ambiguity of past and present events and motives is falsified. This might be called "regression in the service of the national ego": more precisely, its narcissistic glorification. It is a variety of what John Mack calls "the egoism of victimization,"[8] in which the memory remains bound to the injustices done by others, and the shadow of the ego's actions remains unseen, thus prompting the victimization of still other persons. In this form of memory, individuals, groups and nations assume simultaneously the roles of Victim and Executioner. Together with this egoism, there is also a *literalism* of victimization. When we become victims, we are just that: literally victims. In victimizing another, we again become literal: literally treating the other as a victim. Because victimization takes place literally, it is particularly difficult to step back from the process, and the memory, of victimization, and recognize its more metaphoric dimension.

The egoism (and literalism) of victimization is strikingly apparent in national war memorials and monuments, where members of one's own national group—and no others—are commemorated. While the memorialization and commemoration of war and its victims is a phenomenon far too complex to subsume under the category of "egoism of victimization," this latter has nonetheless pervaded such collective memorializing, as even a brief recall of whatever war memorials come to one's mind will make clear. The danger is not in the memorializing of a given nation's war dead *per se*—this serves important psychological, cultural, social and even religious functions—but in the concurrent forgetting-to-care deeply about the sufferings and dyings of those in other groups. In the U.S., the Vietnam War Memorial in Washington D.C. powerfully evokes the memory of Americans who died in the war. The sufferings of the Vietnamese are conspicuously forgotten. Nor are there any memorials commemorating the approximately twenty million Soviets who died in World War II in any country other than the Soviet Union. Yet within the Soviet Union, there has been no commemorating of non-Soviet and particularly of Jewish victims of the Nazi Holocaust. This forgetting of the Other, this flowing in collective currents of Un-Care, is a major psychological ingredient in preparations for mass violence cloaked in the rhetoric of prudent remembering of how the Enemy laid one's nation low when it was unprepared.

Hiroshima is not often used, even in Japan, in the same way that examples such as Munich and Pearl Harbor are. (However, surviving victims of the atomic bombing may be subject to a certain amount of egoism of victimization. More importantly, the Japanese as a whole have tended to forget that many thousands of Koreans, against whom there is a traditional Japanese prejudice, also died at Hiroshima.) Yet it is not clear that remembering Hiroshima and Nagasaki alone must necessarily work to attenuate national, or even individual, reliance on the nuclear weapon to ensure security. Instead, as Lifton has shown (see next chapter), the imagery of total extermination evoked by Hiroshima and Nagasaki has greatly added to individual and collective death anxiety while threatening all possibilities of "symbolic immortality" or larger continuity beyond the self. Images of nuclear hell can add impetus to ever-present tendencies to ward off images of death and annihilation. Lifton speaks too of victimization, of "murdering" death in the guise of acts of violence directed against others, and of the tendency to embrace that which is finally responsible for the increased threat of annihilation: nuclear and other weapons technologies.

We require a different kind of engagement with memory. In its deeper prudential sense, memory leads us beyond the idealizations of ego toward a remembering of "what is shameful, base and cruel in a people's past" (together with the remembering of the destructiveness of which each of us is capable).[9] The possibilities of this form of memory and prudence are apparent in recent efforts in the U.S. to remember not Munich, but American use of Nazi war criminals after World War II in the Cold War struggle; and in Soviet opening toward a genuine remembering of what went on under Stalin as well as the Soviet victory over the Nazis in the Great Patriotic War. Such complexly-shadowed remembering, insist John Broughton and Marta Zahayevich, is essential if the individual is to resist manipulation by the nation-state, and by narrowly nationalistic and chauvinistic appeals. (Moreover, statesmen who are relatively more open to this darker current of memory will be less likely to make such appeals.) For this reason, "Memory is the place where the psychological and political intersect"; and this place of memory is the place where the politics of ego deepen toward a politics of soul, an attentive and prudent concern with non ego and transnational realities. Notice that Lethe is not absent here either; there is in this remembering a letting-go, a forgetting of parochial (individual and/or collective) ego-concerns. (This theme is dominant too in the varieties of the soul's religious concerns; see discussion in chapter 3.)

This deepening of memory also implies a broadening imagination of victimization that transcends its egoism (including the reverse egoism of excessive and literalized guilt, with its focus only on what I or we have done), and opens toward larger realities of destructiveness, suffering and death, starting with a greater depth of compassion and empathy for the sufferings and deaths of those in groups other than one's own. Such will be our movement here: the remembering of Hiroshima and Nagasaki, together with associated images, will become a way of remembering these others in a more careful way. It will become, too, a way of remembering those Others of imaginal realms who appear and personify previously cited primary or archetypal realities of the soul's fate.

The realities of Hiroshima and Nagasaki only become fully real with the closest possible engagement with nuclear images—an active engagement such as is cultivated by the art of memory. Rather than fending off death anxiety, we shall move toward its shadowy realities, proposing intense and immediate encounters with figures of the nuclear imagination that deepen and amplify the entwined powers of memory and prudence.

This form of imagining goes deeper than the usual prudential view that remembering nuclear images is primarily a means to the avoidance of a nuclear end. The *intensity* of this remembering of images reveals it as a form of *commemoration*, the root meaning of which is precisely "an *intensified remembering*" (*R*, p. 217).[10] It is thus a close relative of the commemorating of the war dead cited and criticized above. However, two critical differences between these forms of commemoration need mention here. First, this practice of memory is explicitly aimed at the commemoration of those *outside* of the particular (e.g., national) group with which one most immediately identifies. Second, this way of memory, while having (in common with collective war memorializing and public commemorations of Hiroshima and Nagasaki) an important interpersonal aspect, is more specifically a form of what Casey calls "intrapsychic memorialization" (*R*, pp. 239–43), involving also the commemoration of imaginal or psychic figures alien to one's ego.

The intensity of the remembering proposed in this book opens into a deeper dimension of prudence, of paying careful heed to what is present in the psyche that reveals the presence of the place of Hiroshima. Earlier I asserted that one aim of this work is the revaluing of memory for its own sake (hence not only for *ours*). Just so, the images we remember in connection with the place of Hiroshima, with whatever horror and suffering they may embody, have an intrinsic value. They are worth remembering for their own sake, quite apart from their role in strengthening efforts to prevent actual nuclear holocaust. In opening ourselves to these particular images, we allow a place in imagination for the careful exploration of their psychic depths. We will remember presences here that have a permanent place in our psychic lives. From this perspective, our efforts to prevent nuclear holocaust become a way of acknowledging the enduring claim of the first place of nuclear destruction on our awareness. As the images associated with this place are memorialized in the psyche, the fascination they evoke opens to reveal a curious love, a devotion echoing that with which Dante and others remembered the medieval hell.

In this careful heeding of imaginal powers, there is a deep forgetting of conventional views on what sorts of images are acceptable and valuable, and which are not. But, as in traditional forgettings of habitual or ordinary perspectives, this forgetting becomes also a remembering of original realities, of mythic and archaic or archetypal origins, when the present world came to be; "this primordial dramatic and sometimes even tragic history must be *known*, it must be continually recollected."[11] Mircea Eliade traces this motif through the retelling and ritual reenactment of mythic or paradigmatic events in archaic societies, through Platonic recollection of the divine Forms, to modern historiography, the aim of which is the revival of *"the entire past of humanity,"*[12] including its pyschic and spiritual heritage. This, says Eliade, is "one of the few encouraging syndromes of the modern world." The encouraging of this *archetypal memory* is a major theme in our exploration of the remembering of the nuclear world and its origins.[13] An example of the deepening of the historical memory of Hiroshima into the memory of the archaic is found in Albert Goldbarth's poem, *History as Horse Light*:

> It ended at the time of Hiroshima. Everything
> ended, the world. Though some of us didn't
> know it, and kept on, like the spasms you see
> in the hips of an animal—small and useless
> telegraph keys—where it's stretched at the edge of the road.
> But it wasn't that slow for the horse
> at Hiroshima: they'll show you it's shadow
> burnt permanently to a wall by the blast.
> Think of such light. In *Guernica*, Picasso approaches light
> like that—flash—a whole horse screaming.
>
> It began in the Paleolithic caves. Something,
> someone, surely happened before that, but
> whatever matters took its first idea
> of its shape in those blindblack passageways.
> Somebody crawled, with a raw lamp, with a wick
> and its fat. Somebody made his way through
> rockgut, crawling on his knees like a beast,
> rising where the space permitted, making his necessary

> Aurignacian way to a place where a horse could be put
> on a wall in the first light's first distinctions . . . [14]

Historical memory and the art of protest lead back through "blindblack passage-ways" of soul to a first vision, a horse-memory, a memory-vision of primordial animal-art.

The foregoing reveals some of the myriad possibilities inherent in working with memory. In our usual vision of memory as concerning only the literal past, we tend to forget that memory also presents images rich with present and future possibilities. In contrast, traditions of memory combine a sense of the past and of possibility, going right back to the primary possibilities of soul and world in myth; time circles back in memory, so that going back is a way of looking for-ward. Despite the despair evident in Goldbarth's poem, the time when "It ended" leads back to the time when "It began," as if to suggest that the despair of the end-time becomes, through memory, a beginning in the dark.

The art of memory elaborates imaginal possibilities of memory, and its Renaissance practitioners, as will become apparent below, remember the orig-inal, world-creative and ordering possibilities of images of memory as they vi-sion societal, cultural and religious reform. Here, too, we seek the ancient rela-tion of memory and possibility through the work of imagination, beginning with the latent possibilities still within the remembering of Hiroshima, Nagasaki and the nuclear world since then.

2

Dwellers in the House
of the Nuclear World

Before going more deeply into traditions of memory and their potential contributions to psychological work in the nuclear world, it will be well to review and reflect on some of this world's major psychological features. For we who dwell in the nuclear world are not alone. There are present with us images through which we may envisage the prenuclear, archetypal powers that must be faced in any psychological exploration of varieties of mass violence.

Robert Jay Lifton has been especially concerned with what he calls *"nuclearism:* the passionate embrace of nuclear weapons as a solution to death anxiety and a way of restoring a lost sense of immortality" (*BC*, p. 369; italics in original). In this "religion," development of ever more weapons is imagined as a way of salvation from the dangers posed by the weapons themselves. Nuclear defense, together with other varieties of high technology (including space) weapons, becomes a way of defending against the imagery of annihilation first given concrete form at Hiroshima and Nagasaki. In an appendix, Lifton stresses that

> There is . . . the deification of not just nuclear weapons but of science
> and scientific technology in general. It is this broader technicism and

scientism that provides the matrix for nuclearism. Within this scientific abberation, "knowing"—the essence of both science and the arts—becomes only solving puzzles or manipulating the environment. Science, the parent, is consumed by its technological offspring. What results is an impulse—never stronger and more dangerous than now—to substitute a brilliant technological vision for the more recalcitrant problems of human continuity.

(*BC*, p. 430)

There is a mythic matrix to this problem concerning the interrelated places of violence and of scientific and technological power in our culture. We begin to discern the outlines of this matrix in a statement cited by William Lawrence, a *New York Times* science writer who, during the 1950s, enthusiastically embraced atomic and hydrogen-bomb tests as the *via regia* to a warless and paradisal world. Lawrence cites Dr. Maurice Tainter, a pharmacologist, who says that

Medicine today is accomplishing greater miracles than, for example, atomic-energy developments. It is because, in this Golden Age of Medicine, we have conscientiously evolved a technique and a scientific philosophy that finally enabled us to wrestle with death itself, and on increasingly even terms.[1]

(quoted in *BC*, p. 375)

It is ironic that a *fantasy of healing* presents itself in a discussion, however enthusiastic, of instruments of nuclear violence. Yet this "medical model" is quite germaine both to the psychology of nuclear developments and of mass violence in general, in which *killing takes place* within a fantasy of healing. Nuclear strategists follow this model when discussing "surgical strikes," while doctors played major roles in Nazi visions of a "cure" for Germany's malaise or "sickness" via the annihilation of the Jews.[2] Imagery of violence gains numinous power through this intimate association with the power of healing. The sickness for which a cure is sought, observes Lifton, is, finally, death in both its actual and its symbolic forms. It is Death and Death's imagination with which nations wrestle, now using nuclear arms.

Violence, healing, wrestling with death—these three appear not only in Lawrence's citation of Tainter; the drama is far older than that. It is subtly portrayed in Euripides's play, *Alcestis*.[3] In the myth which gave rise to the drama, Apollos's son, Asklepios, is struck down by Zeus's thunderbolt for using his powers as a healer-God in order to bring a dead man back to life. Enraged, Apollo kills the Cyclops who had fashioned the thunderbolt with which Zeus had killed his son. In punishment, Apollo is required to spend a year serving a mortal man, Admetos. While in the latter's domain, Apollo grows fond of his master and arranges for him to avoid a fated early death by having someone take his place. Since Admetos's parents refuse to offer themselves to death, his wife, Alcestis, offers herself in his place. It is at the point when Apollo returns to the house of Admetos, on the fated day of death, that Euripides's drama begins.

In the logic of myth, Apollo's servitude in the house of Admetos is itself a sojourn in Death's house. This reality is hinted at by Death himself when he finds Apollo in Admetos's house on the day when he is to take possession of the young wife (hence making the house his own): "Phoebus! what are you doing here?/Why do you haunt this house? (*Alcestis*, p. 43). (The irony of this statement will return to haunt us as we reflect on deadly forms of the quest for immortality.) Death rightly fears that Apollo, having deprived him of Admetos, will now deprive him of another life. For, as Apollo warns, a man will come and "will wrest Alcestis from your hand by force" (Ibid., p. 45).

Like his son, Apollo is a God of healing, an archetypal dominant of medicine which—since the time of Asklepios's miraculous but ill-fated cure of the dead man—has not always been on easy terms with Death and Necessity. Witness the fantasies of "miracles" alluded to by Tainter that inform his "technique and . . . scientific philosophy." The man to whom Apollo refers appears in the fantasy of being able "to wrestle with death itself, and on increasingly even terms." This, of course, is the hero, Herakles (or Hercules). Herakles tells Euripides's audience what he will do upon Alcestis's death:

> The black-robed king of the dead will come to drink the blood
> Of victims offered at her tomb. I'll go there, hide,
> And watch for him, and so leap out and spring on him.
> And once I have my arms locked around his writhing ribs,
> There is no power that can release him, till he yields
> Alcestis to me . . .
>
> (Ibid., p. 70)

Herakles succeeds in his fantasy, and shortly thereafter arrives at the house with a veiled Alcestis, speaking of an athletic contest where the prize for "boxing and wrestling," which he had won, was a team of oxen and the girl (Ibid., p. 75). After Alcestis is revealed to Admetos, Herakles acknowledges that "I joined battle with Death, who rules the world of spirits" (Ibid., p. 79).

Three psychological themes emerge in this drama that can be considered archetypal structures of the nuclear age. The first theme is that of what I will call the "Strong-Armed Ego," for which Herakles is a main image. Second, the *Alcestis* probes, with great sensitivity, struggles that result from one's being threatened by and witnessing untimely death, or the psychology of the "survivor." Third, this drama points toward the deep, pervasive presence of Death's imagination in life: the realm of Hades, the "place of shades."

For Herakles's strong ego, the nuclear stand off (between the superpowers in particular, but also between other nations) takes place within images of a contest of strength and will as if it were a traditional athletic contest with the usual winners, losers and prizes. For this is one of the ways Herakles wrestles with death; and his grip remains strong in this world of strong-armed nuclear powers. Strong-Armed Ego, as a prenuclear, archetypal dominant of our culture, insists on negotiating "from a position of strength," justifying his own reliance on nuclear arms with reference to his opponent's reliance on "force." The history of arms control and disarmament negotiations shows that rhetoric about "mutually advantageous accords" has often masked hard determination to win an advantage for one's nation's "vital interests": again, to win a bout with Death, for which in many ways the threats posed by adversaries (national or otherwise) are finally personae.

The Heraklean, or more generally, "heroic" ego, has been severely criticized in the past few decades, usually for its one-sided masculinity and (fearful) rejection of "feminine" qualities such as emotionality, vulnerability and dependence. This cultural critique, though valid and important for reflections on the imagination of sex and gender, need not be reelaborated here. Rather, I shall let it stand beside the primary focus of this book on places and images of death, which Strong-Armed Ego wards off with his decisive life-activities, his victories over images of enemies.

It is precisely this *avoidance of imagination and death as crucial realities of the soul* that renders Strong-Armed Ego such a dangerous figure. Lifton hints at the consequences of this when he speaks of "false heroes" with "their literalization of death and killing as opposed to symbolization of death and rebirth" (*BC*, p. 289). Here he alludes to the forms of hero mythology, which often (as in the labors of Herakles) imagine the hero as killing a figure or series of figures (monsters or monstrous people, snakes, etc.) that embody death's presence (notice Herakles's reference in *Alcestis* to Death's "writhing ribs"). This is the archetypal aspect of the "murdering" of death which is essential to processes of victimization and violence. It pertains not only to the false heroes of history. It is given with the mythic pattern of the hero, particularly the Heraklean variety, who, as James Hillman observes in reflecting upon "Hercules in the House of Hades" (*DU*, pp. 110–7), is Death's most virulent opponent and may be seen as lacking the tragic connection with the realities of Hades that characterize other Greek heroes.[4] Referring to Herakles's aggressive behavior in Hades, and his inability to recognize its figures as shades—psychic images—Hillman observes that "Rather than die to metaphor, we kill literally; refusing the need to die, we attack death itself." The recognition of multiple imaginal realities by Strong-Armed Ego counters this figure's violent literalism, its murderous defense of one vision of reality against death; "Without imaginal understanding, we may expect killing. . . ."[5]

Strong-Armed Ego is not identifiable with any one mythic pattern or figure (despite its tendency toward single-minded literalism). In its style we can discern memory-traces of a variety of characters in addition to Herakles, for instance, Prometheus, frequently cited for his stealing of the Gods' fire, and the war God, Ares or Mars.[6] And we have already alluded to the role of the Healer—Apollo, together with his son, Asklepios—in violent "cures" for the illness of death. There is also Apollo's association with the clear light of objective, distanced rationality that has characterized the Western scientific imagination and takes on malignant form in the detachment with which nuclear scenarios are contemplated and weapons designed and deployed. Nuclear "rationalism" casts the harsh light of purely instrumental reason: "Think of such light" by which at Hiroshima a horse-shadow was "burnt permanently to a wall . . ." The association, evident from fifth century Greece on, of Apollo's light with the sun God, brings him into relation with the latter's son, Phaethon, the mortal youth who tries to drive the Sun's four-horsed chariot, and nearly incinerates the earth in the process. The myth of Phaethon as portrayed by Ovid indicates the boy's fascination with technological power (in the shape of the bejewelled sun-chariot). Elsewhere I have explored the inherent fascination of harnessing cosmic forces with technological means through the myth of Phaethon's ego.[7] Now this Phaethonic spirit is fascinated by the prospect of space weapons, in which Apollonic detachment takes on truly cosmic proportions: again the substitution of "a brilliant technological vision for the more recalcitrant problems of human continuity."

The image of Phaethon suggests the role of the *puer eternus* or "eternal youth" in our cultural fascination with new technology and its power. This represents a technicized variety of the idealism and boundless energy evoked by myth's imagination of youth. Another character who plays an important role in the constitution of Strong-Armed Ego is discernible in other, more cynically-toned dominant preoccupations of our culture. The nuclear era has witnessed a number of swings between expansive idealism and a narrower preoccupation with national defense and (physical and moral) adherence to national boundaries. This goes together with an emphasis on law, order and authority (reflected prominently in fundamentalist religious movements);[8] and a preoccupation with conspiratorial schemes of national enemies that reflect the paranoid cast of nationalism generally and the structure of the "national security" or nuclear state in particular.[9] All these are concerns of the *senex* or archetypal figure of the old man that always appears in tandem with the puer. In the Western tradition the senex is often figured by the image of Kronos-Saturn, the Old Ruler who must repress threats to his rule, incorporating potentially rebellious children (nascent figures of his soul) into his *system* by devouring them.[10] The mythic behavior of Herakles and Kronos-Saturn together inform the typical psychopathology of Strong-Armed Ego, in the form of *The Authoritarian Personality* described by T. W. Adorno, et. al., during the initial phase of the Cold War:[11] one-sided reliance on images of "strength;" ethnocentricity and national chauvinism; fear of the ambiguous, of change, of inferiority, "weakness" and "femininity" and of whatever opposes one's totalistic idealogical system or group; and a "black-and-white" way of viewing the world. This last, the splitting of the psychic and political cosmos into opposites, such as the United States and the Soviet Union, goes together—as Wolfgang Giegerich and Hillman observe—with psychological monotheism: Strong-Armed Ego's single vision. This oppositional way of seeing has roots in the hero's myth, for he must oppose (and yet remain bound to by virtue of his opposition) Death or the Great Mother.[12] Oppositionalism also reflects the defensive and paranoid moves of the senex ego that must oppose, oppress and repress that which threatens his institution (again, we arrive at death, the final disintegration of one's system).[13] Yet the rigidity of the Old Ruler's system, its stasis, is at the same time a revelation of death and bears within itself its own destruction and decay—is finally corrupted by its own power.

Strong-Armed Ego as described here highlights the archetypal background of prenuclear and nuclear oppression and violence. Because Strong-Armed Ego is obsessed with maintaining and increasing his power (ultimately, over Death) his most terrifying conscious fantasies do not concern the threat of nuclear destruction, but the loss of "vital interests" to outside enemies. He is present in the U.S.-Soviet power plays that have dominated most of the nuclear era, and exerts his power through dictatorships of militaristic fantasies. (The development of the "national security state" with its preoccupations with centralized and secret [e.g., ultimately nuclear] powers, has been a profoundly anti democratic influence in the U.S.)[14] His literalized oppositionalism provides the basis for "enemy images" and what Erik H. Erickson aptly calls "pseudospeciation," or people's immemorial tendency to imagine that members of groups they do not identify with are less-than-human, another species.[15] Surrounded by that which is less-than-human but nonetheless exerts a greater-than-human power of fantasy, groups in the grip of Strong-Armed Ego become themselves dehumanized, justifying the inhuman acting-out of violence via an intense egoism of victimization.

Strong-Armed Ego's psychological life is dominated by fantasies of ultimate control and victory, which have been countered by warnings about the limits of the ego's ability to control that which transcends it. Yet Strong-Armed Ego is itself a power transcending any individual or nation. It is (in Giegerich's characterization of the ego of the modern world generally) "an archetypal power, . . . the modern mode of being of everything that is, the mode of being of God, the world, and man. It is not we who have an ego; the ego or the will has us and our world."[16]

We would appear to have moved some distance from the themes of Euripides's *Alcestis* as we have stressed the complexity of Strong-Armed Ego's psychology, its multiple dominants. However, the imagination of death underlying the struggles of that drama and the life of Strong-Armed Ego points toward our second theme, that of the psychology of the *survivor*. A review of this will reveal how Euripides's drama is played out in the present.

In different ways all the characters of the *Alcestis* are survivors: Apollo, Admetos, Alcestis and the family present, as well as Herakles, all see death but escape its grasp. As Lifton says, "We may define the survivor as one who has come into contact with death in some bodily or psychic fashion and has himself remained alive" (*DL*, p. 479). In a sense we are all survivors, for given with human existence is the capacity to know, to imagine, death as physical reality and as metaphor. Lifton stresses three psychic forms or equivalents of death: images involving separation (v. connection), stasis (v. movement) and disintegration (v. integrity) (*BC*, p. 53). Also involved here is the capacity to survive human mortality by imagining symbolic or nonliteral forms of immortality: the individual finds continuity, for instance, through his or her descendants or other relationships, creative works and various forms of cultural or spiritual connection to the past, present and anticipated future.

The images of nuclear extermination given concrete form at Hiroshima and Nagasaki have profound implications for collective aspects of survivor psychology in the nuclear world. Not only the *hibakusha* or surviving atomic-bomb victims,[17] but in important psychological ways all of us are "survivors of Hiroshima and, in our imaginations, of future nuclear holocaust" (*DL*, p. 479).

The plight of *Alcestis* evokes many relevant themes of survivor psychology. After Alcestis's death, Admetos and his father, Pheres, engage in a bitter argument in which each accuses the other of cowardice in refusing to sacrifice himself to death—Pheres, so that Admetos might live, and Admetos, so that Alcestis might live. Admetos defends himself by saying that "Dying is different for an old man. I am young" (*Alcestis*, p. 65). Lifton observes that the young adult whose life-projects—modes of symbolic immortality—are not yet established "can . . . be stalked by a double image—that of unlived life and premature death—an image expressing one of the greatest of all human terrors" (*BC*, p. 86). This in turn suggests, regarding *hibakusha* and others in the nuclear "world of survivors," the special horror of the spectre of premature, grotesque and pointless mass death that renders all our life-projects questionable.

While the massive death-immersions of twentieth century holocausts differ radically from that undergone by the survivors of *Alcestis*, there are significant themes connecting these that Lifton highlights. Two intertwined themes that are again relevant to the nuclear world are psychic numbing and death guilt. During his argument with Pheres, Admetos tells him that when he (Pheres) dies, "I shall not lift a hand to bury you; I am dead, for all you care" (Ibid., pp. 63–4). This is not only a sarcastic expression of Admetos's anger, but has multiple significances. One way of taking the statement is as an expression of Admetos's psychic state just after Alcestis dies. He himself is in a sense dead, or deadened by the pain of separation and loss. Lifton, speaking of *hibakusha* who suddenly found themselves in nuclear hell, observes that "Very quickly—sometimes within minutes or even seconds—*hibakusha* began to undergo a process of 'psychic closing-off'; that is, they simply ceased to feel" (*DL*, p. 31) as a way of protecting the self from the overwhelming intensity of horror. Admetos's psychic state is not as extreme as this, but reflects the more enduring and less total form of this self-protective shutting down of the soul that Lifton calls "psychic numbing." The latter term has since been used in a somewhat cliched manner to describe and criticize our collective apathy and anaesthetization in the face of the nuclear and other threats to our survival. Often forgotten is Lifton's key point, made with reference to one woman *hibakusha* whose self-reflection after the bomb experience mirrors Admetos's assertion that "I am dead": "Besides the living me, there is another me which has been dead. . . ."[18] For "psychic closing-off is itself a symbolic form of death" (*DL*, p. 34) in which the self dies to the intolerable reality of the surrounding environment of death in order to protect itself from the impact of the horror, as well as from the immediacy of its own possible more final death. This psychic death is present in the varying degrees of numbing, or the survivor's continuing diminution of the capacity to sense, experience and imagine life. In this vein we can understand Admetos's plight as he tells his dying wife that "I cannot live when you are dead" (Ibid., p. 51) and his exclamation, as she expires, that "This ends my life" (Ibid., p. 55). His son, Eumelos, adds: "With her departing our whole house is dead."

What Lifton refers to as psychic numbing is at once a prenuclear reality and a specific evocation of the place of Hiroshima and the psychology of the nuclear dilemma in general. Because of its cliched application, however, many have become numbed to the phrase "psychic numbing" itself. For this reason, I shall in this text refer instead to "psychic deadening" or "deadness." By this I mean to allude more concretely both to the place of this phenomenon of psychic life in general, and to the memory of the place of Hiroshima out of which it first arose as a psychological concept.

The theme of death guilt is crucial in the *Alcestis*, in which Admetos and his parents survive only at the cost of *Alcestis's* death. Lifton's comments with regard to *hibakusha* and survivors of situations of untimely death in general capture the dilemma of the house of Admetos precisely:

> Inseperable from his death imprint is the survivor's struggle with guilt. Since survival, by definition, involves a sequence in which one person

dies sooner than another, this struggle in turn concerns issues of *comparative death-timing*. Relevant here is what we have spoken of as [the *hibakusha's*] guilt over survival priority, along with the survivor's unconscious sense of an organic social balance which makes him feel that his survival was purchased at the cost of another's.

(*DL*, p. 489; italics in original)

From this standpoint Euripides's drama appears as a striking portrayal of ineluctable and fundamental human dilemmas around mortality and survival; the predicament of the house of Admetos is our own.

The argument between Admetos and Pheres can be seen as involving a mutual avoidance of a profound sense of guilt over having survived, and having *wanted* to survive, while allowing inescapable Death to claim another member of the family. Hence the bitter accusations of father and son, while overtly directed at the other, are finally self-accusations. Their largely unconscious power is fueled by the presence, on stage, of Alcestis's body. (This presence can be seen, from a Jungian perspective, as revealing a death of anima or soul, hence as a portrayal of the psychic deadness afflicting and pervading the house of Admetos. Suggested too is a relation between unacknowledged death guilt and a deadening of anima: unanimated guilt.)

Before this event, the chorus anticipates: "When [Admetos] has lost his royal Alcestis,/His life thereafter will be not worth living" (*Alcestis*, p. 50). This hints at the mutual interplay of psychic deadening and guilt. The survivor is haunted by the sense that, because he or she lived while others died, his or her life "is not worth living." This gives additional impetus for psychic deadening, which figures both as punishment for one's survival, and as a way of avoiding the pain of guilt. The deadening also fuels the survivor's (unconscious) identification with the dead, or what Lifton calls "identification guilt" (this is suggested by Admetos's exclamation, as Alcestis dies, that "This ends my life"). This is especially difficult for survivors of holocaust. Suggests Lifton:

Recalling [Elie] Wiesel's phrase, "In every stiffened corpse I saw myself," we may say that each survivor simultaneously feels himself to be that "stiffened corpse," condemns himself for not being it, and condemns himself even more for feeling relieved that it is the other person's and not his own.

(*DL*, p. 496)

In situations of more ordinary death, the psychic wounds of survivorhood can be healed (if partially) through the "work of mourning," as Freud put it, and through various and creative ways of reasserting and reimagining larger continuity that reserve a place in psychic life for the realities of death. The peril of the nuclear world, and the experience of survivors of past holocausts, present situations in which this giving-place to death in life is rendered far more difficult. This encourages totalistic attempts to allay death anxiety and a strengthening of associated problematic tendencies in our culture's collective psychology. In the survivors' dilemma of *Alcestis*, Death is beaten by the figure of Herakles. Here is a paradigm for our current dilemma: Strong-Armed Ego in a "world of nuclear survivors," or Strong-Armed Ego as a survivor. In survival as imagined by this ego, there is an attempt to beat Death rather than give the latter his place. The effects of this cultural psychic complex during the nuclear era have been evident particularly in periods of heightened Cold War tensions (e.g., the late 1940s through the early 1960s, and again in the late 1970s through mid 1980s). We are likely to witness further recurrences or "survivals" of Strong-Armed Ego's way of viewing the world (a rigid holding on to of outmoded fantasies of strength and winning, together with other themes such as Phaethon-like reliance on technological modes of immortality and life-power, and the nationalism and paranoid preoccupations of the senex). But such occurrences may be avoided (or at least attenuated) through a careful remembering of precisely those images and psychic situations of which Strong-Armed Ego remains unaware, encased in his armor of forgetfulness.

Work with psychological dilemmas of the nuclear world must involve the entwined defensive systems of Strong-Armed Ego and the survivor. Here, as is often the case in psychological work, our approach to these defenses will be somewhat indirect and engaged with an effort to acknowledge their psychic values as well (the place of these and what they are will become evident by the final chapter). A clue to our way of proceeding can be found by returning to the *Alcestis* to observe the play of the third pattern which, along with Strong-Armed Ego and the survivor, characterizes the soul's nuclear situation. This is the place of shades: the House of Death.

To stop with a consideration of the relevance of the *Alcestis* for issues of *human* survival would neglect the soul's inhuman and archetypal depths, along with the disturbing metaphors within Death's house. We noted earlier that in mythic language Apollo's original sojourn at the house of Admetos was a by-form of a journey to Hades. Only by considering the significance of this language of images do we fully apprehend the irony to which Euripides is pointing.

Before the arrival of his father but after Alcestis's death, Admetos greets Herakles, who has just arrived at his house. Herakles, on discovering that there has been a death in the house, makes ready to go, but Admetos insists on receiving him over the objections of the chorus. For he will not allow that "my house shall be called inhospitable" (*Alcestis* p. 60), and rejoins, "Well, some, no doubt, will think me a fool for acting thus,/And criticize me; but my house has yet to learn/Such conduct as to shut the door in a friend's face" (Ibid., p. 61). It will not do to speak only of Admetos's desire for human contact, or his upholding of the human value of hospitality. Euripides's audience would consider the significance of this host's name: *Admetos*, "The Untamed." Consider also who it is that goes by the name of *Polydegmon*, "Host of Many:" it is untamed Death himself;[19] Death who stands behind the persona of Admetos; and Death's house that lies behind the facade of the house of Admetos. No wonder that Admetos tells his father that "I am dead," and that Eumelos, his son, says that "our whole house is dead." When (after this last statement) the chorus intones: "Death is a debt which every one of us must pay" (Ibid., p. 55) and this is echoed in Herakles's initial refusal to stay with Admetos—"Let me go; I shall still be deeply in your debt" (p. 60)—we realize the final irony of the drama. Death does not let Herakles go after all, and Herakles—thinking he had subdued Death—gives Alcestis back into Death's hand.

Death receives Strong-Armed Ego hospitably in spite of the latter's Heraklean fantasies of immortality; we may say that the whole of Euripides's drama, and in some way our own, transpires in the place of shades, Death's precincts. This casts a shadowy light on life's victories and survivals: Death survives, too, and the Fates weaving the twine of our mortality are not in this end deceived. What emerges is the immortality of Death himself; our psychic deadening in the house of the nuclear world deepens so that we realize ourselves as shades. the personae of the House of Hades. Whatever our human struggles for survival, we inhabit a house of shadows; and the realization of this, as Hillman insists, is essential for the therapy of our culture and its killing.

This returns us to the work of remembering. For, as is evident in the great *nekyiai* or underworld journeys of literature (e.g., Odysseus's [*Od.* XI] and Aeneas's [*Aeneid* VI] underworld meetings, and Dante's descent into Hell), the House of Death, where one encounters the shapes of myth and history, is also the House of Memory.

Part II

Images in the House of Memory

3

Sources of Memory

Throughout this work we are concerned with what Gaston Bachelard calls "the synthesis of immemorial and recollected" (*PS*, p. 5), seeking to remember in images of the nuclear world "the inherited possibilities of human imagination as it was from time immemorial" (*CW* 7, par. 101). Having taken an initial look at some possibilities of memory and at the psychological situation of the nuclear world, we return in this Part to traditional images of memory for a more detailed exploration of these. This chapter remains largely within Greek traditions of memory, which provide many of the source-images of the Western memorial psyche, including the art of memory we shall explore in the next chapter. In exploring images of the Greek memorial tradition, we will focus first on its mythic sources and then on certain aspects of Plato's elaboration of memory that have been neglected in most explorations of the latter. The aim of this section is a psychological *anamnesis* or remembering of memory itself, which will serve as a foundation for the more specific work of imaginal memory to be proposed in Part III.

THE HOUSE OF MEMORY

In considering the drama presented in the *Alcestis*, we were led to the place of the House of Death that is also a House of Memory. Concerning Death,

Kerenyi says that "Hades is the most recent form of his name, an older form was Aides, or Aidoneus, and a still older form was Ais, which was preserved only in connection with the word for 'house' or 'palace'. 'The House of Hades' was the Underworld . . ."[1] Death is the place where memory images are housed: hospitably received, given shelter and protection. It is where images can be remembered, where Odysseus, Aeneas and Dante had to go to meet the shades of their relatives, friends and personages of myth and history. And Death too is housed in memory, the memorial imagination.

The *house-motif* also appears in Jung's imagination and Bachelard's reflections on house and memory in *The Poetics of Space* (Bachelard himself cites appearances of the house-image in Jung). Bachelard, "taking the house as a *tool for analysis* of the human soul," observes that "Not only our memories, but the things we have forgotten are 'housed.' Our soul is an abode. And by remembering 'houses' and 'rooms,' we learn to 'abide' within ourselves" (*PS*, p. xxxiii; italics in original).

Bachelard begins by citing a passage where Jung takes as a figure for the structure of the psyche "a building whose upper storey was erected in the nineteenth century" and whose lower stories and cellar turn out to date from the sixteenth and eleventh centuries and Roman period, respectively. "Under the cellar is "a choked-up cave with neolithic tools in the upper layer and remnants of fauna from the same period in the lower layers. That would be the picture of our psychic structure" (*CW* 10, par. 54). This figure is probably based on an often cited dream Jung records in his autobiography and which he says "led me for the first time to the concept of the 'collective unconscious:'"

> I was in a house I did not know, which had two stories. It was "my house." I found myself in the upper story, where there was a kind of salon furnished with fine old pieces in roccoco style. On the walls hung a number of precious old paintings. I wondered that this should be my house, and thought, "Not bad." But then it occurred to me that I did not know what the lower floors looked like. Descending the stairs, I reached the ground floor. There everything was much older, and I realized that this part of the house must date from about the fifteenth or sixteenth century. The furnishings were medieval; the floors were of red brick. Everywhere it was rather dark. I went from one room to another, thinking, "Now I really must explore the whole house." I came upon a heavy door, and opened it. Beyond it, I discovered a stone stairway that led down into the cellar. Descending again, I found myself in a beautifully vaulted room which looked exceedingly ancient. Examining the walls, I discovered layers of brick among the ordinary stone blocks, and chips of brick in the mortar. As soon as I saw this I knew that the walls dated from Roman times. My

interest by now was intense. I looked more closely at the floor. It was of stone slabs, and in one of these I discovered a ring. When I pulled it, the stone slab lifted, and again I saw a stairway of narrow stone steps leading down into the depths. These, too, I descended, and entered a low cave cut into the rock. Thick dust lay on the floor, and in the dust were scattered bones and broken pottery, like remains of a primitive culture. I discovered two human skulls, obviously very old and half disintegrated.

Jung told the dream to Freud but refused his hint "that secret death-wishes were concealed in the dream." But to appease Freud and avoid conflict, Jung answered the former's query about whose the two skulls might be by naming "My wife and sister-in-law." This was a lie, for "I was newly married at the time and knew perfectly that there was nothing within myself that pointed to such wishes." In Jung's own view the skulls and other remains on the cave-floor disclosed "the world of the primitive man within myself" (*MDR*, pp. 158–60).

But this dream-house, which became for Jung "a guiding image," *does* incorporate "secret death wishes" and there is a psychic truth within Jung's lie that the skulls were those of his wife and sister-in-law. For the dream's deepest imagery evokes the Greek or proto-Hellenic imagination of the house that is Death's place, picturing a house of the memorial psyche that is in its deepest sense a house of Death. In the *Alcestis*, the wife of Admetos becomes (like Persephone) Death's bride, reflecting the universal awareness of myth and rite that being married involves a dying as well as a vital continuity. Is Jung's wife also Death's bride? More generally, this house reflects the *myth of Jung's death*, expressed too in what Jung remembers as an early "Unconscious suicidal urge or . . . a fatal resistance to life in this world" (*MDR*, p. 9), and in his later "confrontation with the unconscious" which, says Jung, "corresponds to the mythic land of the dead, the land of the ancestors" (*MDR*, p. 191). And the dream as guiding image is entirely classical, evoking Hermes Psychopompos, the Guide of Souls to the Underworld.

This does not contradict but rather qualifies Jung's experience of the dream as revelation of the archaic psyche and its primordial house, the cave. Remember that Albert Goldbarth's vision of *History as Horse Light* leads to a similar place. The crucial point is the psychological homology, at the deepest foundational level, of House and Hades. From the first, to house memories means to remember the place of Death.

The theme of the house will appear in various ways throughout our explorations of memory and our dwelling-place, the nuclear world. A few further features of house-images of memory are worth noting here. "If I were asked," says Bachelard, "to name the chief benefit of the house, I should say: the house shelters daydreaming, the house protects the dreamer, the house allows one to

dream in peace" (*PS*, p. 6). The house is "bosom" and "cradle," Mother as well
as Death (and the mother of images remembered: images of life that in some
way have "died"). And the house gives precise imaginal shape and location to
memory:

> thanks to the house, a great many of our memories are housed, and if
> the house is a bit elaborate, if it has a cellar and garret, nooks and cor-
> ridors, our memories have refuges that are all the more clearly de-
> lineated. A psychoanalyst should, therefore, turn his attention to this
> simple localization of our memories.
>
> (*PS*, p. 8)

The house of imagination is not confined to that of physical reality; "the
real houses of memory, the houses to which we return in dreams, the houses that
are rich in unalterable onerism, do not readily lend themselves to description [;]
. . . the oneiric house," says Bachelard, "must retain its shadows" (*PS*, p. 13).
Again, Hades is present; evoked here are the dreamlike riches of his house sig-
nified by his epithet, *Plouton* ("Wealth"; see *DU*, p. 28), which yet retain their
shadows. And these "houses that were lost forever continue to live on in us . . .
they insist in us in order to live again, as though they expected us to give them
a supplement of living. . . . How suddenly our memories assume a living possibility of being" (*PS*, p. 56)!
    Another feature of the house emerges in a reminiscence of Loren Eiseley:
"As a boy I once rolled dice in an empty house, playing against myself. I sup-
pose I was afraid. It was twilight, and I forget who won. I was too young to have
known that the old abandoned house in which I played was the universe."[2] But
the house indeed "is our first universe, a real cosmos in every sense of the word"
(*PS*, p. 4), an *imago mundi*, as the history of the religious imagination reveals.[3]
In ways that will become evident throughout this book, *the house of memory is
finally the world, and memory the house of the world*. It is the Renaissance practitioners of the art of memory who explicitly develop the project of placing the
entire world and its various realms in memory, of remembering the world. And
it will become apparent for us that remembering the house of nuclear death is a
way of remembering once more the world, dwelling in it as a house.

MEMORY AND HER FAMILY

The *Homeric Hymn to Hermes* tells how the God, still a child, was ordered
by Zeus to relinquish cattle he had stolen from his half-brother, Apollo. Hermes
charms Apollo by playing his lyre (later given to Apollo), singing of the Gods
and how they came to be.

> And the first of the gods
> that he commemorated [*egerairen*] with his lyre
> was Mnemosyne, Mother of Muses,
> for the son of Maia
> was a follower of hers.[4]

Following Hermes in turn, we shall commemorate Mnemosyne, the Goddess Memory, together with some of her family—her sister, Lethe or "Forgetfulness," her daughters, and the waters (springs or rivers) associated with these. This family reveals another picture of primary sources of memory, or memory itself as a primary source.

First, it is important to reflect upon what this commemorative act itself implies. Because we are following Hermes, Guide of Souls to Hades, our commemorating moves in the direction of death. This movement is implicit in commemoration generally, which evokes the presence of the dead in its intensity of remembrance. The Greek verb *gerairein*, rendered by Charles Boer as "to commemorate," means more specifically "to honor" or "to reward with a gift," with particular reference to the Elders (*hoi geraiteroi*) and Ancestors. To honor and to reward with a gift are basic to the intensity of commemoration and its acknowledgement of the place of the dead. We will acknowledge Memory's place of honor in the ancestral imagination, rewarding the Goddess with the gift of concentrated, careful remembrance. We will do likewise in the commemoration of images associated with the place of Hiroshima.

The present commemoration begins with Hesiod's *Theogony*, where the poet begins by invoking the Muses. These daughters of Memory inspire the poet to tell how the Gods and world come into being. The Muses inspire the poet because, as Gregory Nagy stresses, "they have the power to put his mind or consciousness in touch with places and times other than his own in order to witness" the fundamental memory-making events of those places and times (in this case, the *Theogony*).[5] The witnessing of the *Theogony*, its places and times, begins with the inspiring power spawned by Memory. Memory is this world's grandmother; it is through her that the Gods and Goddesses—the personified powers of the world—are forever recreated in the retelling and remembering of myth and poetry. For the Muses "reveal what is and what will be and what was before" (*Theog.* 38).[6]

Memory (together with her family) forms the foundation of the world—including the world of memory. In meeting this family, we discover foundational powers of memory that will bear in important ways on the practice and perspective of imaginal memory in our time. Exploring this Greek mythic foundation is a way of reflecting on questions of considerable contemporary relevance: the role of truths and falsities in memory, relations between the imagination of myth and that of history, remembering and forgetting, life and death, time and world.

Imagine the setting in which the Muses first appear, in the countryside of Boeotia on

> Helikon, a mountain high and holy,
> as they dance around some spring's dark water of soft feet
> and around the sacred altar of the mighty son of Kronos.
> Having washed their tender bodies in the stream of the Permessos
> or the spring called Hippokrene or the holy brook Olmeios,
> on the topmost part of Helikon they hold their circling dances.
>
> (Ibid., 1–7)

To gain a more vivid sense of this image, the reader might pause to recall whatever images of mountain springs come to mind: their setting, their murmuring, their emotional resonance. A setting not unlike the one remembered may have been the occasion for the springing-forth of Hesiod's memory and imagination.

There are, as Hesiod envisions it, inspiring feminine beings mothered by Memory who dance in mountainous heights, nearest to their Olympian father and by his altar. The dance of the Muses has its own elevation in holiness, is itself a form of elevation, in which the tellers and hearers of the Gods' tales share, forgetting for a while life's usual cares. Yet there are in these heightened realms connections to the depths of Hades. This connection is through water, through the Muses' nature as spring-Goddesses. The murmurings and musings of springs reveal, says Kerenyi, "the experience of 'welling up' recollection;" for "water that springs forth . . . is a primal image of the origin of life and—of memory" ("ML," p. 122). There are springs and rivers of death as well, such as Acheron or Styx, the River Hate (how well we remember what we hate). We find postclassical depictions of springs of Memory and Forgetfulness at the threshold of the House of Hades and in an account of a late oracular ritual. We will return to these springs below. . . .

Truths and Lies of the Muses

The Muses tell Hesiod that "we know how to tell numerous/lies which seem to be truthful, but whenever we wish/we know how to speak the full truth" (*Theog.*, 27–8).

Memory is mother to both truths and falsehoods. This is the mythic source of our immemorial questions about the truths and falsities of memory. How far dare we trust our memories? Plato saw memory, in one aspect, as the way toward knowledge of ultimate truths—the Ideas—but also recognized that memory could house both true and false opinions.[7] Later, Freud found in his patients' recollections "numerous lies which seemed to be truthful . . ." Though historically untrue, these memorial fantasies yet pictured psychic truths: a crucial source of depth-psychological thought. For Freud's realization

> that the stories he was being told were psychological happenings dressed as history and experienced as remembered events was the first recognition in modern psychology of psychic reality independent of other realities. It was, further, a recognition of the independence of memory from history and history from memory. There is history that is not remembered—forgetting, distortion, denial, repressing; there is also memory that is not historical—screen memories, confabulations, and those tales told him of early sexual trauma and primal scenes that had not occurred in the literal historical past.[8]

The psychic reality of memory is duplicitous. Its lies tell their own true stories, and we are deceived if we take truth and falsity in memory only literally and empirically.

If history and memory are independent, they are still in the same psychological family, history-telling (and making) being attributed to Memory's daughter, Kleio.[9] Memory always reveals psychological aspects of, and values in, history (both in the latter's truths and its falsifications). We will witness this displaying of the psyche in vivid precision when we recall and work with historical memories of Hiroshima and Nagasaki. Here it is most important to notice the essential language in which memory reveals the psyche of history: the language of myth. This truth was seen by Euhemeros: historical events and persons are or become *personae* of the Gods, faces of a divine drama. Euhemeros falsified this insight by literalizing it, reducing the figures of the Gods to a presumed origin in historical figures who are retrospectively divinized. But he was right to say that history becomes myth in memory.

Remembering and Forgetting

We have already noticed a close relation between Memory and Forgetfulness. Nationalistic remembering, with its egoism of victimization, we saw (chapter 1) to be also a way of forgetting, and this in turn led to suggestions of a way of forgetting egoistic concerns given with mythic and religious remembrance. Traditional imaginings of Memory and Forgetfulness reveal nuances of this archetypal tandem of remembering and forgetting that will resurface in our work with nuclear images.[10]

We usually imagine memory to be largely under the control of the conscious will or ego. While the deeper reaches of memory give us much cause to doubt this, the role of memory in the formation of individual and collective senses of identity as well as enduring relationships is foundational in human existence (and that of much of the nonhuman world as well). Given this fundamental place of memory, the unwanted appearance of Memory's sister Lethe can provoke a fundamental anxiety, the dread of utter forgetfulness: separation, disintegration, death.

It is important to differentiate between the notion that memory is under the control of the ego or habitual personality, and the place of memory as ontological foundation of the experience of identity, continuity and relationship. Memory in this foundational sense functions in a number of ways outside of one's immediate conscious awareness. (For important examples in addition to the usually-framed psychological concept of unconscious memory, see Edward Casey's investigation of *body* and *place* memory [*R*, chs. VIII and IX].) There *is* a necessary ego-involvement and conscious capacity of control here. But to assume that *primary* control of memory resides in the ego greatly limits its scope, together with one's capacity imagine the place of memory in psychological life.

Given the conflation between the notions of memory as necessary capacity of the will and as largely under the latter's control, it was inevitable that awareness of the psyche outside the ego would emerge, as in the early investigations of Freud and Jung, through the exploration of disturbances in (the ego's) capacity to remember. Forgetting thus became the way toward a deeper remembering. Further exploration of the unfolding of the ancient Greek imagination of memory and forgetting reveals a mythic foundation for the awareness of sources of memory and forgetfulness alien to the ego's habitual identity as well as beyond its control.

Hesiod sings of the Muses' "circling dance" and their origin when Mnemosyne, "queen of the slopes of Eleuther," mingled in love with Zeus and "bore these/powers that make evils forgotten and bring a cessation to sorrows" (*Theog.* 53–5). Notice that his allusion to the powers of forgetting in the family of Memory follows immediately upon the identification of Memory herself as a queen (*medeousa*, She Who Rules). Such acknowledgement from Hesiod, who is constantly stressing the capacity of the Olympians, reveals who rules the power of memory we ordinarily place in the ego.

On certain occasions when our attempts to remember are frustrated, this forgetting may be Memory reasserting sovereignty, an intimation of an altogether different realm of memory. Close attention to one's fantasies at such a time of forgetting may provide clues to what sort of remembering may be going on in the psyche. Forgetting in this way becomes one of the springs of psychological exploration. "By following Lethe," says Hillman of Freud and Jung, "they were led into the underworld" (*DU*, p. 154). There is a death of ego involved here (hence anxiety over forgetting is a form of death anxiety). David

Miller ingeniously illustrates this with reference to the etymology of the word "forget," which comes "from the Indo-European root, *ghed-*, meaning 'to hold,' 'to grasp,' 'to take,' 'to steal,' or 'to seize.'"[11] This suggests ego fantasies of "grasping, seizing and taking." And (the prefix for- means "omission") "'Forgetting,' then would express the experience of letting-go, a for-getting of the getting, the grasping, and the seizing." In short, "'forgetting' names the times when ego-perspective dies."

The death of ego's acquisitiveness allows us to remember Forgetfulness in its archetypal aspect.[12] Hillman's statement that "By following Lethe they were led into the underworld" echoes an episode in the journey of Aeneas to the entrance of Hades. In it, Death's brother, Sleep, visits the ship's helmsman, Palinurus, shaking over him "a bough that drips with Lethe's dew" (*Aen.* V. 1129),[13] so that he falls overboard. Lethe is now "the water of death;" forgetfulness happens on the way toward remembering Death and the dead. When Aeneas has descended into Hades and met his father, Anchises, he sees nearby the river of Lethe flowing through the Groves of Blessedness or home of heroic souls: near Lethe he meets his most poignant memory. And his father, like Teiresias during the *nekyia* of Odysseus, reveals hidden or secret knowledge. Hiddenness, meaning that which is concealed in life, and the final hiddenness of death, is the root meaning of Lethe ("ML," p. 121)[14] Lethe as well as Mnemosyne has hidden sources or springs in those "lost houses" where ancestral characters dwell.

In the world of Hesiod, there is no separate river or spring of Lethe; the waters of remembering and forgetting flow together. But even there they flow on the border of life and death:

So if someone is stricken with grief of a recent bereavement
and is torturing his heart with mourning, then if some singer
serving the Muses sings of past glory and heroes of old and
tells of the blessed immortals who have their homes on Olympos,
swiftly the grief-stricken one is forgetful and remembers
none of his sorrow: quickly the gifts of the Muses divert him
(Theog. 89–103)

The daughters of Memory, "power that make evils forgotten," make the bereaved remember as he forgets. He remembers the ancient heroes and the Gods. The singer of the Muses is, in the original text, their *therapōn* or servant. In this setting, forgetting mortal sorrows is a form of mythic remembrance with a therapeutic value for the bereaved; but also a way of serving the myth-making powers of memory. Through these powers, a world is renewed, a theogony repeated.

The primary flowing-together of the streams of remembering and forgetting through Hesiod's imagination splits apart, in later images, into separate springs of Mnemosyne and Lethe. The latter is then regarded in largely negative terms: by Plato as Ameles or Un-Care, and later by the Christian Platonist, Augustine, who (echoing the notion of evil as a privation of good [*a privatio boni*]) asks, "what is forgetfulness, but the privation of memory" (*Confessions* X. xvi. 24)? This splitting-apart has the value of disclosing different aspects of remembering and forgetting which, as we saw in chapter 1, help us to reflect on psychological undercurrents in the nuclear world.[15]

The relation of remembering and forgetting remains ambiguous and complex. At times the two streams merge and memory and forgetfulness "flow" into each other; at other times the streams, though near each other, appear sharply distinguished or opposed. There is value in each perspective through which we imagine remembering and forgetting; each reflects a different image of life and death, the death in life, the life in death.

There is an image of initiation through memory that saves the ambiguous relation of the two streams as it distinguishes them. It is from Pausanias, who in his travels through Boeotia (second century B.C.E.) describes an oracular sanctuary near the town of Lebadeia, dedicated to the hero, Trophonios (*Description of Greece* 9. 39).[16] Pausanias, who inquired of Trophonios himself, relates that the inquirer must go through a series of purifications and sacrifices. Then, just prior to being taken to the oracular cave, he must drink from the two springs "as near as possible to each other," the waters of Lethe and Mnemosyne. In this way he is able to forget distracting events of the past and of daily life, and to remember the visions he will be given in the cave. Following the visionary experience, which Pausanias describes as being quite frightening, the inquirer is seated on the throne of Mnemosyne where he relates what he has seen and heard.

Here Lethe reappears in its archaic role as the water that initiates one into a deeper or archetypal remembrance as more surface concerns are forgotten for a while. But Mnemosyne takes on a more frightening aspect that the predominantly "positive" one Kerenyi says she plays in the older religion ("*ML*," p. 130). Memorial descents can take us to places of terror, as Odysseus, Aeneas and Dante recall for us. And Trophonios, the "Nourisher," is also an epithet of Death. What hidden nourishment does soul find in terror and in memorial descents into the House of Death?

What the Muses Reveal

The remembering of oracular visions at Trophonios hints as an aspect of memory that is vital for our nuclear and other concerns for the future, but forgotten in the conventional and rational definition of memory as the recall of past experience. If the visions are taken literally, as prophecies, then this conventional definition is ultimately contradicted, for the rememberer recalls not only his past experience of the visions, but what is actually yet to come. "Remembering the future,"[17] however, is also a kind of convention. During their descents into the house of memory, Odysseus, Aeneas and Dante also learn of future events. These episodes can be considered as elaborations of memory's archaic imagination which, as noted in chapter 1, implicates and extends in the direction of, future possibilities.

While I am not concerned here with literal prophecies, such instances of "remembering the future" must be seen in their phenomenological distinctness. In this form of memory, images of the possible and/or anticipated future are made present in the "past" of remembering. This *presence* of images of the future is tightly bound to images of memory in two related ways. First, their relationship is ontologically given: images of the future can endure *only* through being remembered in imagination (this may or may not be true for images of the past and present, which in principle can be perceptually verified). Without memory, continuity in the imagination of the future is impossible. (There could be no continuity of concern about a possible nuclear holocaust without a future present in memory.) Second, this relationship is psychologically inevitable: any images of the future will have a psychological resonance with the past and present.

Conversely, images of the past and present inevitably point to future possibilities. Remember T. S. Elliot's opening lines in *Burnt Norton*: "Time present and time past/Are both perhaps present in time future,/And time future contained in time past."[18] If we recall and explore childhood memories, as in psychoanalysis, we see that these fantasies of the past speak too of what is and will be in our lives (including transformative possibilities), for we are remembering foundational complexes. So too with collective memorial fantasies, which "present" the cultural psyche and its future possibilities. When we address remembrances of Hiroshima and Nagasaki, we will discover ways in which these images tell not only of the past but also of the present and (the imaginal presence of) the future.

It is now evident that Hesiod's assertion that the daughters of Memory can "reveal what is and what will be and what was before" (*Theog*. 38) is relevant in very precise ways to the present and future.

Echoes and Arts of the Muses

Memory is also mother of the artistic and aesthetic qualities associated with her daughters. This suggests a deep-going connection between memory and the forms of aesthetic imagination and sensitivity. Through memory we are given not only artistic talents and works, but the potential for an acutely perceptive imagining of the *world itself* as artistic, as primary place of soul and its aesthetic life.[19] There is an art inherent in remembered images that echoes—and is the echo of—the world. The world resounds in us, echoing in the memory of the imagination. Listen to Hesiod's description of the song of the Muses:

> A single sweet tone melodiously, easily
> flows from their lips, and the house of their father
> Zeus the Lord Thunderer shimmers with joy at the
> piercing-sweet sound of their voices everywhere
> scattered: echoes roll over the peaks of snowy
> Olympos and through the homes of the gods. They
> with voices immortal first in their song offer
> praise to the holy race of the gods from the
> beginning . . .
>
> (*Theog.* 39–44)

We hear in the voices of the Muses another figure: the nymph, Echo, who is "everywhere scattered:" anima, soul, reflected in all things, all memories, all faces of the world.

Echo is an important person in the family of Memory and the memories born within images. As Bachelard says of the "poetic image": "It is not an echo of the past. On the contrary: through the brilliance of an image, the distant past resounds with echoes, and it is hard to know at what depth these echoes will reverberate and die away" (*PS*, p. xii). And "The old house, for those who know how to listen, is a sort of geometry of echoes. The voices of the past do not sound the same in the big room as in the little bed chamber, and calls on the stairs have yet another sound" (*PS*, p. 60). Aesthetic attention to memory means to give an ear to the echoes of soul resonating in the houses of images which are "the homes of the gods." In the words of T. S. Eliot:

> Footfalls echo in the memory
> Down the passage which we did not take
> Towards the door we never opened
> Into the rose-garden. My words echo
> Thus, in your mind.[20]

The Muses' song is one of original wonder, and returns this wonder to us in memory as the mother of primary aesthetic response as well as actual artistic creation. In this vein Hillman speaks of "*aisthesis*" as meaning "at root a breathing in or taking in of the world, the gasp, 'aha,' the 'uh' of the breath in wonder, shock, amazement, an aesthetic response to the image (*eidolon*) pesented."[21] Kleio is originally not so much the celebrator of fame and history in the unsual sense, but of this primary wonder of the world in which the many Gods make their homes. The *remembering of the world's wonder* will be the larger context in which the practice of imaginal memory explored in Part III takes place.

Memory becomes, in the train of the Muses, a celebration of the world's ever-present origins: "what is and what will be and what was before." It is in this polytheistic world, with echoes of soul scattered everywhere, that Memory and her family have their sources.

PLATO'S *PHAEDRUS*: THE LOVE OF PLACE AND POLYTHEISM

A look at Plato's dialogue, the *Phaedrus*, reveals important aspects of memory rarely treated in discussion of Platonic remembrance. In the *Phaedrus* memory is evoked by a *love for a particular place* in the context of the *polytheistic world* just mentioned. Love, Eros, is the God through whom the dialogue's characters, Socrates and Phaedrus, experience both the powers of the place in which *Phaedrus* is set, and the powers of the Gods revealed in the soul's memory of the Pre-existent. Exploring the place of the *Phaedrus* and the many divine figures there revealed, we discern powers basic to imaginal memory, both practiced as it was in earlier times and as proposed in Part III.

The Place-Setting

The dialogue begins when Socrates and Phaedrus meet one summer morning, shortly before noon. Phaedrus has heard a speech by the orator, Lysias, about why a handsome boy should submit to a sexual relationship with a man who does not love him (the lover, being mad, cannot look after his partner in a rational manner as can the non-lover). Phaedrus, carrying a copy of Lysias's speech, wishes to read it to Socrates (in fact, he wants to be able to repeat it from memory). Socrates obliges, and the two go for a walk outside the walls of Athens, by the Ilissos River: an unusual setting for a Socratic dialogue. Phaedrus suggests they head toward a certain resting-spot, by the stream under a tall plane tree. As they walk toward this place, Phaedrus is reminded of a myth telling how Boreas, the North Wind, seized the Maiden, Oreithyia, nearby (*Phaed.* 229Bff).

This myth about the rape of a maiden figures as a foreshadowing of Socrates's own later speech about Love, which acknowledges the power and necessity of this God, and his manifestation in the soul's memory that he seizes with his madness. The mythic image of a love maddened beyond all bounds is an ironic contrast to the rational sophistry of Lysias's speech with which Phaedrus is so taken. Notice, too, the contrast between Phaedrus's superficial and ego-bound desire to remember the speech and the spontaneous surfacing of a deeper memory of myth.

Most crucial is the way this memory of myth that anticipates Socrates's myth of memory is evoked by and implicates the psychic history, or inhabiting powers, of a particular place. In the form of the image of Boreas raping Oreithyia, these inhabiting powers indicate deep connections between the soul's seizure by Love, death and that which the soul remembers. (What the soul remembers is in another world: this Plato signifies by reference to a myth that is a by-form of that of Hades seizing Persephone and taking her to his house.)

When Socrates and Phaedrus reach their resting-place, Socrates shows his aesthetic responsiveness to its sensuous and numinous particularities:

> Upon my word, a delightful resting-place, with this tall, spreading plane, and a lovely shade from the high branches of the agnus: now that it's in full flower, it will make the place ever so fragrant. And what a lovely stream under the plane-tree, and how cool to the feet! Judging by the statuettes and images I should say it's consecrated to Achelous and some of the Nymphs: and the shrill summary of the cicada-choir! . . .

$$(230B–C)^{22}$$

Achelous, the river-God, appears on vases with bull's horns and a serpentine body, struggling with Herakles. He is said to be father of the Sirens, whose lovely voices lead men in their ships to their death on jagged rocks (see Odysseus's encounter with them, *Od.* XII. 184ff). They are akin both to nymphs and (through their beautiful song) to the Muses. Socrates, after his hymn to Love, tells a story that cicadas were once men who lived before the birth of the Muses. When the Muses were born, some of the men so delighted in their gift of song that, forgetting eating and drinking, they finally died (*Phaed.* 259B–D).

These related images—Achelous, the nymphs and the Muses—thus return us once more to the dialogue's major themes of the soul's movement toward death through seizure by irrational eros and of the relation between this death and the power of memory.

It is the *sense of place*, inherent in the setting of the *Phaedrus*, that evokes these powers, which are themselves remembered images. At the dialogue's conclusion, Socrates will offer a prayer "to the divinities here" (279B). At the foundation of the *Phaedrus* and its visioning of memory, is what we can call an "erotic sensitivity" to a particular place and its inherent memory-powers, and a memory sensitive to the erotic possibilities of the place, its movements of soul toward death. Here is an original example of what Bachelard refers to as to-pophilia, literally "love of place" (*PS*, p. xxxi).[23]

The Place of Time

Part of the power of the place in which the *Phaedrus* is set is the time, noon. Socrates is about to leave the resting-spot, having given the first of two speeches in reply to that of Lysias. Phaedrus tries to persuade him to stay and say more: "Don't you realize that it's just about the hour of 'scorching noon-day', as the phrase goes" (242A)? Socrates is persuaded, however, not by Phaedrus, but by Eros himself, in the form of Socrates's divine "sign" or *daimonion*, which keeps him from leaving until he has given a fitting account of the God (Socrates's first speech erred by confusing Love's divine power with merely human passion).

The time of noon has a definite place in this, being itself laden with mythic memory. Noon, the time of greatest heat—especially in the middle of a Mediterranean summer—is a sleepy, spooky time; an in-between time (like midnight) when Gods, ghosts and other Powers may be most active. It is at this time (Ovid, *Metamorphoses* 3. 143ff) that Aktaion, wandering off in the woods, spies Artemis and her nymphs bathing; due to the Goddess he grows staghorns and is torn apart by his own hunting dogs. More, the goat-God Pan—to whom Socrates will pray at the conclusion of the dialogue as one of the divinities inhabiting this place—is said to haunt the hour of noon; if awakened from his noontime rest, the God will send the mad terror for which he is known.[24]

Displayed in this moment of myth is what we may call the "place of time." Memory is indeed time-laden, as Aristotle said, but not in the sense of an empirical or linear past only. Nor is it adequate to speak here of the cyclical time of the Eternal Return; we must imagine more precisely.[25] The point is that *time is "placed" in memory*, given a particular location. We acknowledge this when, in frustration, we say we "can't place" the occurrence of some event in time. Memory, as revealed in the *Phaedrus*, is inherently and deeply related to the particularities of place; the times we remember are set in place-images. And place, conversely, is always "timed"—evokes personal, historical and/or mythic "times-when" (in the *Phaedrus*, for instance, the time when Boreas seized Oreithyia).

Moving through the house of memory we recall such "times-when," each of which has its place, housed in memory. In the *Phaedrus*, time is given a place as the dialogue is timed; and time evokes memories of places and powers (ultimately, for Plato, of the soul's home in the eternal place above heaven [*huperouranios topos*; 247C]).

The immediate relevance of the place of time will be evident when we return, in Part III, to the place of the time "Hiroshima."

The Memories of the Gods

After the noontime intervention, Socrates is prepared to give his second speech in honor of the God, Eros (243E–257B). Socrates begins by describing certain forms of madness that, far from being merely human ailments, come from the Gods (one of these is possession by the Muses [245A]). In fact, it is through madness (*dia manias*) that the greatest of gifts come to us.[26] Next, Socrates defines soul as immortal because autonomous or self-moving (245C–246A). After this prelude, he describes the well-known image of the chariot of the soul with its pilot and two horses—one restrained and one impulsively passionate. If the impulsive horse can be held in check, the soul is able, on the high feast day of the Gods, to rise with these to the realm beyond heaven. The soul whose charioteer cannot control the impulsive horse is, however, dragged down, sinking into forgetfulness and earthly life. The task in this life is then to make the right use of remembering, through which the soul can be reinitiated into divine mystery and truth.

Most germaine for the practice of imaginal memory is the polytheistic form this remembering takes. It begins when the soul falls in love with "a godlike face or bodily form that truly expresses beauty," (251A) and recalls the lover to his celestial origins and his journey with a particular God, of whom the human face is a likeness. The memory through which Eros seizes the lover is thus formed after the fashion of the God in whose train the soul followed in the world above. Those who followed Ares will, if they believe themselves to be wronged by their beloved, "shed blood" (252C) and be ready to kill both themselves and their partners. Love can lead to war (as we know from Aphrodite's affair with Ares, and the Trojan War, which started with the seizure of Helen), and a relationship become a vessel of murderous rage. Again, if one was a follower of Zeus, the emphasis will be on dignity and the search for wisdom. It is the same with the other Gods; *memory thus imagined is fundamentally polytheistic*, and involves what we most deeply love.

Maurice Halbwachs, a French sociologist who studied the social basis of memory, echoes this imagining of memory (although from a quite different vantage-point). Halbwachs asserts that memory is at bottom collective, a function of one's social interactions beginning with birth. This holds true even when one is remembering by oneself:

> Our memories remain collective, . . . and are recalled to us through others even though only we were participants in the events or saw the things concerned. In reality, we are never alone. Other men need not be physically present, since *we always carry with us and in us a number of distinct persons.*[27]

These "distinct persons," as well as being representations of actual others (in Halbwachs's sociological perspective) and embodiments of the psychological qualities of our relationships with these others (as in the perspective of psychoanalytic "object-relations" theories), are *imaginal* presences, characters bodying forth the soul's deepest memories.

Halbwachs observes that, for instance, on his first visit to London he was reminded of Dickens's novels; thus when he took a walk it was "with Dickens." It is true that he was not alone on his walk, but he errs in that it is not Dickens *per se* who goes with him, but an *image* of Dickens intimately related to the novels Halbwachs also remembers. More, the *place* of London is a power here; its features remind Halbwachs of places and images from Dickens's novels. Halbwachs also carries with himself the fictive characters of the novels, not only their historical or actual author. The *imaginal* character of persons and places of various sorts will be a key theme in our exploration of the place of Hiroshima.

Among these "distinct persons" who bear within themselves memory-traces of the Gods or archetypal powers we may, moreover, count the remembering ego. This is also implied by the vision of the *Phaedrus*: lovers, as they seek wisdom,

> follow up the trace within themselves of the nature of their own god [and] their task is made easier, inasmuch as they are constrained to fix their gaze upon him; and reaching out after him in memory they are possessed by him, and from him they take their ways and manners of life, in so far as a man can partake of a god.
>
> (252E–253A)

This suggests a question: when "I" am remembering someone, some place or image, *who* in me is doing the remembering? Because polytheistic memory is polycentric, a radical de-centering of the ego is implied here. Thus, when traveling down streets reminding me of my grandparents' neighborhood where they lived when I was a child, that child stirs within, remembering as I remember. Too, my grandparents, now dead, come to life in this remembering, their ghosts in me remembering what was. I am not alone; many characters are with me, remembering through me. These characters make present crucial relationships, ways of being with others. They are also archetypal powers: the Child and the Ancestors, whose reality is also felt through the deep love (together with a myriad of other emotions) that stirs here.

The powers of place envisioned by the *Phaedrus* thus disclose a polytheistic, many-centered memory. This is basic to the remembering of the many characters we shall meet in the place of Hiroshima.

We have found a wealth of source-images housed in the Greek tradition of memory, springing from the waters of Mnemosyne and her family. These memory images are echoes disclosing the places of soul in the world, witnessing the immanence of Gods in place-images and their resonance within the many families of our memories.

This wealth forms the foundation of the places and images, the "spacious palaces" (Augustine, *Confessions* X. vii. 12) of the art of memory.

4

Places and Images:
The Art of Memory

In *The Memory Palace of Matteo Ricci*, Jonathan Spence describes a "reception hall" of a vast imaginal palace housing the memory images of the life and historical experience of Ricci, a Jesuit missionary to China in the sixteenth and seventeenth centuries.[1] Entering this reception hall—"a fairly large formal space supported by pillars"—one finds in the corner immediately to the right a composite image: two warriors locked in combat. Ricci, learning Chinese and seeking to interest his hosts in his rigorous memory training as part of his missionary effort, composed this image with reference to the Chinese ideograph for "war."[2] When divided in a certain manner, this ideograph yields two other characters, one denoting a spear and the other "with a sense of 'to stop' or 'to prevent.'" This evokes a tradition in which Chinese scholars have seen, "buried inside the word for war, the possibilities, however frail, of peace."

The action of war is stopped, arrested yet also preserved in the entrance to Ricci's Memory Palace: "A warrior, the very picture of martial vigor, holds a spear, poised to strike at his enemy; that second warrior grasps the first by the wrist, striving to stop the blow from falling." The two figures stay as they are in the place of memory. When the need arises, Ricci can visit them and remember information he has previously associated with the image, for its vivid and dramatic character will evoke the memory.

In the art of memory, such striking and dramatic images, housed in various and distinct memory places, serve to keep memory alive, while memory serves the life of images, or the soul's life (and, we shall see, its dying). The art of memory—our main source is Frances Yates's book of that title—is a set of methods by which classical speakers, and oral storytellers before them, remembered information and ordered the imagination, finding places for imagination in memory, and memory in places imagined.[3]

James Hillman calls attention to the psychological importance of the art of memory, recognizing it, together with alchemy, as a "complex [method] of soul making" (*DU*, p. 128).[4] The art of memory is itself a form of alchemy, a work against nature (*opus contra naturam*) in which life's basic experiences and information are rendered into metaphoric images revealing the complexities (and complexes) of the soul. Remember the warriors at the entrance to Ricci's Memory Palace. They reflect a great deal of historical experience of war (in both Europe and China), and suggest Ricci's own ambivalence about war: his respect for its martial art and his horror of its violence.[5] By holding this image in memory—not only visualizing it but also sensing the conflicting bodily positions and movements, thoughts and emotions of the two warriors, we begin to realize that this ambivalence is not Ricci's alone. The "stopping" of war in this image, with its arresting power, gives us pause as we reflect upon the history of military conflict and of conflict about the military. The image now is a complex metaphor, has a deep resonance: this is soul in the making.

The art of memory envisions not only striking but often bizarre and disfigured or otherwise "unnaturally" pathologized images because these are recognized as having the most power to move the soul, to stir memory. Hillman stresses the role of the art in giving place to pathologized images, and these places and images reveal the order of archetypal configurations: the many Gods in psychic complexes. In Ricci's warrior image, for instance, we see Mars in action.

With Yates's historical exploration of the art of memory and the perspectives of archetypal psychology as foundations, we can develop the imaginal sense needed as individual and collective memories associated with the place of Hiroshima (in chapters 5 and 6) are given place and realized as metaphor and image. With this in mind, I shall in this chapter review the foundation and development of the art of memory, reflecting on those aspects of its psychological nature that are of greatest importance for the practice of imaginal memory in general and vis-a-vis the nuclear era in particular. Certain features of the memory tradition will then be considered in greater detail: memory and the "art" of imagination; primary themes of the memorial imagination as displayed in images of the earliest known memory treatise; and the special relation between the art of memory and melancholy. (The interested reader will find in Appendix B a somewhat more involved discussion concerning the relation between memory and the art of rhetoric.) So that the reader may keep his or her bearing in the somewhat bewildering wealth of imagination explored here, the chapter concludes by briefly reviewing the key features of the art of remembering images and comparing this practice to Jung's method of "active imagination." In certain ways the two methods are closely parallel, but we will discover essential differences that will guide us through the developing work of imaginal memory in Part III.

For a more detailed resume of the art of memory, the reader is enthusiastically referred to Yates's book. For here is—in a phrase frequently used by the old authors—a treasure-house of images. In the House of Memory we find many mansions.

THE ART OF MEMORY: MYTH AND HISTORY

Growing out of mythopoetic imagining and the later rhetoric traditions, the art of memory goes through various transformations that Yates traces through the rationalistic philosophical systems of the seventeenth century. Before tracing its development and features, returning to its mythic foundation will prove revealing.

This is embodied in a story told by Cicero, who I follow here, and others about the origin of the art, which I take as its foundation myth.[6] In it, the sixth century B.C.E. poet Simonides is hired to sing a panegyric at a banquet given by a Thessalian nobleman, Scopas. Simonides sings not only in honor of Scopas, but also includes a paean of praise for Castor and Pollux, the twin brothers and sons of Zeus (*Dioskouroi*). Angered, Scopas tells Simonides he will pay him only half the fee agreed upon, adding sarcastically that the poet might obtain the rest from the twins also honored. A messenger then tells Simonides that two young men outside the banquet hall wish to see him, but when he goes outside he finds no one. The roof of the banquet hall collapses at that moment, and all except Simonides are killed. Their bodies, in fact, are so mutilated that relatives cannot identify them. Simonides does so, for he had kept in memory the order in which they sat, and this enabled him to identify the victims in their places. Thus, Simonides discovers the art of memory: the holding in memory of a particular order of places, with a mnemonic image housed in each. And Simonides discerned, says Cicero, the special efficacy of sight, of the visual imagination, to the placings of things in memory. Yates believes that Simonides may have actually codified mnemonic practices of an earlier oral tradition (*AM*, p. 29).

There is, however, more to the story: an absurd, seemingly chance catastrophe involving grotesque death. Disfigured images will be seen as particu-

larly valuable for the memory, which, in turn brings order into a horrifying,
situation of death and loss. While the value of the visual imagination is often
stressed in later *ars memorativa* treatises, there is that which does not meet the
eye here. (Remember that the visual is only one aspect of the imaginal; far more
important is *imaginal vision*—a way of "seeing" the world as a play of images
and metaphors. In our ongoing exploration of imaginal memory, imagination is
understood as inherently *synaesthetic* and *kinaesthetic*, hence involving a variety of dimensions of which the literally visual is only one—and not always the
most important.) In the background are the *Dioskouroi*, invisible to Simonides.
Nonetheless this is an epiphanic moment: the poet is saved by the appearance of
the Unseen. The unseen reality has to do with brothers, one of whom is mortal
(Castor) while the other (Pollux or Polydeukes) is immortal—though the immortal twin shares in the death of the other and vice versa. For the two brothers
spend one day in the tomb, the house of Hades; and the next in heaven. Alterna-
ting between life and death, they are (according to an ancient logic of myth)
moon-brothers. The art of memory at times takes us into an in-between realm,
where one experiences the moon-like—part immortal and part mortal—quality
of the psyche.

   This story embodies the mythic pattern that practitioners of the art of memory must in some way follow. Present here are essential relations between memory, death and human continuity: from death arises the necessity of remembering: the dead must be "placed" in memory if what is essential is to be kept alive.
Simonides's discovery of the principles of the art of memory presupposes his
granting of a place in the remembering of his song to the twins; through his gift
of mythic remembrance a "brotherly" relation of the mortal and the immortal
becomes efficacious, saving the poet as the others sit at table unaware of the
peril overshadowing them. And we are given the gift of the art of memory by
Simonides's having gone back after the disaster and seen death, which seeing
granted a place for the profound sorrow of survivors.

   Yates discerns reflections of the ancient Greek practice of memory in Aristotle's work on memory (*De memoria et reminiscentia*), which asserts that
memory cannot occur in the absence of *images* (450 a 13–4) representing the
things remembered,[7] and speaks of the value of an *order of places*, arranged
mentally, as an aid to recollecting needed information (452 a 4). She also finds
reflections of a traditional practice of memory in Plato's *Phaedrus*, the value of
which for imaginal memory we discovered in chapter 3. This dialogue reflects
a recurrent theme in the different historical transformations of the art of memory
that is directly relevant to the practice of imaginal memory elaborated in subsequent chapters.

   In exploring Plato's *Phaedrus*, we found a tacit contrast between Phaedrus's initial desire to be able to repeat Lysias's speech from memory, and the
surfacing of a deeper memory of myth that foreshadows the dialogue about to

take place. This contrast alludes to the practice of mnemonics as a technical rhetorical skill without regard for the precise knowledge of the soul that Socrates (after his hymn to Love) argues is essential for the art of persuasion. Mnemonics practiced without a deeper awareness of the soul's way of speaking is actually a form of forgetfulness in Plato's sense. This is why Socrates recalls the divine heritage of memory in his second speech. However, the well-known critique of writing as a device that will lead to the weakening of memory (*Phdr.* 274C–285B) seems conversely to suggest an older and deeper art of memory (*AM*, pp. 38–9) that alone can lead to true wisdom.

There is a tension running throughout the history of the art of memory between its use as a largely technical aid in the recall of information for speaking and other activities, and as a way of ordering psychological, ethical and religious inquiry emphasizing the value of memory and imagination. These two trends are not entirely separate, and are synthesized in the medieval and Renaissance forms of the art of memory to be outlined below. In these forms, the technical and pragmatic aspect of the mnemonic art becomes the vehicle for profound explorations of fundamental psychological and religious powers that transcend the ego's capacity for manipulation of remembered images. In Part III, we shall be confronted with this tension once more, probing the necessity as well as the limits of pragmatic methods of remembering images. Such methods can be developed in a way that deepens, rather than constricts, one's appreciation of the power of the place of Hiroshima.

The earliest-known works explicitly addressing the art of memory arise from the Latin rhetoric tradition. The first of these is the anonymous treatise *Ad Herennium libri VI* (III. xvi. 28–xxiv. 40), probably written around 86–82 B.C.E.,[8] to which most later works on memory refer. Cicero treats the art more briefly, though with much enthusiasm, in *De oratore* (II. lxxxv. 350–60), but an equally important contribution to the tradition in his treatment of memory, together with intelligence and providence or foresight, as a part of Prudence.[9] This is the major source for a later Scholastic stress on the ethical value of memory. A more sceptical treatment of the art of memory is given by Quintilian in his *Institutio oratoria* (XI ii. 1–23).[10] Quintilian, while providing a clear account of the mnemonic practice, prefers more traditional methods of memorizing and omits the role of striking images detiled in *Ad Herennium* and cited by Cicero.

Before describing later transformations of the art of memory, a more detailed account of the "rules" for its practice is in order. Memory, says the author of *Ad Herennium*, is "the treasure-house [*thesaurum*] of the ideas supplied by Invention" . . . (III. xvi. 28). The orator seeking to improve his "natural" memory through the use of "artificial" memory should learn a set of rules for mnemonic places (*loci*) and images (*imagines*). First one must search for memory loci, seeking out buildings with easily remembered places, for instance "a house, an intercolumnar space, a corner, an arch, or the like" (III. xvi. 29). The precise details of these places are then memorized in an order appropriate to the images (with their associated information) that will inhabit each. This is best done in relative solitude, since the distractions of crowds tend to weaken the impression of the (place-) images. Having memorized the loci, one can move through them starting from any place and find the images, with their embodied information, in the right order. For the loci are like wax tablets and the images like the letters impressed upon these; the images can be removed or effaced so that the "tablets" of loci can be "written" upon again.

The places should be well-lit (but not too bright), so the images will stand out sharply. They should be spaced at moderate intervals, "approximately thirty feet; for, like the external eye, so the inner eye of thought is less powerful when you have moved the object of sight too near or too far away" (III. xix. 32). They should likewise bear distinguishing features in order to avoid confusion, and for the same reason one may mark every fifth and tenth place with a special feature, starting for instance with a golden hand or an image of an acquaintance named "Decimus."

Memory places need not be limited to actual buildings; "we may in our imagination create a region for ourselves" (III. xix. 32). Later authors extend this suggestion in various ways. The place of memory may be partly actual and partly non-actual, "as in the case of a building one knew well and through the back wall of which one broke an imaginary door as a shortcut to new spaces, or in the middle of which one created a mental staircase that would lead one up to higher floors that had not existed before."[11] Another variety of "higher" places cited by Quintilian in connection with a certain Metrodorus of Scepsis (XI. ii. 22) is the zodiac, with its twelve signs and their further divisions (see *AM*, pp. 39–41). He is sceptical of this zodiacal memory system, but Cicero (without mentioning the zodiac itself) exclaims that Metrodorus's powers of memory are "almost divine" (*De or.* II. lxxxviii. 360). The remembering of "higher" or divine realities will be taken up by various religious and astrological memory systems in the medieval and Renaissance periods. The rules for places were varied by the Middle Ages in another direction as well, alluded to in the exhortation of Boncompagno da Signa with which we began. Together with Heaven "the places of Hell, varied in accordance with the nature of the sins punished in them, could be regarded as variegated memory loci" (*AM*, p. 94). Certain Renaissance Neoplatonists constructed memory "theatres," probably based on actual architecture, which carried cosmological symbolism, displaying the Great World of Memory.

In each case, the art of memory involves a direct experience of psychic interiority, or of the *soul as place*—or many places—"within" which one moves as one remembers. The remembered places of soul constitute a kind of pre-Freudian psychic topography, but there is no overarching topographical model.

Instead we find a numberless variety of imaginal places in which the soul's images, with their immemorial strangeness and fascination, can be housed.

As we have seen, the mnemonic figures should take on bizzare, emotionally striking shapes.[12] In learning to practice memory, *Ad Herennium* advises, "nature herself teaches us what we should do" (III. xxii. 35). Marvelous or horrible events; weird, distorted or fabulous images are most effective in stirring the soul, its emotions and memories, while "we generally fail to remember" the ordinary.[13]

> We ought, then, to set up images of a kind that can adhere longest in the memory. And we shall do so if we establish likenesses that are as striking as possible; if we set up images that are not many or vague, but doing something; if we assign to them exceptional beauty or singular ugliness; if we dress some of them with crowns or purple cloaks, for example, so that the likeness may be more distinct to us; or if we somehow disfigure them, as by introducing one stained with blood or soiled with mud or smeared with red paint, so that its form is more striking, or by assigning certain comic effects to our images, for that, too, will ensure our remembering them more readily.
>
> (III. xxii. 37)

These are *imagines agentes* or active images, agents of imaginal activity; "it is clear that [the author] is thinking of human images . . . dramatically engaged in some activity—doing something" (*AM*, p. 10). But what teaches us here is the *psychological* nature of memory with its primary processes: distortions, displacements, overdeterminations. Bachelard's reference to imagination as "the faculty of *deforming* the images offered by perception"[14] well characterizes this art, as does Hillman's reference to the "exact pathological details" that "are an inherent part of fantasy figures" (*MA*, p. 199).

The warriors in the reception hall of Ricci's Memory Palace give one example of an active, "dramatic" memory image. *Ad Herennium* gives three rather complicated examples of memory images, the first of which will serve as a good illustration of the classical Latin art of memory. It is well to preface this with the insistence of *Ad Herennium* and many subsequent memory treatises that one should allow images to arise out of one's individual inventiveness, rather than relying on others' specific suggestions. Though it will be modified by medieval and Renaissance memory practitioners (and in a different way by Part III), this stress on the inventiveness of the individual psyche is significant, echoing Jung's assertion that active imagination best begins with whatever images present themselves in connection with one's psychic situation.

Ad Herennium's initial image is for a legal case. Following Yates, I will call it the "lawsuit" image. This image shows how a defense attorney might remember a case in which the defendant has been charged with poisoning another man to death in order to gain an inheritance, with many witnesses to testify for the prosecution (III. xx. 33–4). This information is rendered into a composite image in the first memory place: the poisoned man lies ill in bed, with the defendant at bedside holding a cup in his right had to remind the attorney of the poison, and holding tablets in his left hand (the will or inheritance). On his fourth finger are a ram's testicles, by which one remembers the witnesses (*testes*) who will *testify* in the case. The imagination of "unnatural" deformity or "displaced" sexuality and death, through quite precise associations, moves one to remember. Yates observes that these images "appear to be completely amoral, their function being solely to give an emotional impetus to memory by their personal idiosyncracy or their strangeness" (*AM*, pp. 16–7). The requirement, in Cicero's words, is that there be "images which are active, sharply defined, unusual, and which have the power of speedily penetrating the psyche [*animum*]" (*De or*. II. lxxxvii. 58). The moral question on which Yates touches will come up at various points in our exploration; here we may note that literal moral strictures on images must be suspended if the power and the pathology of soul is to fully engage the memory.

The strange, often strikingly beautiful or grotesque and horrifying image, plays a key role throughout the history of the art of memory, but it is reflected differently in the classical, medieval and Renaissance worldviews. The use of these *imagines agentes* as practical mnemonics appears foremost to the Latin orators (though Cicero, for instance, may have recognized their prudential or ethical value). In the Middle Ages the memory image was viewed in the mirrors of Christian theology and Aristotelianism. In the Renaissance it is revalued by Neoplatonic and Hermetic imaginings.

We will find that each perspective makes an important contribution to remembering images associated with the place of Hiroshima.

The Scholastic practitioners of memory, such as Albertus Magnus and Thomas Aquinas, justified the remembering of strange images with reference to the authority of Cicero (who said that memory is a part of Prudence, and to whom the Scholastics attributed the authorship of *Ad Herennium*) and Aristotle (who said images are necessary to memory and thought). This remembering of images is now carried on for ethical and devotional purposes. They aid these pursuits because, says Albertus (conflating Aristotle and Cicero), striking images or *metaphorica* "move the soul more and therefore better help the memory."[15] Thomas, on a similar basis and as a concession to the weakness of human soul, which cannot grasp pure and abstract principles without some aid, says that in order to best remember the virtues and vices, "It is necessary . . . to invent similitudes and images because simple and spiritual intentions slip easily from the soul unless they are as it were linked to some corporeal similitudes."[16]

In this way, bizzare and pathologized images gain a foothold in lay devotional treatises and in the art and iconography of medieval Christianity, sanctioned by the most rationally-minded theologians. The places for these images, as mentioned before, can be found in Heaven and Hell. Yates suggests (*AM*, p. 95) that Dante's *Divine Comedy* may be structured in the manner of the three parts of Prudence: the *Inferno* as memory; the *Purgatorio* as intelligence; and the *Paradiso* as providence or foresight. As an example imagine Dante's protrayal of the fate of fortune tellers and diviners, in the fourth Bolgia of the eighth circle of Hell:

> And when I looked down from their faces, I saw
> that each of them was hideously distorted
> between the top of the chest and the lines of the jaw;
>
> for the face was reversed on the neck, and they came on
> backwards, staring backwards at their loins,
> for to look before them was forbidden. Someone,
>
> sometime, in the grip of a palsy may have been
> distorted so, but never to my knowledge
> nor do I believe the like was ever seen.
>
> (XX. 10–8)

As with all the figures of the *Inferno*, these distortions stand in an exact symbolic relationship to the sins committed in life. "Thus," as John Ciardi comments, "those who sought to penetrate the future cannot even see in front of themselves; they attempted to move themselves forward in time, so must they go backwards through all eternity; and as the arts of sorcery are a distortion of God's law, so are their bodies distorted in Hell."[17] Such figures, placed in Hell—*memoria*—with their specific associations, would remind one vividly of the features of the vices of fortune telling and sorcery, and so of one's own prudential "spiritual intentions" to avoid such sins. This is entirely in keeping with both medieval Christian morality and the classical rules for the art of memory.

It is a strange devotion we are remembering here. That Dante's remembering of these images is deeply devotional is evident not only through the context of his medieval theology and cosmology; it is also revealed by his awe in the face of their strangeness: "nor do I believe the like was ever seen." *To be devoted to the remembering of images in deepest pain:* this form of devotion may appear not just strange but grotesque; "the mediaeval love of the grotesque" (*AM*, p. 104) is rarely remembered. But it has its place in memory: a place shared with deep ethical and moral concern. This ambiguous place of history and religion testifies that something in "the soul is moved most profoundly by images that are disfigured, unnatural, and in pain" (*RP*, p. 95).

The Renaissance, with its flowering of Neoplatonic and Hermetic philosophies and psychologies, witnessed the further transformation of the *ars memorativa* into an occult discipline, a way of ascending in imaginative contemplation to the supercelestial realm of the One, and of realizing the cosmic and divine powers latent in the soul. The soul is itself realized both as the reflection of the world in humanity, and as a presence in the world itself—an awareness reflected in the Renaissance valuation of memory and imagination. For now "The emotionally striking images of classical memory, transformed by the devout Middle Ages into corporeal similitudes, are transformed again into magically powerful images" (*AM*, p. 157). Arranged in certain ways and with certain features seen as corresponding with celestial realities, memory images become talismans or magical means of drawing into memory the divine powers of the planetary Gods or astral daemons.

Marsilio Ficino, the fifteenth century Florentine whose works can be seen as talismans by which archetypal powers were drawn into the Renaissance imagination,[18] asks in his book, *On Making Your Life Agree with the Heavens*, "Why not make a universal image, that is, an image of the universe itself?"[19] This would participate, if formed at the right astrological time (the Sun's entry into Aries, which corresponds to the start of the universe), in a process of renewing the imaginal world. We see again how soul, house, world and memory abide together. Suggests Ficino, "Deep inside your house you might set up a little room, one with an arch, and mark it all up with these figures and colors [of the universe and the planetary Gods]. . ." This is precisely what the memory systems of the Renaissance Magi—Giulio Camillo and Giordano Bruno from Italy (sixteenth century) and Robert Fludd from England (seventeenth century) attempt to do: form "an image of the universe itself," in all its particulars as well as its larger patterns, and house this in memory.

So complex are these memory-houses of the world that a detailed account of them lies beyond the scope of this essay. Here I will outline their general features as these pertain to the practice of imaginal memory to be developed in Part III. As we recount this Renaissance of memory, its envisioned place—the *world*—will begin to emerge as the ultimate foundation of our contemporary work of memory. "Think of it: memory not in brain or mind but *in the world*, and thus in the things that belong to the world such as lived bodies, places, and other people" (*R*, p. 310; italics in original).

Giulio Camillo's Memory Theatre

Camillo's Memory Theatre (*AM*, chs. VI–VII and pullout facing p. 114) was an actual wooden structure, a miniature ampitheatre (it could hold two or three people at a time). This place of memory presents a multitude of images whose careful differentiation suggests the possible depth and complexity of imaginal memory in the nuclear context.

Camillo believed that his Memory Theatre concentrated within itself the interrelated Powers of the Great World. The Great World, the Macrocosmos, is in the Renaissance imagination composed of supercelestial, celestial and sublunary realms, with all things in organic correspondence. Camillo's Theatre "seated" images arrayed around the stage according to the order of seven stages of creation and seven planetary Gods. These in turn correspond to seven Sephiroth or Cabbalistic powers of the supercelestial world, which are represented on the stage by "the seven pillars of Solomon's House of Wisdom" (*AM*, p. 137). Those who wished to view this World Theatre could enter, look upon, and remember the vast "audience" of Creation from the vantage-point of the stage, as one might view an entire forest from the top of a hill.

The classical rules for order of memory places are transformed into a complex web of archetypal configurations. The Theatre is divided into seven sections issuing from the Pillars of Wisdom and planetary Gods (the latter on the first stage or "grade" of creation), and these in turn are traversed by the divisions of the succeeding six grades. The successive activities and features of each grade are governed by the archetypal and affective properties of the God of each section, for instance "the tranquility of Jupiter, the anger of Mars, the melancholy of Saturn, the love of Venus" (*AM*, p. 144). The second grade is the Banquet, named after Homer's depiction of the feast given the Gods by Ocean (*Iliad* 1. 423–5). This Camillo interprets as the first day of creation: the Ideas (Gods) in their primordial place (Ocean), or the newly emergent and as yet uncombined elements of creation. The third grade is the Cave, named after the cave of the nymphs by the shore of Ithaca (*Od*. 13. 102ff) where bees bring their honey and nymphs weave on great looms. At this stage elements are woven together to form created things. In the next stage the interior aspects of the soul, ordered by the properties of each God or planet, emerge. This is the grade of the Gorgon Sisters, whose images represent the soul (which like the Gorgons is triple and has an [inner or imaginal] "eye"). (Camillo makes an error here: It is the Gorgons' sisters, the Graiai, who have one eye between them). On the fifth grade, "Pasiphe and the Bull" join and represent the coming-together of soul and body. Next, humankind's naturally given capabilities emerge, figured by the Sandals of Mercury; finally, culture, arts, religion and sciences are created on the grade of Prometheus.

This arrangement gives a quite precise and complex array of interwoven archetypal patterns. For example, in the Jupiter series, the creation of "useful things" proceeds on the Cave grade under the image of the three Graces, while the same image on the fifth grade discloses "beneficent nature." Next, the capability of exercising beneficence emerges. In the Mars series and on the third grade "Two Fighting Serpents" show discord among elemental things. When soul and body are joined (fifth grade), the serpents make for man's "contentious nature." This gives rise to contentious behavior on the sixth grade, while on the final, Promethean grade, we find the corresponding cultural institution, "military art."

The Gods here are emotionally stirring memory images, and the soul of the world their theatre. As in the *Phaedrus*, memory is essentially polytheistic. Again, there is a time (in the work of creation) for each place; the theatre has its own imaginal topography "whose intrasystemic complexity serves to specify archetypal dominants to a rare degree of precision, and, above all, to provide for these dominants places in the total scheme of things."[20] All the "times" of this placescape "take place" simultaneously, so that many images are involved in any given activity. Military activity, for instance, involves a Promethean endeavor as well as a martial anger; there is also an elemental contentiousness here, two serpents fighting. When nations contend, there are two serpents fighting.

Giordano Bruno

Giordano Bruno traveled through Europe during the latter half of the sixteenth century as an ex-Dominican friar and messenger of an imminent universal religious reform to be based on the return of the ancient "Egyptian" (Hermetic) religion of the world, one that would involve universal religious tolerance and recognition of the divine powers immanent in all things.[21] In an era of brutal religious warring and persecution, Bruno preached his message through a variety of writings. These include several forbiddingly abstruse words on "magic" memory: the remembering of the world in its divinely intricate harmony. Unlike his predecessors (e.g., Ficino and Camillo, who cautiously developed their Neoplatonic and Hermetic schemes within a Christian framework) Bruno boldly challenged Christianity through the practice and advocacy of *daemonic* magic (the use of talismans and other vehicles to draw down powers of *personified* astral daemons rather than merely impersonal celestial forces) as an agent of historical, political and religious change. Bruno made the mistake of returning to Italy in 1592, and was imprisoned by the Inquisition shortly thereafter, to be burned at the stake in 1600. In one of his works written during a stay at the French embassy in England (1583–1586), Bruno says of himself: "We see how this man, as a citizen and servant of the world, a child of Father Sun and Mother Earth, because he loves the world too much, must be hated, censured, persecuted and extinguished by it."[22]

The interface of Bruno's memory works with politics is of particular relevance for the present work. Like Bruno, we are concerned with imagination, memory and an active engagement with the world, even though we may not share his belief in the imminence of Hermetic religious reform and unity. Memory systems, as Peter Bishop points out, "are active in evoking responses at a depth level and then organizing these in an archetypal fashion for a particular purpose, conscious or unconscious."[23] Such Renaissance figures as Bruno, he notes, "were aware of the social significance of memory systems for reform or the stabilizing of society." We too take our place at the boundaries of soul, society and culture, religion and politics, remembering the place of imagination in each of these realms.

Bruno seeks to act in and upon the world through the right organizing of the daemonic images which are, in the (partial) title of one of his works, *Shadows of Ideas*, "shadows of reality which are nearer to reality than the physical shadows in the lower world" (*AM*, p. 216). They are intermediaries between the elemental world and the ultimate reality and power of the supercelestial One. The influx from Ideal realities can reach, via the "shadows" (astral memory images), and the work of the Magus himself, into the world and effect a reorganization of its (political and religious) realities, bringing these into harmony with the Gods and the One. This is strong magic: Bruno rejects the notion that concentrating exclusively on one's inner or subjective harmony (with oneself and/ or a larger Self) is an effective way of changing the world. He insists on the importance of being *in* the world; while essentially renouncing his Catholicism, he stresses the place of good works. His magic consists in the *bringing-to-bear of imaginal realities on one's work in the world*, rather than restricting imagination and memory to a private, subjective realm.

In addition to the characteristic Renaissance imagining of soul and memory as inherent in the world, there are two further themes in Bruno's work of particular relevance here. One is his understanding of how memory images become archetypally powerful; the other has to do with an interplay between what may be called the "moving" and static or "motionless" qualities of memory.

In his work, *Images* (see *AM*, pp. 293ff), Bruno envisions a complicated architectural memory system that houses all knowledge of the world, about minerals, animals, vegetables and human endeavors. In the surrounding heavens are placed a series of talismanic memory "statues" of the Gods, which through their imaginal proportions and markings draw down corresponding celestial powers and associated magic images. These animated "statues," according to the Hermetic account to which Bruno refers here, were the means by which the ancient "Egyptians" realized divine powers in terrestrial matter, using theurgic, or *God-making*, magic.[24] I do not take this literally, but understand it as suggesting the importance of *close concentration on the precise form of images held in memory*. Through this concentration they are sensed as powerful, precise metaphors of the psychic situation one is in—realized as "Gods" or archetypal powers. An example of this was our initial concentration upon the warriors in Ricci's Memory Palace, through which we sensed the power of

Mars. Concentration upon images associated wth the place of Hiroshima will provide many more instances of this "talismanic" power.

The next theme, that of the "moving" and "motionless" qualities of memory, becomes apparent in a contrast between *Images* and Bruno's earlier work, *Shadows*. In *Shadows*, Bruno combines the classical rules for memory with the Art of Ramon Lull (*AM*, ch. VIII). Lull, an important thirteenth and early fourteenth century figure, devised a system using revolving wheels marked with letters and geometric figures. Its different combinations were meant to disclose the features of the "ladder of being" and make possible a contemplative ascent to the true God. Yates describes this as a "revolutionary . . . attempt to represent movement in the psyche" (*AM*, p. 176). In *Shadows*, Bruno envisions memory as a system of concentric revolving wheels on which are to be placed all the images of the history of the world (*AM*, pp. 199ff). Until this effort, memory images had remained "firmly anchored to a building" (*AM*, p. 198); Bruno brings into memory the dynamic movement of Lullian wheels. In *Images*, however, this movement (represented by the heavens encircling the architectural memory system) is combined with the classical stress on images which, while active, yet remain "statue-like" in buildings or other places. Memory seems to require the differentiations of places and architecture: "places to stay," even if these are encompassed by the Great Round. The Circle must be Squared. There is a "static" quality of memory revealed by the classical rules for places and images, something "lifeless" about these realms.

This *death-like* quality of memory will warrant further comment below. Bruno himself, for all his dynamic movement, was, in his love for the world, "extinguished" by an institution that wished to remain static. In the practice of imaginal memory, we too, in our love for the world, will in some way have to "die" in a place of religious cruelty.

Robert Fludd

The final great monument of Renaissance memory is again a "theatre," envisioned by the English Hermetist Robert Fludd.[25] As in Camillio's theatre, memory is imagined from a dramatic perspective, one which will come into play as we remember the drama that began with Hiroshima.

"I call a theatre," says Fludd, "[a place in which] all actions of words, of sentences, of particulars of a speech or of subjects are shown, *as in a public theatre in which comedies and tragedies are acted*" (quoted in *AM*, p. 331). Though imagination is very important for Fludd, he is against the use of fictitious places in the art of memory. Supported by this view, Yates contends that Fludd's Memory Theatre is "a reflection—distorted by the mirrors of magic memory—of Shakespeare's Globe Theatre" (*AM*, p. 321).

There are for Fludd two sorts of artificial memory: the "square art" (*ars quadrata*) and "round art" (*ars rotunda*); while both are essential, the round art is by far the superior. The square art uses actual theatres, with their stages and sets, as memory loci. In certain recesses in this setting images of corporeal things are to be placed.

There are two main theatres, the "eastern" or Day Theatre and the "western" or Night Theatre. Yates believes these are to be placed in each sign of the great "common place"—the round of the zodiac. "The eastern theatre is to be light, bright and shining, since it will hold actions belonging to the day. The western theatre will be dark, black and obscure, since it will hold actions belonging to the night. Both are to be placed in the heavens, and refer, presumably, to the day and night 'houses' of the planets" (*AM*, p. 331). Alongside these theatres in the Great Round are images of the round art: the magical and talismanic astral images, Gods and "statues" representing celestial rather than corporeal things. As in the system of memory buildings encompassed by the heavens in Bruno's *Images*, in Fludd's system the round and square, macrocosm and microcosm, eternal and temporal, are brought together in an "image of the universe," a house of the world.

Fludd's memory treatise opens with a diagram that well summarizes the Renaissance vision of memory images. It pictures a man with a third eye, the *oculus imaginationis* or "eye of imagination" (reproduced in *AM*, pl. 15), the "rays" of vision of which stream back beyond the brain toward images of memory. While we have seen that to imagine memory only in *literally* visual terms is far too narrow a vision, there is a *seeing of the world as place of imagination* that is crucial in the work of imaginal memory as presented in this book. For the renaissance of memory is given with the world itself.

The places and images of memory are seen very differently by the classical, medieval and Renaissance practitioners of the art of memory, but memory's embodiment in places and images is common to the mythopoetic tradition, the classical Greek and Latin stress on rhetoric, the medieval focus on devotion and ethics, and the Renaissance vision of imaginative contemplation of daemonic realities. And, from the start (as in Hesiod, Plato and Cicero), Memory is a goddess or "almost divine," yet a vision of death (Simonides, the lawsuit image, the *Inferno*, Fludd's Night Theatre). I speak in the present tense to suggest that the history of the art of memory is also myth and dream, that all of its transformations can be seen as simultaneously present, all happening at once and belonging together in an archetypal configuration.

Taking the art of memory in this way, let us more closely consider those of its themes and images most pertinent to imaginal memory in the present.

Memory and the "Art" of Imagination

The relation of memory and art or aesthetic sensitivity to images, is present in a primary myth of memory: Mnemosyne as mother of art through the Muses. Memory and art, or artistic perspective, form an archetypal tandem. This leads us to consider the soul's response to the art of the imaginal, or memory as "art" of the imagination.[26]

In his hymn to Love in the *Phaedrus*, Socrates says that the soul here below most easily remembers the Idea of Beauty (250B–D). Beauty personified is Aphrodite, who with Eros provokes the madness of memory. The art of memory requires an Aphrodisiac sensibility, a loving engagement with the sensual surfaces of images, or an awareness of the Aphrodisiac qualities inherent in imagination. As suggested earlier, imaginal memory is synaesthetic. It involves a discerning sense of "taste" and "feel" for places and images and a love of their metaphoric shapes as well as a careful eye as to their features and placing. Through Aphrodite the *structures* of imagination elicit an awe-filled love. This is reflected in Yates's reference to the art of memory in Augustine's time, just prior to the sacking of Rome in the latter part of the Bishop's life: "To one who saw the buildings of the antique world in their fullest splendor, not long before their destruction, what a choice of noble memory places would have been available" (*AM*, p. 48)! In the halls of memory we "hear" the echoes and resonances of fine and ancient houses.

And there is beauty in the striking images peopling these. Listen again to the evoking of the *imagines agentes* in *Ad Herennium*: here are images of "exceptional beauty or singular ugliness," with "crowns and purple cloaks," some even disfigured, "stained with blood or soiled with mud or smeared with red paint," or with "certain comic effects." These images imply and call forth an acute sense of the art of imagination, through which imagination is rendered strikingly memorable.

Part of the beauty of this art of imagination, however, is that it does not exclude "singular ugliness," "blood," "mud" and the obscene. Beauty itself need not be literalized, as Aphrodite herself is prone to do. The synaesthetic response also embraces ugly, bizzare, grotesque images. Aphrodite is also said to have given birth to the monstrous child, Priapus, who sports a huge phallus (sometimes imagined as bending toward the rear), belly and tongue: he is an archetypal Freak.[27] Though Aphrodite rejects him, she is still his mother: the love of the beautiful is archetypally bound to the "love of the grotesque," which deepens Aphrodisiac consciousness not by moving *beneath* image-surfaces (e.g., toward "deeper" psychological or intellectual significance), but rather erotically toward those surfaces, shapes and faces scorned by a too literal or ideal notion of beauty. There are ugly, grotesque, painful and freakish images that bring soul to beauty and render aesthetic sensitivity psychological. This is well-illustrated by Dante's art of the *Inferno*, and by the beauty we will find in the hell of Hiroshima.

IMAGES OF *AD HERENNIUM*

Ad Herennium discloses, like the myth of Simonides, basic patterns of the *ars memorativa* tradition. These patterns are figured by the image of memory as a *treasure-house* and the three examples of memory images given by the author. An exploration of these will give further precision to the present work of imaginal memory.

The Treasure–House of Memory

Memory, says *Ad Herennium*, is the treasure-house or thesaurus of "the ideas supplied by Invention . . ." Quintilian, though more sceptical of the value of the artificial memory, nonetheless agrees, calling memory the "treasure-house of eloquence" (*Inst. or.* XI. ii. 2). Augustine—himself a rhetoric teacher most likely trained in the *ars memorativa* tradition (*AM*, p. 46)—marvels at "the fields and spacious palaces of my memory, where are the treasures of innumerable images". . . . (*Conf.* X. vii. 12). Matteo Ricci's memory likewise takes on the form of a vast palace, and there are the treasures of images envisioned in the Renaissance world-memories.

Images of memory as a vast thesaurus display the wealth of psyche. Jung, citing the numinous effect of archetypal ideas, points to the emergence of these from "the treasure-house of primordial images". . . . (*CW* 7, par. 110). As Hillman observes, Jung's imagery of the unconscious "appears hardly to differ" from Augustine's *memoria* or *thesaurus inscrutabilis* (*MA*, p. 171). From *Ad Herennium* through Augustine to Jung, *memoria* appears as a treasure-house. Displayed here is the wealth in images, often portrayed in the guise of treasure buried or otherwise "hard-to-attain," or the Philosopher's Stone or Gold of alchemy. Hidden in the treasure-house too are associations to Death's house with its wealth (*ploutos*): the richness within images and reflections on death, the shit in the gold, the decay in what is deposited in images, the decomposition of literal events into imaginal compositions.

These relatively familiar aspects of images of the psychic treasure-house need further qualification in terms of the root-word *thesaurus*, which is derived from the Greek *thēso*, the future of the verb *tithenai*, with the primary meaning of "to place" or "to put." The treasure-house of memory is always in some way a *place*, as we saw in the *Phaedrus*, where the mythic memories shaping the dialogue are evoked by the place-setting on the Ilissos River. The necessary relation of place and memory is also displayed by the loci of the art of memory, which present the "localization" of memory in a "house." Memories are always attached to, or inherent in, places; place is the house of memory and memory is the house of place in the soul. As Quintilian put it,

> when we return to a place after a considerable absence, we not merely recognize the place itself, but remember things we did there, and recall the persons whom we met and even the unuttered thoughts which passed through our minds when we were thee before. . . . Some place is chosen [for the artificial memory] . . . such as a spacious house divided into a number of rooms.
>
> (Inst. or. XI. ii. 1708)

The image of a house of memory-places immediately springs to Quintilian's mind; for place and the house of memory imply each other and co-inhere as part of a basic phenomenological pattern. Place is the house of memory because, as Casey observes in his exploration of place memory, "it serves to contain—to shelter and protect—the items or episodes on which the act of remembering comes to focus" (*R*, p. 188). Housed in place, memories are treasured.

The Lawsuit Image

Memory, as the treasure-house of ideas and invention, is displayed in three particular images in *Ad Herennium*. There is surprising wealth in the first or "lawsuit" image cited above. To reiterate: the poisoned man lies ill in bed (he should be someone we know, or who is in some way familiar to us), with the defendant at the bedside holding a cup in his right hand and, in his left, tablets. On the fourth finger of his left hand are a ram's testicles. The cup reminds us of the poison, the tablets of the will or inheritance, and the ram's testicles of those to testify for the prosecution.

Illness or pathologizing and death we have already witnessed in connection with the art of memory. The Accused brings before us the spectre of a psychopathic thief and murderer: an active agent in the movement within memory toward death. The inheritance he seeks is part of the treasure-house of ideas and invention. There is a sexual aspect or potency in the art of memory—in this image an animal sexuality.

The man ill in bed can be imagined as the Victim of Memory. In the case presented by *Ad Herennium*, he is already dead; in the image, he is ill; in either case, he is immobilized. In the logic of image-talk, the Victim's being at once dead and ill is no contradiction. For his illness is a form of death, and his death a form of illness. His pale persona reminds us that all illness is a movement toward death or contains death within it. Death is not only literal, but an immobilizing illness, as in those complexes whose disturbances never seem to move, those people of the soul who never go anywhere, as if forever bedridden, permanently poisoned. Yet in this ill death is the profound necessity of memory we recognized at the scene of the disastrous banquet: by death the soul is moved to remember.

There is a particular quality of death suffered by soul in memory that is vital to the present work. This is expressed by the *immobilization* of the ill and dead Victim. Consider the usual and contrasting view of soul as the animating principle, that which impels to movement. In the *Phaedrus*, we recall that Plato defines soul as immortal by its self-moving nature. The principle that all is movement and therefore deathless is also found in the *Corpus Hermeticum*[28] and is vital to Renaissance Neoplatonism. Where there is movement there is life; to imagine soul as movement means to imagine it as in essence life.

But Plato himself allows that opinions become knowledge by being "fastened up" by the "reason of cause and effect," and that this "is remembering" (*Meno* 98A–B).[29] This fastening up of memory leads the soul toward the unchanging Ideas, which movement Plato sees (in the *Phaedo*) as a way of practicing death. Says Bachelard: "Memories are motionlessness, and the more securely they are fixed in space, the sounder they are" (*PS*, p. 9). Memories remain in place if they are to remain as memories. We have noticed the static quality of the "moving" images of the art of memory; witness the lawsuit image still fixed in place two thousand years after the writing of *Ad Herennium*. This necessity gives rise to the inability of Bruno and Fludd to do without fixed buildings with loci for memory images; the dynamic revolution of wheels, or the zodiacal round, has to be countered with places to which images are, in Yates's phrase, "firmly anchored." The round art may be superior according to Hermetic tradition, but memory requires the square art as well.[30]

Lifton, focusing on imagery of life and death, contrasts movement and stasis, which latter is one of the "death equivalents" (*BC*, p. 53). The art of memory is likewise a psychic equivalent, or form, of death; memory kills by immobilizing images. Yet this stasis is a way of moving. Images move the memory even as memory renders them motionless. The Chain of Memory is also the Chain of Being. Placed in memory, soul is at once killed and kept alive; images remain. Rendered motionless, soul is moved, remembered.

Ad Herennium imagines us as preparing to speak in defense of the Accused. This is in effect what we have been doing with our psychological reading of the Victim's fate in memory. Let us continue our argument, focusing now on the Accused, showing not his innocense, but the necessity of his psychopathic action. He takes his place by the side of the Victim, holding his poison cup and tablets, with the ram's testicles on his fourth left finger. The poison cup and tablets can be imagined as features of the art of memory. The art contains the death-taint or poison of the soul's pathologizing, dying and death in its variegated un-

natural and disfigured images. Poison is a traditional vehicle of death, as with
Medeia's potions or Socrates's hemlock. Memory is a container for this agent.
The tablets, as we have already suggested, are the inheritance from the treasure-
house of memory. The Accused holds these together. There is vast wealth in the
poisoning immobility of the soul, and the wealth of images is poisoned, tainted
with death. To practice imaginal memory will signify the holding-together of
the poison cup and treasures of soul, to remember that Plouton (Pluto) is Hades.

To what, then, do the ram's testicles bear witness? The translator notes an
anatomical tradition according to which a nerve extends from the heart to the
fourth finger of the left hand. The art of memory, like, like traditional memorizing, proceeds by way of heart; the heart of the art of memory is in a ram's testes.
The finger is the executive organ, the ram's horn. The sexual heart of memory
is not human, but animal and therefore divine. Ficino says that the forms of the
soul are "seminal" reasons or fantasies[31] behind which lie the ideas in the divine
mind. Our image testifies to the seminal or generative fantasy of the art of memory. The translator comments: "Of the scrotum of the ram purses were made;
thus the money used for bribing the witnesses may perhaps also be suggested."
So here is a generative, phallic organ which is also a "purse," containing, in
seed-form, the wealth of memory.

The image is dreamed onward, amplifying itself, in a vision of Albertus
Magnus's. Albertus, somewhat altering the classical memory rules, says that
when we wish to reminisce in a spiritual and devotional manner, we should
"withdraw from the public light into obscure privacy" and "imagine and seek
out dark places having little light . . ."[32]

> For example, if we wish to record what is broght against us in a law-
> suit, we should imagine some ram, with huge horns and testicles,
> coming towards us in the darkness. The horns will bring to memory
> our adversaries, and the testicles the dispositions of witnesses.

Here the art of memory reveals its dreamlike reality, becoming a nightmare
which as Hillman says is the revelation of the "natural God."[33] Notice the precision of the dream-work: the persona of the Accused has been taken on by the
human subject, unmasking a horned God. It is to be expected that Albertus, the
pious Scholastic, would stand accused here, since in his worldview all men are
guilty before God. This helps inspire an attitude of devotional worship. But
what we witness is an epiphany, in the dark of nightmare, of a pagan God, of the
Horns and Balls of the Ram of Memory.

The huge nature of the Ram is also apparent in its astrological character.
Yates, in discussing the early use of zodiacal signs as an order of memory
places, wonders why the testes are those of a ram. "Could an explanation of this
be that Aries is the first of the signs, and that the introduction of an allusion to a

ram in the image to be put in the first place for remembering the lawsuit helped to emphasize the order of the place, that it was the first place?" (*AM*, p. 41). Ficino recalls, in his instructions for making an image of the universe, that the time of the Sun's arrival in Aries "is, as it were, where the universe was when it first started . . ."[34] The First Place of Memory is under the sign of the Ram, the sign of Beginnings or First Awakenings; Albertus's nightmare envisions an awakening in terror to the power of memory. This is a sexual power, a celestial animal-power with horns to penetrate and a "purse" to contain the wealth of generative fantasies—indeed, the whole cycle of the heavens *in statu nascendi*.

The Sons of Mars

The second and third examples of memory images appearing in *Ad Herennium* show how each word in the following line may be remembered (III. xxi. 34): "And now their home-coming the kings, sons of Atreus, are making ready" [Iam domum itionem reges Atridae parant]. In the first locus, we might put an image of

> Domitius, raising hands to heaven while he is lashed by the Marcii Reges—that will represent "Iam domum itionem reges" (And now their home-coming the kings,"); in the second [locus], Aesopus and Climber, being dressed as for the roles of Agamemnon and Menelaus in *Iphigenia*—that will represent "Atridae parant" ("the sons of Atreus, are making ready").

The translator comments here that this verse and play are otherwise unknown and perhaps made up by the author of *Ad Herennium*. The actor Aesopus was a historical figure, a friend of Cicero, and the translator thinks Cimber was a historical actor popular at the same time.

Like the association of witnesses [*testium*] with testicles [*testiculos*], that between the first of these two images is carried by sound: *domum itionem reges—Domitius Reges*. More important here is the dramatic character of this image; Yates suggests that Domitius, as he is lashed by the Marcii Reges, may be "bloodstained to make him more memorable". . . . (*AM*, p. 14) We are reminded of the first image in Ricci's Memory Palace—that of two warriors struggling, with one trying to ward off a spear-strike from the other—in which we discovered a reflection of the war God Mars. Again, we are faced with an image of conflict in the place of memory. Mars is present in *Ad Herennium* too. Albertus Magnus, using a corrupt text of *Ad Herennium*, makes an error that gives an archetypally correct reading of this scene, imagining "someone being beaten by the sons of Mars". . . (*AM*, p. 65).

Images of wars and warring images, both in history and art, strongly move the memory; memory seems drawn to Mars, enacting the mythic love of Venus for the God. We are stirred by the God's fiery rage and violence, and cannot but remember this. War awakens and initiates memory; in memory we go, or go back to, war. (Images of conflicts in our individual lives—our times of raging and battling—similarly strike the memory.) Here is one of the psychological functions of Memorial Day alluded to in chapter 1. There I stressed the egoism of victimization that characterizes national war memorials and commemorations. The inherent connection between memory and Mars suggests a way out of this egoism through a deeper imagining of war in memory (not through refusing the memory of Mars). Imagine: war memorials honoring not only the nation's war dead, not only "our own," but also War itself: giving a place in Memory to a Power transcending individual and national egos, the God Mars.

The Play of Memory

Finally there is the third image of *Ad Herennium*: "Aesopus and Cimber, being dressed for the roles of Agamennon and Menelaus in *Iphigenia*," to represent the phrase, "the sons of Atreus, are making ready." In this image we see the "play" of memory; its dramatic context, later developed in the Renaissance memory theatres, is evident in the primary text of the *ars memorativa*. The actors in this play are the *imagines agentes*, striking and often familiar human faces. But who are they really, and of what theme of this play do they speak?

The actor Aesopus is a friend of Cicero, and Cicero suggests that whatever things we wish to remember "we can imprint upon our minds by a skilful arrangement of the several masks [*singulis personis*] that represent them, so that we may grasp ideas by means of images and their order by means of places" (*De or*. II. lxxxvii. 358; *AM*, p. 18). Yates, wondering about the "use of the word *persona*," asks

> Does it imply that the memory image heightens its striking effect by exaggerating its tragic or comic aspects, as the actor does by wearing a mask? Does it suggest that the stage was a likely source of striking memory images? Or does the word mean in this context that the memory image is like a known individual person, as the author of *Ad Herennium* advises, but wears that personal mask only to jog the memory?
>
> (*AM*, p. 21)

We have noted that it is not actual nature but the nature of the psyche that teaches us the art of memory, and we have seen memory images as masks for divine persons (e.g., Mars through the warriors of Ricci's Memory Palace). Such memory images, though with familiar *personae*, do not refer finally to actual, historical persons; they are masks of transhuman realities. "In dreams," asserts

Hillman, "we are visited by the *daimones*, nymphs, heroes and Gods shaped like our friends of last evening" (*DU*, pp. 61–2). Dreamlike, the art of memory reveals the transhuman through human *personae*. The third image in *Ad Herennium* reveals the art of memory as a kind of classical theatre, the *imagines agentes* playing their parts in a drama involving the Gods.

The images of *Ad Herennium* richly reveal the treasure-house of memory and the drama within. The themes and patterns we find displayed here will be essential to the practice of remembering images associated with Hiroshima. Remembering that context, we can recapitulate: the House of Memory is a place in which memories are treasured, their value disclosed. Soul is "kept" by memory—kept alive, moving, yet still, dead. The Great Ram of Memory is its animal-power: active, penetrating, containing soul's seminal fantasies, a nascent world. Memory is the sign of Beginning. In the First Place or entrance to the palace of Memory we find images belonging to Mars and psychic conflict. It is all a drama in the making, a theatre of soul in which appear the faces of the dream-work of memory.

MELANCHOLY

Ficino's friend, Giovanni Cavalcanti, replying to a complaint Ficino had made about the influence of Saturn's oppressive melancholy in his life, points out the virtues of this planet, including the gift to Ficino of "a comprehensive memory, in which all things are present in correct time and place."[35] Albertus, relying on (Psuedo-) Aristotle's *Problemata*, had noted a few centuries earlier that not only was melancholy—being of a hard, cold and dry nature—the temperament best for ordinary memory, but that there was a special kind of melancholy which favored "reminiscence," Albertus's term (from Aristotle's *De memoria*) for the art of memory.[36] This special melancholy has elements of the sanguine and choleric temperaments, or, as Yates puts it, "it is the dry-hot melancholy, the intellectual, the inspired melancholy" (*AM*, p. 69). Of those who have this condition, Albertus says they are moved most by *phantasmata*—the fantasy images required by the art of "reminiscence." It is the dry heat within the leaden blackness of Saturn that inspires melancholy and the art of memory. And this involves a special sensitivity to fantasy images.

It is not necessary to recount in detail the psychology of Saturn, the exemplary senex (whom we have already seen in the persona of Strong-Armed Ego).[37] But certain of the senex's traits are essential to the practice of memory, inspired as this is by melancholy and its fantasy images. The connectuion between melancholy, the senex and the art of memory does not begin with Albertus and Ficino; rather, it is implied at the start, in *Ad Herennium*. In addressing the rules for memory places, *Ad Herennium* advises us: "It will be more advantageous to obtain [loci] in a deserted than in a populous region, because the crowding and passing to and fro of people confuse and weaken the impress of the images, while solitude keeps their outlines sharp" (III. xix. 31). This evokes a particular state in which the memory is most receptive to images of places: a preference for deserted places, away from people, in solitude. Such a state may be preferred by Saturn's melancholy spirit, whose contemplative activities involve being distant, cut off, isolated, alone. "Saturn," says Ficino, "is the enemy of men who lead an open, public life, and the friend of those who choose to escape the company of public. . . . In fact, he is such a friend to the minds of men who are set apart that he is almost their kinsman."[38] To practice memory as *Ad Herennium* advises is to evoke the spirit of Saturn.

In Yates's words, "the rules summon up a vision of a forgotten social habit. Who is that man moving slowly in the lonely building stopping at intervals with an intent face? He is a rhetoric student forming a set of memory loci" (*AM*, p. 8). The practice of memory requires slow going, frequent stopping and being in a lonely place: contemplating and imagining places. All these are valued by the senex spirit, and are psychic values within the leaden and lonely nature of his melancholy. The senex makes order and boundaries, essential to the differentiation of memory places. Or, as Edward Casey puts it, "place provides its own boundaries—'regionalizes,' we might say—because it possesses an immanent power . . . "[39] Evident here is the senex-quality of place, its power to provide boundaries. The art of memory reveals inherent connections between sensitivity to places and images, images of places, and Saturnian melancholy. It draws out a special quality, a dry heat of inspiration, from within melancholy; in the art melancholy finds its special inspiration and its place.

Both the places and images of the art of memory thus come under the sign of (or signify) Saturn, whose focus renders places into images so that images may be placed. It is good to remember, as Cavalcanti wrote to Ficino, the gifts that may come from working *with* melancholy, rather than fending it off or engaging in a manic denial of our melancholy predicament. Saturn is the planet of good memory, and his melancholy may bear within it special gifts of inspiration and the capacity to be moved by fantasy images. And his lonely contemplations bring places and images to memory, marking out the bounds of the halls and rooms of its treasure-house. The practice of memory is—to use and somewhat alter a phrase of Freud's—a work of melancholy.[40]

DEVELOPING A PRACTICE OF IMAGINAL MEMORY

"Imaginal memory," as defined in the preface of this book, connotes both an "imaginal perspective" on memory that focuses on that realm in which memory and imagination commingle (memory as "a phenomenon of imagination that presents the awareness of what-has-been"), and a specific "practice" of re-membering images. A closer look at what this entails will be helpful. As a prac-tice, imaginal memory draws upon the *ars memorativa* tradition (together with its sources described in the previous chapter) and Jung's method of active im-agination, but takes on its own distinctive features. A brief comparison and con-trast between the art of memory and active imagination will help us discern these features.

Active Imagination and the Art of Memory

Active imagination and remembering *imagines agentes, active* images, are both forms of engaging psychic activities. The art of memory moves, at times, into the witnessing of a direct dialogue between two (or more) imaginal figures. The most obvious examples of this would be the underworld descents of Odys-seus, Aeneas and Dante, each of whom both speaks and is spoken to, by shades: remembered images. Another example is found in the first of a series of dialogues Bruno wrote, set in London.[41] In it, Bruno and two companions un-dertake what turns out to be a difficult journey through places in London at night, to a supper at which Bruno describes his Hermetic philosophy in the course of a lively debate with the others present. Yates believes that the places and images of the journey are memory places and images through which Bruno remembers the themes of his occult philosophy; the dialogues presented have "lively and well characterised interlocutors". . . . (*AM*, p. 311). This is the most direct link between the practice of the art of memory and an imaginal meeting, or *active imagining*, of well-defined characters.

Active imagination involves a meeting of imaginal figures (among whom Jung counts the ego) in which both (or all) parties actively participate. This ac-tivity is initiated when one's habitual self concentrates upon a fantasy image, carefully noticing its spontaneous changes and allowing it its own autonomy and intentions. Then one speaks with the figure in some manner and listens to what the figure may have to say to oneself. Both ego or usual self and image thus assume active roles. While this is going on, another aspect of the self ob-serves the play of imaginal activity, recognizing it as an enactment of the theatre of soul: the drama within the individual's psyche. In some cases a direct dialogue takes place, and one may write the imaginal conversation down or otherwise record it (this is in many ways parallel to what Dante did). Various other enactments (such as dance or other bodily movements, different forms of writing, painting, sculpting, etc.) can also allow the images to express them-selves. Allowing the images the fullest possible expression is an important part of the activity of the ego. Thus, envisioned, active imagination can be a power-ful means of coming to terms with unknown and sometimes threatening aspects of the psyche, and is intended to prompt an inherent tendency in the personality to move toward greater psychic differentiation and individuation.[42]

There are a number of significant parallels between the art of memory and active imagination that bear mentioning here. The first is that both involve the *dramatic play* of images we have already seen in action in *Ad Herennium's* image of the actors Aesopus and Cimber and in the Renaissance world-theatres. Jung specifically likens the work of active imagination to the play of drama.[43] After one has concentrated for a time on an image and observed how it begins to change, "A chain of fantasy ideas develops and gradually takes on a dramatic character: the passive process becomes an action. At first it consists of projected figures, and these images are observed like scenes in a theatre" (*CW* 14, par. 706). In both the art of memory and active imagination the theatre becomes a place expressive of essential psychic activities. There are important differences between the use of the theatre-image in each case, but they have in common a dramatic *perspective* on events occuring in imagination. This qualifies and deepens one's sense of the complexity of what one is remembering: the play within the drama of images, the forms of acting with their stirring power, the character and dimensions of the "inner stage."

Second, the art of memory and active imagination are both ways of facilitating much greater differentiation of psychic images. The art of memory is, as Hillman describes it, a way "of soul making": remember the striking precision of images and of the topography of memory places. The art of memory is particularly effective in developing a sense of *place* in the soul, and in moving toward the exploration of places remembered and imagined. There are also the complex interrelations of images we glimpsed when looking at Camillo's Memory Theatre and Bruno's memory systems. The differentiation of images is likewise implicit in Jung's above description of the development of active imagination. This unfolds as one develops a sense of the specific character of the images and their close, often unexpected relation to one's individual life.

In closely parallel ways, the art of memory and active imagination both involve concentrating upon images in order to allow their peculiar power to take effect. In the art of memory, images are powerful because they are emotionally striking (as in the classical Latin art), figure as "corporeal similitudes" that move the soul to remember abstract principles (the medieval art); and, when rightly formed and imagined, function as talismans drawing into one's memory celestial and supercelestial powers (the Renaissance art).

Recall in this regard Bruno's use of the *statue* figure from the Hermetic account of theurgic or "God-making" magic. Jung uses a similar figure in one of his analogies for active imagination:

> In antiquity when a man had to direct a prayer to the statue of the god, he stepped upon a stone that was erected at its side to enable people to shout their prayer into the ear, so that the god would hear them; and

then he stared at the image until the god nodded his head or opened or shut his eyes or answered in some way. You see this was an abbreviated method of active imagination, concentrating upon the image until it moved; and in that moment the god gave a hint, his assent or his denial or any other indication, and that is the *numinosum*.[44]

Here too the image becomes talismanic through one's close concentration upon it. It is now imbued with archetypal power, is animate in the sense of being ensouled. And the magic of images, in both the Renaissance and active imagination, facilitates change, a reforming of existence. For Bruno the magic of the Gods working through the power of images leads to world religious and cultural reform, and for Jung archetypal powers encountered in active imagination present (mainly) possibilities of individual psychological change.

Comparing the art of memory and active imagination highlights a fourth point, not always noticed with regard to the latter: both ways of working with images involve one in profound remembering—a remembering of the most basic powers of soul and the religious imagination. It is through such remembering of images that the vision of a Renaissance of memory of celestial and supercelestial realities emerges. In the work of active imagination, one remembers foundational realities of one's personal and intimate life, and through these, larger archetypal realities that have come into play.

A fifth important point is that the art of memory and active imagination are both *methods* of psychological exploration. In both, the conscious self or ego takes an active role in entering and moving in imaginal realms. In both, the use of method opens up a dimension of psychic activity far transcending the ego's capacity for technical manipulation (although there is a greater tension within the art of memory between its technical aspects and its recognition of the intrinsic value of imagination).

A sixth and final point relevant here is somewhat more elusive. In several contexts, we have described the art of memory as having an inherent structure of places and images. Though it is not elaborated in the same way, the experience (and particularly the *remembered* experience) of active imagination shows, on close examination, the same structure: one "moves" in and through a series of imaginal places, noticing and engaging with particular images. Again, Dante's journey through the *Divine Comedy* and Bruno's above-mentioned journey through London places illustrate this parallel. In active imagination, one's attention is mainly focused on engaging with images. The placescape often remains tacit, but it is present nonetheless and is crucial in the "taking-place" of the imaginal encounter.

There are also important differences between the art of memory and active imagination that need mention here. In the art of memory, images are always in some way active, powerful. This can come close to Jung's understanding of images as active quite independently of the ego, as autonomous psychic factors with their own intentions that most precisely express the psychic situation in which the individual finds himself. However, the depth-psychological perspective views images more precisely as *metaphors* whose power consists in the ability to express a complexly variegated psychic situation. Our work with nuclear images in the following chapters will be aimed at revealing this metaphoric power. By contrast, the occult perspective of the Renaissance views images more from the perspective of *spirit*: they are links to greater spiritual powers beyond the imaginal and its metaphoric shapes. They represent beings whose intentions may or may not parallel those of ourselves, but the locus of these intentions is not in the image *per se*.

Moreover, the talismanic images of memory are not in most cases developed as *characters* (important exceptions are in Dante's work and Bruno's *Italian Dialogues*, where memory images are subtly characterized). In active imagination, one attends closely to the character of the figures with whom one meets, because here may be hidden characteristics of one's personality with which it is important to come to terms.[45]

In important ways, then, active imagination is more psychological, strikes at a deeper level, than the art of memory as explicitly conceived by its major practitioners. Yet the phenomenology of the art of memory—of places and images—points, conversely, toward a still greater psychological depth than is usually reached in active imagination. This depth has to do with the "motionless," dead or static qualities of memory images "firmly anchored" in their places. Think about the lawsuit image, the image of Domitius raising his hand to heaven as he is lashed by the Marcii reges, of Aesopus and Cimber making ready for their parts in an unknown play, and of the warriors still locked in combat in the reception hall of Ricci's Memory Palace. Memory is a murderer of soul: there are the images, still, in the same place.

Yet such images do move us: they are unmoved movers of the soul, actively embodying in their still-ness the presence of what is most enduring, what remains always. This unchanging depth of imagination does not contradict an awareness of life's irrevocable changes; it deepens one's perspective on these latter. Precisely as these changes are felt as irrevocable, we sense the presence of permanence, of what endures despite our desires, of what will never change.

This deep death of soul is largely forgotten in the moving encounters figured in active imagination, which is oriented toward the soul's movement and change. The art of memory discloses the unmoving *structure* inherent in imagination; active imagination quickens its *movement*. In developing a practice of imaginal memory, it will be important to give place to these both.

The Work of Imaginal Memory

The work of imaginal memory involves an interplay between the psychological qualities of the art of memory assayed in this chapter, and the engagements with images characteristic of active imagination. Here I will briefly outline the features of this psychological interplay and illustrate them with reference to the image of the warriors in Ricci's Memory Palace.

Imaginal memory approaches images as talismans (following the Renaissance view of images as making present cosmic or archetypal powers) and as metaphors expressing a complicated and ambiguous psychological situation (drawing upon the perspective of depth psychology). Recall again our concentration upon the warrior image. Forever locked in combat, the warriors signaled an archetypal presence, the God Mars. This archetypal power of the image was made present precisely in its capacity to *speak*, as metaphor, to multitudinous dimensions of reality. Here is the image's capacity to stir our memories. The talismanic power of the image does not depend only on its literal proportions or markings, but becomes evident through one's psychological concentration upon it, as with images engaged in active imagination.

This concentration could extend to the acknowledging of the autonomous qualities of the image, and to a probing of the *characters* of the two warriors. Let us imagine as if Ricci were alive to explore these dimensions of the image. He might wish to speak to each warrior, to find out something about their biographies and what brought them to this position; this would deepen his empathy for them as imaginal persons. This deepening could be quite frightening as, let us say, the warrior holding the spear ready to strike the other one dead expressed his battle-rage, or Ricci could feel this warrior stirring within himself. The warrior trying to ward off the blow might be able to speak of the intense terror—or perhaps the psychic deadness—he feels in his anticipation of being killed. Ricci might write down what occurred during the dialogue, feeling his conflicts about war with much greater immediacy: the warriors would now be more deeply housed in his psychic life.

As Ricci concentrated upon the scene, he might also notice some movement; perhaps the war would come to life, quickening in the movement of imagination. The scene might change; other characters could join the battle; one warrior might kill the other as the drama was played out on the stage of memory. Or a series of movements could take place within Ricci's field of visual imagining, while in another, "behind-the-scenes" image, the warriors remain in their permanent embrace. Imaginal memory can involve a complex interplay between the moving and unmoving aspects of imagination, in which these are present simultaneously.

A more precise way of describing such interplays of imaginal memory involves distinguishing three forms of imagining: active, inactive and archetypal. In reflecting upon the static aspects of the *imagines agentes* we touch upon a quality of the art of memory which Hillman aptly calls an "*in*active imagination" in which events are carried, held and digested "inside" so that "space is created to contain them" (*RP*, p. 94; italics mine). The *inactivity* of images in the memory house, their deathlike stillness, turns out to be a profound form of psychic activity, a giving-place to imaginal presences without necessarily engaging in active imagination. One may hold an image, or a series of images, in a place of memory for years; it may appear forever unchanging and yet deepen into an important presence in one's psychic life. Thus, Ricci could hold the image of the warriors in quiet contemplation and it might work inactively to produce a slow alchemy of changes in his attitudes toward war *per se* and his own intense battles as a Jesuit missionary in China.

Edward Casey, in turn, names the "archetypal imagination" with reference to Camillo's Theatre, as a further extension of imagining into a realm of imaginal placescapes presenting differentiated orders of archetypal images. Inactive and archetypal imagining are connected in that both involve the holding of images of (and *by*) place, in the primary service of Memory, of developing a more differentiated apprehension of memorial placescapes. The distinction between "inactive" and "archetypal" imagining signifies a shift of perspective and value: when the static figures of inactive imagination are sensed as significant and potent images, they are realized as talismanic, as carriers of archetypal values. Then the inactive imagination is discerned as archetypal, and inactivity as the *unchanging* aspect of the archetypal.

Imaginal memory moves in the realms of active, inactive and archetypal imagining, and does so in intricate ways that are best revealed in the course of a close exploration of specific images. This is the aim of Part III. The images encountered in association with the place of Hiroshima will help us to more deeply imagine that which moves and that which remains still.

The work of imaginal memory may, but need not always, involve the more specific work of active imagination. The perspective given with active imagination, however, is crucial to imaginal memory: images, however imagined, are the shapes of intentions, values and visions that can range quite far from what we identify as our own. If the core of imaginal memory is, as defined in the preface, a practice of remembering images, this means not only that we are remembering images, but also that images are *themselves* remembering. Memory is inherent in the being of images, and our work involves giving images a place within which they can carry on *their* work of remembering us. Approaching the place of Hiroshima, we thus know ourselves to be remembered as well as remembering beings: to be ourselves images in the House of Memory.

Part III

Remembering the
Place of Hiroshima

5

Hiroshima as Place of Imaginal Memory

In the remembering of images from the art of memory, the latter appears as a practice of death, of crafting images of the ever-dying soul. This is evident from our initial recognition of Hades as the House of Memory, from the other sources of the Greek memorial tradition explored here, and from the "tortured" (*AM*, p. 104) *imagines agentes* of the art of memory itself. We remember too the horrible deaths in Scopas's banquet hall, on which the art is founded, and the poisoning, illness and death of the Victim in the lawsuit image. This is the context of the close relation between memory and melancholy that emerged in the previous chapter. This melancholy will deepen here as we engage an art of remembering *nuclear* death, starting with the moving yet "motionless" images arising from the place of Hiroshima. The melancholy of memory becomes, in the time of Hiroshima and the world since then, a way toward the "profound sorrow," in the U.S. Catholic bishops' phrase, with which this book opened.

James Hillman points to the connection of memory with the martial imagination, saying that "The nuclear imagination," in contrast, "is without ancestry."[1] From the perspective of Hiroshima as a place of imaginal memory, it is more precise to say that the nuclear world has forgotten its ancestors. It is time to give these ancestors and their profundity of sorrow a place in memory. The practice of imaginal memory in this context implies, as noted in previous chapters, a form of commemoration ("intensified remembering")—specifically of what Edward Casey terms "intrapsychic memorialization." Most precisely, this can be called "psychological commemoration." This combines aspects of intrapsychic memorialization with a specific psychological perspective and a way of remembering our nuclear ancestors and their dwelling places.

I will offer a more precise description of psychological commemoration toward the end of this chapter, but two of its features bear mentioning here. The first of these emerged in connection with Hermes's commemoration of Mnemosyne. There we saw that commemorative remembering implies honoring the elders and the ancestors, or rewarding them with a gift. Through the work of imaginal memory the world's nuclear ancestors are acknowledged and given a place of honor—rewarded with a gift of memory. More, we honor and give a gift to the precise ways in which these images embody their wounds, dyings and deaths—a gift of life to Death.

Second, the special intensity of commemorative remembering means that the images remembered (and remembering) gain new power in our psychological lives. Referring to Freud's notion of the "deferred action" (*Nachtraglichkeit*) of certain memories in the context of new circumstances, Casey points toward instances of remembering in which "the later vision is inherently stronger—more lasting, more forceful—than the first vision" (*R*, pp. 274–5).[2] Through the work of imaginal memory, images associated with the place of Hiroshima become more potent than when they were first impressed on our imaginations; their effects will thus become "more lasting, more forceful." Recall that through Hesiod, we recognized Memory as a theogonic power; and that Giordano Bruno alludes to a power of theurgic magic or "God-making" through the correct remembering of images. Through the "deferred action" of imaginal memory, the ancestral images of the nuclear world become archetypally powerful. In the place of Hiroshima, a theogony takes place; in the images dwelling there, we apprehend the presence of Gods or basic psychological potencies.

Just how this occurs will be evident after this chapter's elaboration of imaginal memory vis-a-vis the place of Hiroshima. Before entering into this work, however, there are several preliminary topics that warrant discussion, beginning with a consideration of how we may invite the presence of nuclear images.

INVITING IMAGES FROM THE PLACE OF HIROSHIMA

We may say of these images what Hillman says concerning dreams at the conclusion of *The Dream and the Underworld*: "our attitude toward them may be modeled upon Hades, receiving, hospitable, yet relentlessly deepening, attuned to the nocturne, dusky, and with a fearful cold intelligence that gives permanent shelter in his home to the incurable conditions of human being" (p. 202). Taking a hint from the reality that there is no defense from the nuclear bomb, we shall seek shelter not *from* but *with* the disfigured images of nuclear horror, housing them in memory, bringing them home. And to "house" here carries all the implications we have noticed in that most basic structure of the memorial psyche. In the first chapter, we spoke of remembering Hell, and in the second realized our place in the House of Death. Here we grant images of nuclear hell a place in Death's house, which means to realize their qualities as ghosts, ancestral shades of metaphor. Hell will be housed, kept alive in Death. We will return in chapter 7 to the distinction between Hades and Hell, and to what in the soul of our culture renders death a hell. But here and in the next chapter we are engaged in a reverse movement, returning Hell to its primary context: the place of shades, Death's hospitable house.

Gaston Bachelard says "the house shelters daydreaming, the house protects the dreamer, the house allows one to dream in pece." "Receiving" nuclear images, we shall invite them to find shelter in the dream-day of our memories, where we ourselves are protected. Thus sheltered, we, together with the other images, can remember nuclear war in peace. Motherlike, we must find ways too by which the soul may cradle and nurture these images of our collective dwelling. Modeling our practice upon Hades requires our hospitality, a receiving in imagination of those who we in our ordinary forgetfulness and uncare would shut out from the houses of our lives. For Death's doors are closed to no one.

Following the tradition of the *ars memorativa*, we will carefully entertain images arising from the place of Hiroshima; the art of imagination will allow us to entertain details of images that may be painful and grotesque, but in which a strange beauty and love can be discovered. In the course of this exploration (in the following chapter) a number of specific examples of places and images will be given as illustrations of this practice of memory, and the possibilities for psychological work to which it gives rise.

In the comments on psychological commemoration made above, I mentioned how we would be following the traditions of Hesiod and the Renaissance in concentrating upon memory images so that their lasting, that is, archetypally powerful, qualities may be revealed. But no attempt will be made here to envision any given *system* of nuclear memory images, though the systems of Giulio Camillo, Giordano Burno and Robert Fludd become treasure-houses of ideas and inventions as we begin to work seriously with these images. They suggest possibilities of configuration and can help us note some dominant patterns of imagination in the nuclear world that we may wish to keep in mind for our individual work (for example, images that are likenesses to Mars, Prometheus, and Two Serpents Fighting, as in Camillo's Memory Theatre). But, though the focus is mainly on our collective nuclear dwelling, we shall, like the author of

Ad Herennium and like Jung, insist throughout that the starting-place be with whatever places and images appear as most powerfully present in one's individual experience. The examples given here are intended as "seminal fantasies" that can aid in the attunement of one's archetypal sense of things; they are not intended to suggest *guided* fantasies in which specific images are imposed on the soul's experience. As the spirit of Bruno urges: "If you know any other way, try it."[3]

In this way, our invitation to the images present may be kept open.

"MISERABLE IMAGES"

The memorable character of images associated with the place of Hiroshima—whichever of them strike the reader's mind—is spontaneously evident. It may be helpful at this point to pause, notice these images and concentrate upon their memories, in whatever form they present themselves. These can be the images with which one's individual work of imaginal memory begins. Holding these images in memory, we find that they begin to take hold; their power begins to stir. Thus, they may be kept in mind for when the actual practice of imaginal memory proceeds further.

It will also be helpful to briefly recall the memorial experiences of actual *hibakusha*, when images of the atomic bombing first took hold.

Outside witnesses of the bombing of Hiroshima and Nagasaki, as well as *hibakusha*, often speak of horrifying images burned, engraved or otherwise impressed in memory. The authors of *Hiroshima and Nagasaki* say that "Certainly the most sweeping and searing destruction ever visited upon mankind left an enormous, abhorrent, and lifelong impression in the minds and memories of its victims. . . . Despite the passage of time, the memories of these survivors are strikingly vivid and concrete."[4] Lifton, writing of his interviews with survivors seventeen years after the bombings, remarks that "what impressed me throughout the work was the vividness of recall, the sense that the bomb was falling right there in my office—a vividness which seems to reflect both the indelible imprint of the event and its endlessly reverberating psychological repercussions" (*DL*, pp. 9–10). One image suggesting the "indelible imprint" of the experience appears in Masuji Ibuse's novel, *Black Rain*.[5] The marks left by the "black rain" that fell from the atomic cloud upon a young woman's hands will not wash off and remain "firmly stuck on the skin." Remember too Albert Goldbarth's vision of the Hiroshima horse-shadow "burnt permanently to a wall by the blast." Such "imprints" of memory remind one of the impressions of seal-rings in wax—a key figure for memory from Plato (*Theaetetus* 191D–E) and Aristotle (*De mem.* 450a 29–b 1) on, which is cited by all three classical Latin sources for the art of memory. The "endlessly reverberating psychological repercussions" cited by Lifton evoke for us the connection between Memory and Echo, the reverberations or echoes of memory. An echoing image is found in Robert Jungk's description of one *hibakusha's* being haunted by voices and cries of other victims at the time of the Hiroshima bombing: "Memories of 'that day' quite simply refused to be silenced."[6]

Speaking of the moment the bomb fell—of a red dragonfly, the sound of a B–29, his brother reaching out to catch the dragonfly and a flash—a boy, one of Osada's *Children of Hiroshima*, muses: "It is strange. These fragmentary scenes remain fixed in my mind like photographs."[7] "Even now," says a girl, "the sight of Father coming up the road toward us, his head wrapped in bandages, using his one good eye, and walking with a cane, is engraved in our memories."[8] In commenting on a picture he drew for the volume, *Unforgettable Fire*, a collection of pictorial memories of survivors, a man writes of "a charred body of a woman standing frozen in a running posture with one leg lifted and her baby tightly clutched in her arms. Who on earth could she be? This cruel sight still vividly remains in my mind."[9] Another man, who lost his own son to the bomb, tells of a "miserable image" of a junior high school boy, burned and dying as he pleads for water, which "always haunts me."[10] (Psychologically, this man is perhaps "father" to this image—the image serving also as his lost son, evoking endlessly reverberating grief.)

The boy whose memories are "fixed" in his mind adds: "I shall maintain forever in my mind the memory of this brutality and I am determined to help pave the way to true peace."[11] We sense an undertone of rage and sorrow in the boy's words. Too, there is an effort here to master the overwhelming experience of the bombing through an attempt to render inescapably present memories into a willed determination to remember. This then becomes part of the boy's struggle to discover moral meaning in the horror and its memory. There is an echo of this psychological pattern in Elie Wiesel's recollections of his Nazi concentration camp experience: "Never shall I forget these things, even if I am condemned to live as long as God himself. Never."[12]

The moral imperative that the world "never forget" what happened to the victims of the mass violence at Hiroshima, Nagasaki, Auschwitz and other places of twentieth century horrors suggests an ongoing hell of conflict: being haunted by memory regardless of what he wills, the survivor yet fears the forgetting of this memory. Often immersed in currents of uncare, the world would like to forget; somewhere, so does the survivor, so he or she can find "true peace." But the horrifying images—like impressions struck in ancient wax—are "fixed" and "engraved" in memory, remaining strikingly vivid and concrete like the "tortured" *imagines agentes* of the art of memory. Miserable images continue to haunt the soul.

While these wounded and disfigured images of Hiroshima evoked here thus figure the "unforgettable fire" of nuclear hell, those of us who are indirect witnesses of Hiroshima can more easily leave them forgotten, uncared for. Though we may acknowledge their presence at times (e.g., on the anniversaries of Hiroshima and Nagasaki, and when the nuclear peril is perceived as growing), we usually leave them without place in our imaginations. Yet they haunt us too, claiming a place within our psychic lives. As with other haunting figures, it is well to ponder what they want. Edward Casey, with reference to Camillo's Theatre, speaks of the need "to *provide places* for a mass of archetypal figures that would otherwise remain homeless . . ."[13] Lifton observes that: "Those killed in Hiroshima were thought of as homeless dead: they had died violently, in many cases lacking fulfillment and frequently without posterity, inevitably in the absence of proper death rituals" (*DL*, p. 492). These homeless figures have long enough haunted the souls of actual survivors, intensifying and complicating death guilt and other struggles. Perhaps what they want is an invitation from the rest of us: to be given a home in memory.

THE DISASTROUS BANQUET AND LAWSUIT IMAGE REVISITED

Engraved in the imagination of memory, the disastrous banquet that gives rise to the art of memory, and *Ad Herennium's* initial image of the lawsuit scene are still present with us. A reconsideration of these first images of the art of memory reveals their strangely precise relevance in the nuclear context.

The gruesome banquet disaster discloses, we saw, that the art of memory involves a movement toward death and disfiguration. As a myth of origin it shows us the pattern we—like previous practitioners of imaginal memory—will follow. On the morning of August 6, 1945, the people of Hiroshima went about their business, not knowing the peril hanging over their heads. The bomb fell; the roof fell in, leaving a site of horrible, grotesque death. The "world" of the house of Simonides is destroyed. To this site we must return, and, through the placings of memory, seek restoration of order, meaning and human continuity, giving the dead their place. But this requires a prior acknowledgement of the hidden or unseen relation of mortality and immortality in the soul, a way of dwelling like Castor and Pollux in heaven and in the house of Hades. Simultaneously, there is a movement away from the position in which we remain, for practical purposes, unaware of the peril hanging over us. Without this movement there can, in fact, be no art of memory.

The lawsuit image further specifies the relations between the art of memory and the soul's dying—relations whose presence will be felt in the movement toward a practice of imaginal memory in the nuclear age. Entertaining images arising from the place of Hiroshima, we find ourselves simultaneously in the positions of Victim, Accused, Witness and Accuser (or, more precisely, we find these figures present in certain psychic conflicts this practice is likely to involve).

The Victim is present in that we are, as discussed in chapter 2, all victims, in an important psychological sense, of the world's first nuclear tragedies and their reverberations. Part of this reverberation involves our anticipation of ourselves as victims of a future holocaust. (Victim consciousness in a more general sense has become particularly prominent in the 1980s, with increased focus on how certain groups of people have been abused. The abuses are real enough, but it has remained curiously difficult to address the universal victimization implicit in the nuclear threat.) But in remembering images of victimization we discover that one Victim in all this is the life of the soul—and that soul must be poisoned, ill, dying, dead. This much (though not the egoism of victimization and its literalism) is essential to memory's practice of death, to the gaining of the soul's inheritance, of the treasure-house of ideas and invention. And the horrifying images of victims, realized psychologically, become a source of profound wealth; through remembering images of Hiroshima, a wealth of psychic possibilities will emerge.

At the same time we stand accused in this remembering. In practicing imaginal memory we are thieves and murderers. We steal from the wealth within images of extreme suffering and death; in memory these images are kept alive by being killed, and held motionless in place.

The "survivor psychology" of the nuclear world adds a dimension to the way in which we stand accused. In chapter 2 we noted the patterns of death guilt Lifton found in *hibakusha* and Holocaust survivors: guilt over having survived, and having wished to survive, while so many others died; guilt over being relieved that it is the other and not oneself who is dead. Conflicts involving death guilt may reverberate through us as we approach the place of Hiroshima. Indeed, the remembering of Hiroshima has an inherent guilty or criminal association. Some voice will accuse one of using the dead for impure or ulterior purposes, thieving from the wealth of their suffering for the sake of one's own not-wholly-justified survival.

Such conflicts (which have emerged strongly in my work with nuclear images) may be an inevitable part of this practice of memory. But whatever the extent of their presence, it is important to move beyond the egoism of literal guilt. Here it is helpful to reflect on the archetypal element in the feeling of *indebtedness*, the sense that one must *pay* for what one has done, which is essential in guilt. We may recall in this connection the final debt that must be payed to Death. Herakles unwittingly acknowledges this in the *Alcestis*, when he says to Admetos (Death's persona) that "I shall still be deeply in your debt." More, one must pay *in order* to die: Charon demands his coin before he will take the soul across the river of death. Lifton's concept of death guilt here gains mythic resonance; guilt becomes the dying of ego and its innocence: not only the beginning of moral awareness and responsibility but also the necessary payment to Hades, or debt owed to the house of shadows. We must pay as we pass in memory into the house of the nuclear world.

Making this payment, we are forced to acknowledge imaginal realities. We are forced to remind ourselves that there is a difference between the imaginal characters we remember in association with the place of Hiroshima (whether or not these arise from historical persons), and the actual victims of the bombing. Anxiety over guilt leads to a keener awareness of both realities, of what is present in imagination and what actually happened in the atomic bombing.

Returning to the lawsuit image, we also find an image of the Witness. Our practice involves witnessing: recalling the testimonies of *hibakusha* and other nuclear witnesses, together with the *psychological* witnessing given with imaginal memory and active imagination (see discussion in chapter 4 above). In the lawsuit image the witnesses are remembered through the ram's testicles. Ours is a witnessing that engages the qualities of this organ recalled in chapter 4: a witnessing that engages both the striking, active, penetrating qualities of the nuclear *imagines agentes*, and their capacity to contain the soul's nascent world, its riches and its deaths. The moral aspect of witnessing, seen from the vantage point of the lawsuit image, thus gains psychological differentiation and depth.

In the remembering of Hiroshima we revisit the primary places of the *ars memorativa* tradition, discovering their psychological structure within an ongoing remembering of images.

HIROSHIMA AND THE PLACE OF TIME

In reflecting on "the place of time," an image of time quite different from the usual abstract and linear conception of the temporal emerged. Time in place partakes in the qualities of that place; inherent in places are qualities of times. It became evident through these reflections that the *place* of Hiroshima is also an image of *time*. When we consider this particular time more closely, we find it to be composed of many different times and their varying qualities.

We can discern these various times by returning to the foundation of the memory tradition in Hesiod, which tells us that the Muses "reveal what is and what will be and what was before." This was seen to disclose the archetypal qualities of remembrance, the mythic patterns present since the theogonic time (and embodying this time's presence), which will continue in the future (and are present in the current imagination of the future).

The time "Hiroshima" reveals not only "what was before," what took place on "that day" or at "that time," as the Japanese refer to it, but also "what is and what will be." Hesiod evokes the "timeless" time of myth, and this will be present at times in remembrances of Hiroshima. Mythic or archaic time is present in Goldbarth's poem when the Hiroshima horse-shadow opens to the primordial appearance of the horse on a cave wall. The remembrance of what historically was thus opens into another avenue of time; now the time when "It ended" and the time when "It began" are present at the same time. The image of each time is made more vivid, penetrating, active and emotionally striking, by its jux-taposition with the other.

The presence of archaic time within Hiroshima—a first place of the nuclear world—is also suggested by the epithets "that day" and "that time," which have a resonance to Eliade's description of mythic or paradigmatic events as having taken the place *in illo tempore*, "in *that* time."[14] "*That* time," in both the place of Hiroshima and in the imaginings of archaic cultures, is at once irrevocably past and irrevocably present. Hiroshima as first place of the nuclear world is also its first time, a paradigmatic time; its images of horror and destruction are yet of a "world-creating" character.

Yet the presence of what-has-been in the place of Hiroshima is in another way quite distinct from the essentially ahistorical time of archaic myth; the his-toricity of Hiroshima has its own particular quality. The what-has-been of the place of Hiroshima evokes and echoes all the places and times of history that have witnessed the human capacity for violence and killing in action. For the nuclear bomb concentrates in its being all the destructiveness, the *inhuman* power, of human violence. This is part of the reason for the profundity of sor-row one senses in the remembering of Hiroshima: its totality of destruction points toward a still deeper and broader remembrance of "what-we-have-been," of our collective psychic heritage of cruelty and killing. The time of the place of Hiroshima reveals this heritage of cruelty as an archetypal reality, now claiming its place in memory.

Hiroshima is also a first place of the nuclear end-of-the-world time, a time that is both past and future. In its concrete horrors there is a vision of this end, an echo of remembering of mythic visions of past and future ends-of-the-world.[15] "What was before" at Hiroshima may point to "what will be" for us all: an end both feared and fascinating, a future made present in images of the past of Hiroshima. This is why, in Jonathan Schell's words,

> The Hiroshima people's experience . . . is of much more than histori-cal interest. It is a picture of what our whole world is always poised to become—a backdrop of scarcely imaginable horror lying just behind the surface of our normal life, and capable of breaking through into that normal life at any second. Whether we choose to think about it or not, it is an omnipresent, inescapable truth about our lives today that at every single moment each one of us may suddenly become the de-ranged mother looking for her burned child; the professor with the ball of rice in his hand whose wife has just told him "Run away, dear!" and died in the fires; Mr. Fukai running back into the firestorm; the naked

man standing on the blasted plain that was his city, holding his eyeball in his hand; or, more likely, one of the million corpses.[16]

Again, Hiroshima becomes a paradigmatic time, a time which must forever be remembered—remembered as "omnipresent."

There is another way in which the time of Hiroshima reveals "what will be." Images arising from this place of time speak to us of the inevitability of death and of pathologized, disturbing psychic images. The nuclear threat compels us to imagine that the time of Hiroshima prefigures the literal time of the world's end. But from the perspective of imaginal memory, we can envision these images as prefigurings of a quite different sort of future. We may remember and imagine instead a future in which pathologized images from Hiroshima and other instances of historical catastrophe and violence are actively imagined, given their place in memory not acted out in literal annihilation.

In the work of imaginal memory, actual past and anticipated future are both made present so that we may apprehend the *presence* of soul in places and images figuring our nuclear history. The latter part of Schell's above-quoted passage reminds us of the distinct *imagines agentes* of memory. These remember for us as well as the psychic present, together with the presence in soul of future possibility. An archetypal sense of memory, as suggested in previous discussions (chapter 1 and 3), frees one from a too literal notion of time and the past, so that we can see the past's present and future. A narrowly literal concept of remembering invites, as Hillman observes, a displacement of the psychic present onto the historical past. Thus, he points out that "The Holocaust wasn't in the 1940s only. It's going on now. . . . We are living in a psychic concentration camp, in the sense that we are passively accepting the soulless world."[17] So too with remembering Hiroshima and Nagasaki. The "living hell" of which *hibakusha* speak is living in the soul of our culture, in images that speak too of the world's present pain, dying, disfigurement. Hiroshima reveals *what is*.

UNHEALING WOUNDS

Dr. Takashi Nagai, a survivor of the Nagasaki bomb (he died in 1951), writes of himself and his fellow victims: "We carry deep in our hearts, every one of us, stubborn, unhealing wounds."[18] This can be amplified in an unexpected manner by the experience of Father Wilhelm Kleinsorge, of John Hersey's *Hiroshima*, who begins to feel symptoms of radiation sickness during a walk through the ruins of Hiroshima. A few days later, back at the Novitiate outside of Hiroshima where he is staying, "the rector, who had examined Father Kleinsorge's apparently negligible but unhealed cuts daily, asked in surprise, 'What have you done to your wounds?' They had suddenly opened wider and were swollen and inflamed."[19] Let us consider this opening of wounds caused by the damage done by radiation to the body's reparative capacities as an image: what are the effects of nuclear images on the soul's imaginal body? Returning to such images and placing them in memory will mean opening and amplifying, or *un-healing*, wounds. The soul opens wider in pain to the stubborn wounds of its heart, its tissues now "swollen and inflamed." The experiences of Father Kleinsorge—who, as a figure in one of the primary stories of Hiroshima, can be taken as a kind of mythic character of the nuclear age—resonate in us all. We who were not present at the bombings of Hiroshima and Nagasaki drink often of Lethe's safe waters, and tend to consider the damage of these events to our individual and collective psychic lives as relatively superficial and minor, like Father Kleinsorge's cuts. Yet "We carry deep in our hearts, every one of us, stubborn, unhealing wounds" which are only "apparently negligible." And they will open wider and deeper when we return, like Father Kleinsorge, to the site of destruction.

This practice of imaginal memory involves a therapeutic perspective in which the emphasis is less on healing and health than on the "un-healing" of the soul. Here we give open attention, and are open, to the unhealing wounds and inflamed tissues of nuclear images.

Yet this practice has its prenuclear traditions: the art of memory with its disfiguring operations, and the similar work of alchemy. (Here is another way in which Hiroshima and Nagasaki reveal "what was before.") The third century alchemist, Zosimos, records for us a vision of the un-healing wounds of alchemy. In it, he sees a priest standing upon a bowl-shaped altar who proclaims that "I submit myself to an unendurable torment": dismemberment by a figure with a sword "in accordance with the rule of harmony.

> And he drew off the skin of my hand with the sword, which he wielded with strength, and mingled the bones with the pieces of flesh, and caused them to be burned upon the fire of the art, til I perceived by the transformation of the body that I had become spirit. And that is my unendurable torment." And even as he spoke thus [relates Zosimos], and I held him by force to converse with me, his eyes became as blood. And he spewed forth his own flesh. And I saw how he changed into the opposite of himself, into a mutilated anthroparion, and he tore his flesh and sank into himself.
>
> (quoted in *CW* 13 par. 86)

This "unendurable torment" is, according to Jung, "the torment of hell" (*CW* 13, par. 94). Jung observed the typical motifs of archaic sacrificial imagery: flaying, dismemberment, torture, burning, "death, and transfiguration" (*CW* 13, par. 139).[20]

Notice, however, the priest's words: "that is my unendurable torment." Despite his being rendered as spirit, the torment does not go away, but remains simultaneously present. Despite the spirit-fantasies of alchemy, which tend toward wholeness and "transfiguration," the wounds imagined throughout its tradition remain unhealed, in a state of *dis*-figuration, bodying forth the still living hell that is fundamental to the deep movement of soul. Hillman, speaking with reference to Zosimos, and the general role of the motifs of dismemberment and torture in Jung's alchemical psychology, connects these with Dionysos, whose epiphany lies precisely in this painful horror and suffering (this is shown by the name of the God's unwitting double in Euripides's *The Bacchae*: Pentheus, "He Who Suffers").[21] "Dismemberment," he says, "refers to a psychological process that requires a *body metaphor* . . ." He cites a number of bodily-based symptoms (e.g., psychosomatic and sexual) and fears (such as those of aging, pollution and disintegration) as belonging archetypally to this constellation. We may add to these the damages, and damage-fantasies, radiated by nuclear weapons: burns due to thermal radiation and fires, disfiguring and even dismembering injuries from blast effects, and the disintegrative processes in the body resulting from radiation sickness.

We shall further explore the wounds of nuclear images as we develop our practice of memory. Here we notice the pschological connections between woundedness, openness and depth. To be wounded is to be "open," with deeper structures and tissues laid bare. Hillman cites a dream in which

> A young potter's hand is cut open down to the bone. He is horrified and fascinated by the sight. The dreamer can now see that his hand which forms itself formed by deep, hard, ancient structures and that the shapes he makes have a preformed interior pattern. The dream has released an archetypal sense of what he is doing.[22]

The un-healing wounds opened at Hiroshima and Nagasaki also horrify and fascinate; placed in memory, they help us remember the archetypal sense of what we are doing.[22]

THE PLACE OF HIROSHIMA AND THE PLACE OF MEMORY

"The place of Hiroshima" and "the place of memory" are two main themes of this book. The phenomenological relation of place and memory (or place as the house of memory) has been discussed with reference to the place setting of the *Phaedrus*, and the imagination of place in the art of memory. I have often spoken of the place of Hiroshima, but so far have not addressed an important question: Just what kind of place is Hiroshima in our imaginations?

In order to discover the specific nature of the place "Hiroshima," some further discussion of the more general psychological nature of place will be helpful. Edward Casey, in a discussion of how soul inhabits place, refers to the "memorability" of specific, unique places such as San Francisco. With regard to the particular attractions of that city, he observes that

> it is just the sort of place you can leave your heart in. And "heart" is the the *most juste* since the heart is the ultimate place of human attach-ments: "you have a place in my heart," meaning that you and more par-ticular memories involving you belong to me, constitute me in the most intimate way. . . . Place-heart-memory: here is a genuine *mys-terium coniunctionis* which yields heart as the place of memory, mem-ory as the place where heart is left, heart as what is left of remembered place.[23]

The "intrinsic memorability" of place, notes Casey, is a disclosure of its power. For vivid examples of this we may turn to the phenomenology of sacred places, for these are where the divine is remembered, experienced and placed in imagi-nation. This is illustrated in the *Phaedrus*, where the sacred grove by the Ilissos evokes myths essential in the religious history of Athens. The relation of place, memory and the power of the sacred is also shown in the story of Jacob's dream in which he sees a ladder connecting heaven and earth upon which angels are as-cending and descending, and in which he is spoken to by God. Upon awaken-ing, Jacob exclaims, "How awesome is this place! This is none other than the house of God, and this is the gate of heaven" (Gen. 28:17). Jacob then sets up the stone he had used for a headrest as a marker, a monument witnessing to and commemorating the divine power there housed. We remember that place still.

Also displayed in different ways by these two sacred places is what Casey describes as the "verticality" inherent in the structure of place.[24] This is most ob-vious in Jacob's dream, with its ladder and its themes of ascent and descent. It is present too in the place of *Phaedrus*, suggested by the constellation of myths around Oreithyia and Boreas. The former is a mountain-maenad who in one version of the story is swept off the Aeropagus to fall to her death, and the latter is the cold mountain wind that is also the breath or spirit of Hades, the under-world. Again, in ancient Shinto ritual, the *kami* or sacred reality was invited "to come down and take up its residence temporarily in the sacred place. . . . Around the sacred spot were placed stones."[25] The *kami* originally descended to a sacred tree, the place of which was later taken by the Shinto shrine.

Memory in place is a means of experiencing vertical connection between worlds, the connection and striving of spirit. Remember the vertical connec-tions present from the outset of the *Theogony*, the linking of the heights and depths through Mnemosyne and her daughters. The relation of memory loci to lower and upper realms is evident in the medieval and Dantean descent into *memoria* and in the celestial and astral connections of Renaissance uses of the art of memory. An imaginal sense of place always apprehends and considers its heights and depths, heeding one of its basic powers.

Cities are also displays of the memorable power of place. They too embody the vertical imagination; they bear within themselves memory-traces of the first places of connection between the human and the divine: trees, mountains, temples and shrines, which are places of contact betweeen earth and sky; and underground places, which connect surface and depth. In addition, cities extend *horizontally* and create boundaries—both between city and outside realm, and between distinct precincts within the city itself. The horizontal or boundary-making power of place emerged in our discussion (previous chapter) of the relation between memory and melancholy, and was seen as expressive of an archetypal power, Saturn or the senex. The vertical dimension of place embodies that direct connection with spirit for which the puer or eternal youth seeks. Cities are particularly powerful places because they are *meeting-places* of senex and puer, of horizontal boundaries and openings to higher and lower realms.

Returning to the nuclear context, we find that this power led American planners during World War II to omit Kyoto—considered uniquely rich in religious, historical and cultural memories—from their list of atomic-bomb targets. This was done out of a combination of respect for the place (especially on the part of Secretary of War Henry Stimson) and concern for the reaction of the Japanese were it destroyed;[26] in both considerations, the power of place is fundamental. We resist remembering Hiroshima and Nagasaki not only because of our tendencies to deny and avoid death, and also the nuclear reality; this resistance can also be imagined, not as *ours*, but as the resistance of *place itself* to the destruction of its memories, of its distinct boundaries and its openings to the vertical.

Casey draws a sharp distinction, interesting in this regard, between place and site.[27] Site lacks the particularities, the specific characteristics of place that disclose the latter's power, its place in dream and memory, soul and heart. "Think of the difference," suggests Casey, "between being in a cityscape or landscape and becoming sensuously attuned to it, versus gazing at a map of the same placescape." Site, by contrast, is a "modification" of place, in the sense of being "non-unique and replaceable." It is without differentiation, lacking soul, power and memorability.

Nuclear weapons are an extreme expression of aesthetic insensitivity to the qualities, the soul, of unique places. Think of the computer maps guiding strategic planning. Robert Sardello, speaking of the neglected importance of remembering a city's past history, criticizes ill-considered projects of "urban renewal," quoting the architect Arthur Erickson in this context: "There is no greater machine of aggression against the city and against one's fellow man than the bulldozer."[28] "With the exception," Erickson prefaces his statement, "of the nuclear warhead."

Remember what Hiroshima and Nagasaki looked like after the nuclear fires died down. Casey observes that: "Sites modify places by leveling them down, razing them, making them indifferently planar, so that horizontality comes to count for more than verticality."[29] When Father Kleinsorge returns twelve days after the bombing to near the explosion's hypocenter, he finds "the few standing, gutted buildings only accentuating the horizontality of everything else . . . "[30] Listen to Yoto Ota, a woman *hibakusha*, tell of her wandering through the destroyed city when

> I reached a bridge and saw that the Hiroshima Castle had been com-
> pletely leveled to the ground, and my heart shook like a great wave.
> . . . This destruction of the castle gave me a thought. Even if a new city
> should be built on this land, the castle would never be built and added
> to that city. The city of Hiroshima, entirely on flat land, was made
> three-dimensional by the existence of the white castle, and because of
> this it could retain a classical flavor. Hiroshima had a history of its
> own. And when I thought about these things, the grief of stepping over
> the corpses of history pressed upon my heart.
>
> (quoted in *DL*, p. 86)

Such landmarks as the castle, revealing the historical heart of Hiroshima, are unique and irreplaceable; their leveling stirred Miss Ota's heart and memories at a time when she had become to an extent "used" to destruction and human corpses.

The leveling of Hiroshima (the memory of which is present in feared images of nuclear holocaust, where the destruction of cities remains a dominant theme), in addition to serving its vertical connections, destroyed what is basic in place's horizontal imagination: distinct boundaries, enclosures, habitations. Nuclear destruction—as is often said—knows no boundaries (nor, Chernobyl reminds us, does nuclear radiation).

"The place of Hiroshima," in the context of the preceeding discussion, seems a paradoxical if not oxymoronic phrase. Yet Hiroshima *is*, and *lays claim to*, a quite definite place in our individual and collective imaginations. More, it is a place with remarkable staying power, an archetypal image of the nuclear age. The place of Hiroshima endures through the vicissitudes of public concern about nuclear weapons; so deep is its impression on memory that we can be certain it would remain there even if nuclear weapons were abolished.

For *Hiroshima is the place of no place*, revealing a deep lacuna, a *placelessness*, at the heart of postindustrial culture. To this place we must nonetheless repair; within the place of memory we may allow the imagination of place itself to once more stake its claims. Then Hiroshima's power as place will be present, distinctly bounded, expressive of that which is highest and lowest in history and soul.

Conversely, nuclear devastation and plans for it are the final expression of indifference to place, and its importance to the memorial heart—a form of total forgetfulness, annihilation of all memory. Just here we grasp part of the reason why nuclear devastation is a horror "beyond imagination"; it leaves no place to remember.

APPROACHING HIROSHIMA AS PLACE OF IMAGINAL MEMORY

It is now evident that the forgetting of the place of memory discussed in chapter 1 goes in tandem with the forgetting of the memory of place implicit in the unfolding of the nuclear age. Approaching Hiroshima as the first place of imaginal memory implies the remembering, the reconstructing of our cultural imaginations of place and memory themselves, as we work explicitly to give place in memory to nuclear realities. For it is this that is most basic to the practice of imaginal memory: place and memory are primary aspects and powers of the world, the structures which render the world a house for the soul's imaginings, a place where images dwell.

The practice to be proposed here consists essentially in the imagining of a house of memory whose inhabitants are images and figures associated with the place of Hiroshima. Its basic structure follows that of the art of memory: places and images. In the remainder of this chapter I will elaborate a frame for beginning this work, starting with a few suggestions that may be helpful for first approaches to places of imaginal memory.

Imaginal memory is, as stressed in previous chapters, synaesthetic and kinaesthetic: memory images may or may not be primarily visual, but other sensings of the imagination are always at least tacitly present. Remember or imagine, for example, the experience of writing down one or two words while bearing down hard with the writing implement. A visual image arises; but at the same time, there is a distinct tactile or bodily impression of bearing down hard on the writing surface. Without actually engaging in bodily movement, one's body is fully engaged in this remembering as its imaginal weight goes into the effort of writing. A sound associated with writing (differing according to the type of writing implement and surface) may be present as well.

There is more to the image. Is it a memory in the sense of an actual experience that occurred sometime in one's personal past? Or is it an unfamiliar image composed, nonetheless, of elements of various remembered experiences of writing something down? A particular emotional tone, a mood or atmosphere, may become noticeable; a number of other memories associated with that emotional atmosphere may also come to mind. Any emotional atmosphere is likely to be related in some way to the word or words being written down. Whatever the verbal image is, it is likely to have multiple connotations, pointing to a variety of associated remembrances engaging the many senses of imagination. Other features of the image as a whole are apparent: what are the writing implement and surface being used? Is it oneself who is using them, or someone else? If it is oneself, where is one's remembering consciousness placed? Is it within one's imagined body, mimicking the actual experience of writing? Or is this body viewed from some other perspective (e.g., front, back, above or below)? If it is another person doing the writing, is it someone familiar or not? Together with the active image of writing, there is also a particular place setting. Where is this activity taking place, and what is that place like? Is any connection evident between different facets of the image (e.g., word, imagined bodily posture, place, or writing implement)?

The complexity of this imaginal remembering is now at once more apparent and more obscure; we wonder why the image appeared in a particular way and not another, and what meanings it might conceal. Notice, however, that there is an intricate complexity *prior* to any attempt at an in-depth psychological or other analysis. This is the complexity of imaginal presence in its various dimensions. Within the place and image as present in the field of imagining and remembering, there are suggestions of many other places and images. It will be helpful to remember this suggestive complexity as one's imaginal remembering develops.

Another first approach into the realm of imaginal memory would involve in some way mimicking the rhetoric student summoned up by *Ad Herennium* (*AM*, p. 8), who moves slowly in a lonely building, pausing at intervals with an intent face as he concentrates upon memorizing one place after another. If, following his example, one were to begin remembering places, what might be a good place to start? This might include actually going to and moving through a series of places—say, a room or series of rooms in one's dwelling-place—in an effort to memorize the distinct features of each. If so, what would seem the best way to go about the actual work of remembering? If it is, instead, a place one visits in one's mind, the same question presents itself, though with a different set of possibilities and limitations (e.g., it would be possible to view the place from the vantage-point of above, over one's head—which would be physically impossible—while it would not, of course, be possible to actually run one's hand over some feature of the place). One way of remembering would be to concentrate on, and visualize, the features of each given place, perhaps returning to the place several times in order to make sure of remembering its features as precisely as possible. However, the features of the place call for a different kind of noticing as well, an aesthetic response, a taking- or breathing-in of its qualities. Now the place has a place within one's sensual imagination, at the same moment as one realizes oneself as fully in the place.

There is a give-and-take of relationship between one's body and the given place that also warrants noticing. For, as Edward Casey observes, "it is by bodily movement that I find my way in place and take up habitation there. My body not only takes me into places; it habituates me to their peculiarities and helps me to remember them vividly" (*R*, p. 180). The body remembers a place in its own way, responding to the place through its positioning and movements, so that the place becomes embodied. An important aspect of remembering the place involves carefully noticing the body's own remembering responses.

There are a number of possible ways of entering into and exploring the memory of place. Here I will cite two of these. One involves an emotional exploration, starting with the apprehension of the particular mood present in the place. Concentrating upon this mood of the place, a number of associated memories and images may begin to emerge. These can be seen as the powers inhabiting the place: this way of noticing reminds us of Socrates's awareness of the powers and Gods inhabiting his and Phaedrus's resting-spot by the Ilissos River. The place itself may be, or become, emotionally striking, an active image; then it will more deeply penetrate and impress itself upon the memory.

The second way of exploring places of memory concerns the possibilities of remembering nonactual places. These may be places from a work of literature, a painting or photo; places imagined or created for the specific purpose of housing memories (such as envisioning a room added onto an actually existing house); or historical places, past or present. Each of these places will have its own distinct power and way of making its impression upon the memory.

There are many other possible ways of entering into the realm of imaginal memory. To quote Bruno once more: "If you know any other way, try it." The above examples provide a glimpse of the possible range and complexity of this method (or set of methods) of imagination, which will help orient us as we approach the place of Hiroshima.

The first necessary move of our work may be simply to recall the largest context of the art of memory: to remember the world, to call forth whatever images of the world one finds most powerfully present in imagination. Remember Augustine, who, "in that vast court of my memory," finds "present with me, heaven, earth, sea, and whatever I could think of therein, besides what I have forgotten" (*Conf.* X. ix. 14). When remembering the world, what images appear "present with" one in memory? The images recalled may arise from the human world, as well as the nonhuman natural and cosmic realms; from places where we have traveled, or from those we have never actually seen. Nor need we exclude images of worlds usually labeled "imaginary": in landscapes of dream, fiction and fantasy the cosmos makes its presence felt also. Moving through these various places and images of what Robert Fludd called the great "common place," we sense, become aesthetically attuned to, the presence of world in imagination.

Open to and mindful of the world, we may turn more specifically to the practice of remembering images arising from the place of Hiroshima. Having mused over images of the greater world, the musing mind now begins to focus more specifically on the nuclear reality. Places and images associated more directly with that reality begin coming to mind, stirring in the memorial heart. It becomes evident that the prior step of ranging through places and images of the world has rendered the ability to sense the immediacy of these nuclear images more acute.

Musing over places and images associated with Hiroshima, it can be helpful to pay close attention to the sensual yet mindful *imagination of the body*, whose role in the work of memory we have just seen. The body has its own mind, its own intelligent imagination.

Particular bodily sensations or images may now become apparent: where in the body might they be placed? Bodily sensations contain and embody images—particularly difficult, sensitive and painful ones resisted by the ego's mind. For instance I feel a nervous tingling in my hands as I ponder the nuclear situation, then become aware of an urge to dance and jump. I imagine myself doing so, or, if I choose to actually embody this urge, I imagine myself *as* I dance and jump. In this movement of bodily imagination, I notice the presence of an image. It is a picture drawn by a *hibakusha* of a victim whose hands were badly burnt, so that the skin hangs in strips from the fingertips. I now feel this image and its exquisite pain with and *in* my fingers and yet, as I feel it, it becomes distinguished from "my" self. Now "pictured," it gains a separate place in the soul while still very much present in the body. A number of possibilities—of significance and imaginal enactment—are released and come to mind with the image; the memory of the actual bomb victim becomes more striking, makes a deeper impression with its felt immediacy of presence.

Through these opening movements of memory, one experiences Hiroshima as a quite definite place within one's imagination. In more closely approaching this place, the art of memory provides a helpful thematic structure, the "rules" for places and images. The use here of these rules need not, of course, be taken literally; they are instead an opening framework. We begin with them to feel our way into the memorial structures of soul and history, which always present themselves in terms of places and images.

Remembering the place of Hiroshima in this manner leads to the question: precisely what place, or places, of imagination will be right for the images arising from the place of history? There are a variety of possibilities for such houses of memory. A building one frequents, or has visited in one's travels, may come to mind. It could be an actual house one remembers: one's own present, past and/or childhood home; the home of a friend or other acquaintance, or one from an earlier historical period. Following *Ad Herennium*, ancient Rome could be the setting for one such place; or one might imagine a cave (the first house of humankind?), or a house of a God. Various combinations of actual and nonactual houses may be imagined (if an actual house appears altered or distorted in imagination, it is important to notice and remember the distortion, rather than to try and remember the place "correctly"). Or is the original nuclear drama to be imagined in a memory theatre? Other places and terrains are possible: that grove one remembers by the river, a place on the beach, some new circle of Dante's *Inferno*. (It is important to remember the distinction between traditional images of hell and the underworld, which are made up of often highly differentiated places, levels, dimensions; and the undifferentiated character of the site of nuclear destruction. Imaginal memory provides a place for this site and thus "re-places" it.)

The place of Hiroshima may be recollected from that city, and/or Nagasaki, as these actually were (just after the bombing?) or are. Would it then be a place in the Peace Park at Hiroshima—say, the Peace Museum or the Memorial Mound, in which the ashes of some 70,000 bomb victims are said to be housed? Perhaps the "A-Bomb Dome," the partially destroyed remains of an industrial exhibition hall left as a monument to the destruction, comes to mind.

Other places may be associated with that of Hiroshima. Where, for instance, is the place of Chernobyl (together with other civilian nuclear power plant accidents) in memory? A variety of associated places may appear in memory: images of the area surrounding the power plant, of Kiev, of Moscow's Hospital No. 6. Such places (and times) as Chernobyl and Three Mile Island inevitably become associated with Hiroshima and other nuclear bomb-related images; their psychic topography may become evident through one's imaginal exploration of the latter.

Memory provides "a large and boundless chamber" (Augustine, *Conf.* X. ix. 15) of possibilities for places in which the place of Hiroshima can be housed. Yet the places are precisely bounded; the practice of imaginal memory involves an exact noticing, we have seen, of the particular features of the various loci. This noticing may follow *Ad Herennium's* suggestions that the places be spaced at moderate intervals, be relatively well-lit, and provide a space proportionate to the images each will house. Again, one need not literalize these rules; they are metaphors, *archai* or first principles of imagination: what we need to notice most closely is how the psyche is always present in particular places, to remember place itself. One may find the recommendation of Albertus Magnus congenial: "Imagine and seek out dark places having little light." One may also pay attention to the sensuous *quality* of whatever light is given with a particular place, to where the light comes from, and to the darkness and shadows of the place. Different places evoke different moods, textures, associations, sounds and smells. These particularities reveal important psychological nuances of the way one is remembering the place of Hiroshima: or, how the *place itself* is re-membering through one's imagination.

Some examples of imaginal places of Hiroshima will reveal the formative power of place in this work. One man who recently left the Navy after serving five years remembers a particular hallway in the Naval College at Newport, Rhode Island, which appears to him as a fitting place for nuclear images. The hallway is about fifty yards long and is well-lit, for one side of the hallway, fac-ing east, is largely glassed in. Set in recesses in the opposite wall are six exhibits, copperplated and three-dimensional, of famous episodes in major wars, such as the Civil War (with cannon), World War I, World War II (a relief of soldiers emplacing the American flag on Iwo Jima), and others the man does not distinctly remember. It is in this place of war memorialized that an imaginal character dying from the Hiroshima bomb will appear.

A woman, politically active in disarmament and other antiwar efforts, re-members a particular dark hallway in her former elementary school; the school nurse's office opens into this hall, and may be able to provide some shelter to a terrified little girl who comes running through the hallway. Hanging on the wall next to the nurse's office door is a painting: *The Scream*, by Edvard Munch.

Another hallway—this one entirely nonactual—appears to a woman who has recently become interested in the nuclear dilemma. The woman walks down the corridor, onto which many doors open. There are two rooms about which she is especially curious—the Night and Day rooms, as she calls them. She first looks into the Night room; on the ceiling all the stars and constellations are vis-ible. It is a black starry night, with no air or movement. On the walls are black shadows that are all that is left after people—victims of nuclear holocaust—walked through the walls into blackness. The woman only takes one step into this fearful room.

We will come back to this place, and look into the Day room, when (in the following chapter) we look more closely at the psychology of places and images remembered. One more example is from a man, trained as a scientist and now devoting his time to disarmament efforts. He remembers the old house of a friend whom he admires and looks up to. He decides that it should be called "House of Desire," which refers to his belief that his friend has more completely fulfilled his desires than he has been able to do. When asked what room in the house might be right for images associated with Hiroshima, he names the mas-ter bedroom.

There is a particular power in each of these different places, and a kind of rhetoric: each place speaks eloquently to essential themes in the individual's life history and response to the nuclear threat. Each place speaks, too, to psycholog-ical factors transcending the individual, though with varying emphases. (The collective and impersonal dimension is more apparent in the imagery of the

Night and Day rooms than in the other three places, but our exploration below will indicate that these too have transindividual features.) The rhetoric of these places will warrant a closer hearing below, but their power to make a deep impression upon the memory, to provide a place for remembering images, and to evoke a number of psychologically potent themes, is evident even from a brief recounting.

After allowing enough time for the places one remembers to make a deep and vivid impression upon the imagination, one's attention turns to the images that will inhabit these houses. Recall *Ad Herennium's* observation that emotionally striking, perhaps disfigured or bizarre, images "can adhere longest in the memory." Previously, I noted the inherently memorable character of images connected with Hiroshima. Which of these now come to mind, are most impressive? It is probably well to begin with images spontaneously appearing (allowing them, as with the places, to be present as they are, not trying to force them to appear as one may think they "should"), though it may also be helpful to read or reread historical, pictorial and/or fictional accounts of the atomic bombings. These are the images that may find shelter, a place to stay in the house of memory.

The images may appear as alive, dying, dead, or as ghosts—perhaps in between life and death in a way not easily defined. They may be well-known, like Father Kleinsorge of *Hiroshima*, or unknown and unnamed. They may emerge from other sources of imagination, places of fantasy and dream we remember in connection with Hiroshima. Whatever their sources, we may find them altered or distorted by the fantasy so as to better reflect the nature of the psyche. Like Dante's figures, for instance, they may reflect historical persons, and may greatly deepen our empathy and compassion for the sufferings of actual atomic bomb victims; but, as I have emphasized in several contexts, the *images* are not literally and actually these persons. It is essential to notice that history and fantasy—although ineluctably bound together—are also distinct. Keeping in mind this distinction allows us to further notice the distinct presence of each in the other. In the present work of memory, images are given a place where the truth and precision of fantasy take precedence over literal historical fidelity even as we seek to remember what, historically, is and has been. What is needed here is a *psychological* fidelity, a careful noticing of what is present in imagination rather than a whimful constructing of images according to the ego's conscious wishes or preconceptions (historical, empirical or otherwise).

Strangely, this insistence on psychological fidelity enables one to sense most keenly the presence of history in fantasy. The image, seen as an autonomous figure of soul engaging yet distinct from the ego and history, is the most precise expression of the situation present in memory. For instance, no atomic bomb victim with skin hanging from his or her burned fingertips would wish to dance; accounts of this horror depict persons holding their arms still in front of them as they walk slowly, trying to avoid any friction that would add to the pain. In fantasy, though, the urge to dance, which this image presents to me, seems a way of accentuating both the pain and its awareness; this I get in touch with through the fingertips. The fantasy figure seems to want this, to want to articulate a dance of pain, a movement of suffering in ritual, which opens into the felt woundedness of image *and* of actual history. (Images of things, says Bruno, are nearer to reality than their physical or empirical "shadows" [*AM*, p. 228]; curiously the realization of the nonempirical nature of image leads also to a keener sense of physical realities, which themselves are then seen psychologically, not as empirical facts only.)

What position do these "miserable images" take? What are they doing in their places? Though fixed in memory, they are active images; their torments move us in unforgettable ways. What do they look like? If they have visible disfiguring images, what do these look like? Because "exact pathological detail" inheres in the movements and figurings of the soul, it will be important to notice precisely where and how these figures are wounded, to see with the acuteness of nightmare: the walking ghost with no hair, the naked girl searching for her lost mother, the father who has lost his left eye, the woman whose face, disfigured by burns, now resembles "a comic mask."[31] Are any smells noticeable, or remembered in association with a particular figure? Smell is an important carrier of memory and many *hibakusha* vividly remember the overwhelming stench of wounds, disease and death. (See *DL*, p. 23 on this olfactory imagery. The "stink" of nuclear wounds will be further imagined in the following chapter.) Are there cries, voices or other sounds echoing in these halls? Perhaps some kind of music comes to mind, whether placed with particular images, given as a kind of overall quality of a place, or simply remembered in association with one's imaginings.

More important than actual auditory imagery may be our sense of metaphoric hearing, an attunement to a mute rhetoric of the images, the precise ways in which they *speak* to us. There may be no blatant physical wound, scar or disease visible, but a figure's eyes, facial expressions and bodily positions may tell of sufferings we do not directly envision, or perhaps of joys remembered.

Like the memory rules for places, the rules for images are not seen only literally in this work; the psyche itself defines what makes the deepest impression, is emotionally striking and strange. One afternoon, for instance, I remember the aforementioned image from *Unforgettable Fire*, of a dying boy crying out for water, recalled by a man whose own son was lost to the bomb. I remember an intense, haunting sadness through which I enter the imagination of this man's grief. He is wearing what at first seems an indistinct, Japanese-style robe, but this resolves itself into what unmistakably a a *tallith* or fringed prayer-shawl traditionally worn by Jews when praying. It is like the one the rabbi of the synagogue I attended as a boy wore when he conducted services.

"But that's bizarre," says some voice within me—a voice at once expressing bewilderment and issuing a kind of mocking challenge to me in my work of remembering. I am challenged to remember what in this instance is *really* bizarre, hence truly *real* in imagination. The voice now appears to have confirmed the reality of this strange new—yet also not new—presence with which I am faced: a man with a Japanese visage, a *hibakusha*, head bowed in what I sense is a kind of "religious sadness," wearing a *tallith*. The voice is a kind of affirmation: "Yes, this *is* bizarre. Remember." I am left in the presence of this sad, yet prayerful, father, whom I must now face in a place I would not have thought to call a synagogue.

As the remembering of images proceeds, it becomes important to reflect on the question, discussed in the previous chapter: Just *who* is doing the remembering in this house? If *images* truly remember; if throughout our existence we are remembered as well as remembering beings, we are *being remembered* when in this house as in all the other places of our lives. The implications of this reverberate in the depths of soul and being. Not only do we come to know the images present; we are also known by them. They each have their own perspective, their own specific way of remembering. Here no less than in the grove by the Illissos where Socrates describes the role of the many Gods in memory, memory is fundamentally polytheistic, a many-faceted complexity of places and images each with its own power and subjectivity. The awareness of ourselves as remembered *by* images opens into possibilities of a far greater depth of dialogue or other forms of meeting with the inhabitants of this house of memory.

Two further implications need acknowledgement here. First, we must extend the question, "*Who* is remembering?" to ourselves. When I am in the presence of the sad father who lost his son, who is it that through my persona is recalling this man? Is it possible that it is that son, remembering his father? The different characters who inhabit our selves have, like the Gods in the *Phaedrus*, their own distinct ways of remembering and imagining. Grandfather and Mother react differently when remembering in the House of Hiroshima; more, the different images we face in this house evoke different characters, as the sad father calls forth his (or perhaps another's) son; and as the terrified girl in the elementary school described above calls forth a nurse. We move deeper into memory as we become able to trace the variegated imaginal characters who are housed within us, and who respond to those housed in the place of Hiroshima.

The second implication of the realization that we are being remembered is thoroughly ontological: we *are being*, remembered in the House of Hiroshima by those imaginal beings who point toward a reality, and a possibility, of nuclear *non*-being. In this house, as in those visited by Odysseus, Aeneas and Dante, there are shades who find in our entry an occasion to remember Being itself, as well as the many different beings constituting our, and others' existences. And the Being being remembered here is the world itself; as these images of Hiroshima force us to remember and reflect upon our beings in essence, so we, by being there with them, allow them a chance to remember the world. We embody not only our personal being, but the being of the world, which being is being remembered in us by the ancestral images of the nuclear age. This is an occasion for us as well: an occasion to sense how the world might be remembered in a way quite different from what we *ourselves*—without these images—could ever imagine.

The *place of time* discussed previously is also important here. Each image and place has, and takes, its own time, or may embody different times simultaneously. How long has it been, for each figure, since the bomb went off? It could be immediately after, or later "that day," or days, months, years, or even an indeterminate time later. In what ways do these different times find place, make themselves present? An image may appear just as when the bomb went off, while it has yet been forty-five years since "that time." (This would echo classical imaginings of the underworld, where the dead may bear fresh wounds but are aware that much time has passed since their deaths.) One may become aware that an image has a time extending far beyond the historical event of the bombing to other events in human history. As we witnessed in this chapter's previous discussion, the place of Hiroshima as a whole opens back into the remembering of all the mass violence witnessed in history. Again, as in the case of Goldbarth's vision of the horse-shadow imprinted on a wall in Hiroshima, an image may extend further back, into the "timeless," transhistorical realm or *illud tempus* of the soul; in this way the image is *eternalized*. Another time which may appear in connection with some images is the anniversary-reaction, in which the bombing is remembered and relived with particular intensity on its anniversary date.[32] But some of the images living each day in nuclear hell may recognize no special anniversary time; for them, the anniversary of the bomb takes place eternally. And some images may take their place in a time just before the bombing, as with the boy's recollection, cited earlier, of his brother reaching out to catch a red dragonfly as a B–29 sounds above.

In these and other ways, myriad times are given a place in this house of memory.

How do we respond to such figures and their suffering? Do we seek to avoid them out of some deep dread that we might be infected with the taint, the pollution, of their suffering and death? Historically, *hibakusha* have suffered additionally through discrimination due to this archaic fear. (This is closely related to the "pseudospeciation" and other defensive operations aimed at keeping death at a distance that were examined in chapter 2.) Perhaps the psychic figures we meet have been avoided for a similar reason, so that their suffering is compounded by isolation. But at the same time we are drawn to these figures: can we feel our secret fascination with woundedness and death as we move through their places? We may be horrified, indignant, or feel guilty and desire to take on the images' suffering as our own. Something in us surely suffers *with* them, and we in our compassion may want to help or to heal these figures. But perhaps—as Dante learns in the *Inferno*—there is no hope, help or healing here; and the most we can do is give care and attention to suffering itself, providing a place in our hearts for these unhealing wounds.

Throughout this book, I speak of images "associated with," or "arising from," the place of Hiroshima. This is to indicate that the present work of imaginal memory cannot literally be limited to images from Hiroshima and/or Nagasaki *per se*. In this house there is likely to be a variety of images other than those of human victims of the bomb, and many images associated with this place do not, literally and actually, arise from the atomic bombings of 1945. Thus, for one of the women cited above, Munch's painting, *The Scream*, is associated with the terror of Hiroshima, and she thinks too of an image of her younger sister with leukemia. The scientist-turned-activist remembers an image of a block of sand melted into glass by the heat of the first nuclear blast at Alamagordo, and a bird about to be shriveled and burnt in a nuclear test at Christmas Island. Someone else first remembers a photograph of a victim of Chernobyl whose hair has fallen out, sitting in Hospital No. 6. Images may appear from various literary and artistic treatments of the nuclear dilemma, such as *Dr. Strangelove* or *On the Beach*, or from such political and historical events as the Cuban Missile Crisis. All these images appear here as figures of the soul in its nuclear plight; they speak of the connections between the most intimate affairs of our hearts and the reality of nuclear weapons, showing how close to home lies our peril.

In this house there may be figures from "non-nuclear" times and places of massive killing and death: the Black Death, Auschwitz and starvation in Africa, or other images of individual and collective memory. One man remembers, in association with images of lines of bomb victims walking slowly in and out of Hiroshima, the figure of a little girl from a photo of the Vietnam War that appeared in *Life* magazine. The girl, her face contorted by grief and panic, flees, naked, from the scene of an explosion down the road. It is this same little girl who appears, terrified and screaming, in the elementary school hallway with *The Scream* hanging on the wall remembered by the woman who thinks of her younger sister ill with leukemia. The presence and juxtaposition of these images show the wounds of Hiroshima and Nagasaki opening wider, sensitizing the soul to many dimensions of human pain.

It will be helpful to notice the positions and movements of our (actual and imaginal) bodies as we move through these memory places: do we walk slowly, diffidently, with hands in pockets, for instance? Or is there an urge to reach out, to embrace? How closely do we approach different figures? Or if we imagine ourselves as stationary, where do we stand vis-a-vis each image? Reflecting in imagination, we begin to feel qualities of relationship between the images and ourselves, and among the images themselves. Our gestures and expressions may mirror those of images; we may become aware of a mute dialogue of imaginal bodies, of ways memory here is embodied. Different images carry and implicate (hence allowing us to apprehend and discern) numerous emotional and effective qualities (in this regard the memory of Camillo's Theatre is relevant). An image may embody terror and panic, deep and gentle compassion, a slow and melancholy endurance of unendurable torment, bitter rage at the violence and horror of history. These places and images are indeed "emotionally striking"; sheltered here are unfathomed hate, loneliness, wonder; eyes flashing, tearful, vacant; hands reaching, stroking, miming the world's dance of pain.

We may want or need at some point to share our responses to the images and their realities with actual persons, or notice instead a reticence among the residents of this house: an urge to keep quiet and contained. This practice carries its own risk and prudence: unexpected depths of threat may open up and emotional support may be essential, or one may find oneself not ready to meet a certain image. (Needed emotional support, it should be noted, can come from the imaginal characters as well as from actual persons. Thus, the school nurse provided some calm and comfort for the terrified Vietnamese girl in the elementary school hallway, and for the woman to whom both figures appeared.) And yet one will often find strange shelter among the images, a subtle house of strength in one's vulnerability to their melancholy realities.

When we grant these figures of woundedness, illness and death their place in memory, many possibilities for further psychological work open up. These involve the interplay of imaginal memory described in the previous chapter, between "moving" and "unmoving" images, or active, inactive and archetypal imaginings. A figure may wish to tell his or her story, so that the imaginal encounter becomes a direct dialogue. One can write the ensuing conversation down, or otherwise record it. One may feel a desire—the desire of the images—for some other form of realization involving active imagination. This may lead to enactments of memory scenes in poetry, dance or other bodily movements, drama, painting, drawing or sculpture. On the other hand, it might be important to sit quietly at times with the images, not yielding to a desire to do anything to or with them. Then they work inactively, as deepening impressions in the soul, where they are held, housed in the place of memory. The next chapter will explore examples of some of these possibilities of the work of imaginal memory in more detail.

Another possibility is to engage this work in a workshop or other group setting (e.g., with friends and/or family). Exploring and working with nuclear images in a group with a supportive and trusting atmosphere can allow for a mutual opening to and experience of, the power of these *imagines agentes*. In my own experience leading workshops, I have found that the sharing of a powerful image is what leads to the group's discovery of itself as a community:—a community of rememberers and remembered. In one workshop, when the Navy veteran cited above related the image of a dying man on a stretcher, the rest of us realized more deeply our dwelling in a world of nuclear survivors. As the man on the stretcher became a felt presence in the group, the group was *opened* by his woundedness, and the members more openly related to each other. There are hints in this of how imaginal memory could contribute to community building in a larger and finally worldwide context (further observations in this regard will be offered in chapter 7 below).[33]

Yet, although this work of imaginal memory can be fruitfully begun and carried forward in a group, it cannot be completed in that setting. For the work of memory involves time, repetition and psychological movements that go on in the soul's deeper places. Through time, places and images may change in their appearance and/or significance, or perhaps remain entirely static and unchanging. The remembering of the place of Hiroshima not only takes more time than could be spent in a group; it takes a variety of different *qualities* of time (both personal or individual and collective) that may best be discerned in quiet, contemplative aloneness.

Two interwoven themes characterize the ongoing work of imaginal memory: *forgetting* and *psychological commemoration*. Working through time leads to reflections of the place of Lethe in this practice of memory. We require a draught of Lethe as we enter into nuclear *memoria*: a forgetting of distracting details, ego's usual desire to forget death and hold onto life, and habitual strictures on images, including moral judgments and conventional convictions regarding the unreality of fantasy. We may at times even have to forget present-day nuclear concerns in order that we may concentrate on a deeper nuclear, ancestral presence. In this forgetting we, in fact, remember the root-significance of Lethe—the "hiddenness" of death. We are forgetting daily life so that nuclear death, which usually remains hidden from our lives, may be remembered.

Furthermore, if, as I have insisted, images have their own ways of remembering, so must they have particular ways of forgetting. Our curiosity is stirred by what they may remember of other places and times; what have they forgotten? As we are remembered by and through them, so too are we forgotten. On the far side of a current of Un-Care, these images may care little for the memories of our daily lives in which we are usually immersed; instead they are focused on the unhealing wounds of hell. How different must our lives appear from their view. And these images of a nuclear realm of the dead, like others of our ancestors now on another shore, have an essential quality of hiddenness, are never fully revealed. In this sense they belong finally to Lethe in her presence as the hiddenness of death.

But what happens when, after a plunge into this world of images, we return to life's other concerns? We must of course forget the place of Hiroshima to a significant degree in our regular lives, but that assertion as it stands is far too obvious. There is something else hidden within this forgetting. Recall Bachelard's statement that "Not only our memories, but the things we have forgotten are 'housed.'" Having housed in memory nuclear images, these figures now inhabit a house even though our attention is far more frequently focused on other affairs. What happens after an initial series of explorations of (and with) images arising from the place of Hiroshima? Having been housed, they abide with us even when we do not notice. They are now in place, cared for and attended; we will periodically visit this house (for it is also, in one aspect, the house in which we all live) and/or be reminded of these images; and certain of them may in some way become a more overt presence in our lives than others. But their remaining housed in memory does not require our constant, or even frequent, recollective attention.

The forgetting I am attempting to specify here is quite different from the usual forgetting of nuclear realities, in which the images are given no place to dwell, like the homeless, uncared-for dead. Rather, this forgetting is essential to the work of imaginal memory, because *it is a basic aspect of psychological commemoration*. In order to more carefully describe this way of forgetting I refer again to Casey's adroit discussion of what he calls "intrapsychic memorialization," or the commemoration of the presences of others within the psychic sphere. Following Freud, Casey distinguishes between "recollective [and conscious] remembering" and an "Ongoing, steady remembering" which for the most part proceeds outside of conscious awareness, and is basic to commemoration within the psyche (*R*, p. 242). There is an essential part of the work of memory that, far from requiring a continual and all-inclusive (ego-) consciousness, requries a degree of hiddenness; it goes on behind the "scenes" of recollective (and, as usually imagined, visual) remembering. A "forgetting" of recollective memory (including here its synaesthetic aspects stressed in this book) of the place of Hiroshima is necessary not only (and perhaps not primarily) so that we "may get on with life." Instead, the images—themselves rememberers—must be given space so that they may impress themselves in their own ways, or set up their own houses, in memory. They are then present with us, largely hidden, invisible, yet potent and lasting, powers dwelling within our lives.

How do these ancestral *imagines agentes* become such relatively permanent though (on most occasions) invisible presences within the world(s) of our being? Through another facet of psychological work common to both intrapsychic memorialization in general and psychological commemoration in particular. Again with reference to Freud—his work on "Mourning and Melancholia," which is particularly apposite in the present context—Casey describes the psychological processes of *incorporation* of others into one's psychic sphere, hence of the *identification* of aspects of oneself with these others, and finally of their establishment as fully *internalized* presences "hidden" within our identities. And "Each of these presences brings about a new place in the psyche—a new memorial location that, far from freezing the past into fixity, opens ever more expansively into the future" (*R*, pp. 239–43, 247). In this way the *imagines agentes* become, and remain, effective within our ongoing lives.

Psychological commemoration as understood here is based also on the premise that these "others" of the soul are archetypal or ancestral Others as well as internalized presences or impressions made through relationships with actual persons. There are several other features specific to psychological commemoration that bear mentioning here. First, while a forgetting of recollective memory is essential, one's ego or habitual self does play an active, deliberate role: we *intend* to entertain, in a house of awareness, images associated with the place of Hiroshima. Second, we are specifically cognizant of the activity (together with the *in*activity) of these images, and may choose to engage them in forms of active imagination that acknowledge their particular claims upon us as well as their psychic autonomy. Third, imaginal memory as developed here connotes an exploration (whether or not through active imagination *per se*) of multiple levels of metaphor through which the talismanic or archtypal power of these images, and their ability to speak to our situation, become more fully present. It is due to this *attunement to metaphor* that the images become *more* lasting and potent within our lives than our original (vicariously) remembered images of the place of Hiroshima. The "internalizing" of the images then refers not only to our incorporation of them in our individual (and interpersonal) psychic lives, but also to our grasp of and relationship to *their* inwardness, their ultimately fathomless, depths.

A fourth feature of psychological commemoration has to do with its connotation of giving honor, or the reward of a gift to the Elders and Ancestors. Who, and what, does the work of imaginal memory in the context of the place of Hiroshima, honor with a gift? In part, it honors the same ones commemorated in public observances on the anniversaries of Hiroshima and Nagasaki: the actual victims of the bomb. In this work we honor as well, and reward with the gift of our concern, the archetypal presences that these images also are. Finally, we are honoring, and rewarding with that same gift, the inhuman realities of Death's house. With our attention, we will in the next chapter be "rewarding" quite specific features of nuclear wounds, the precise ways in which these images are in pain, probing their forever-opened depths of metaphor. In this way the wounds with which the nuclear age opened become lasting, forceful impressions upon the world's memory.

These lasting impressions do implicate the (largely unconscious) ways in we are all survivors of Hiroshima, and hence have to some extent incorporated, identified with, and internalized the sufferings of actual *hibakusha*. In the next chapter we observe the interplay of this actuality with that stressed by Jung who, in speaking of how possession by dangerous psychic forces may be avoided, urges that one put the unconscious "clearly before [one] as *that which one is not*" (*CW* 7, par. 112; italics in original). The emotions stirred by the remembering of images are not only "mine," private and subjective; and not only "ours," a property of our human collectivity. They inhere in the images and their places themselves, revealing these as talismanic powers playing their parts in a renaissance of soul, a strange Renaissance of Walking Ghosts.

6

Imaginal Memory in the Nuclear World: Further Explorations

Giordano Bruno, in his treatise on *The Shadows of Ideas*, speaks of the power of images "to form the inform chaos," of "a figurative art that . . . will help not only the memory but also all the powers of the soul in a wonderful manner."[1] Imaginal memory in the nuclear world starts with the "inform chaos" revealed at Hiroshima, and seeks the form inherent in the "figurative art" of its images, in this way helping and attending to the powers of soul. In the destruction of Hiroshima we remembered a "world-creating" event, a foundational event of the nuclear world. Further explorations of this place and time—and configurations of place and time since then—will move us into deeper, more detailed awareness of places, images and powers of soul hidden in this world of "after Hiroshima."

Once more we will follow the "rules" of the art of memory, beginning by looking more closely at four of the examples of places imagined that were cited in the previous chapter: the hallway of the Naval College, the Night and Day rooms (together with the hallway off of which they open), and the elementary school hallway. (The master bedroom of the House of Desire will also be considered, in a later section.) Next, we will get to know three "fascinating" *imagines agentes* from the atomic bombing that are relatively well-known; first, however, we shall have to reflect on the *image of fascination* itself as it arises from the place of Hiroshima. This will lead to further exploration of the possible interplay within imaginal memory between "active," "inactive" and "archetypal" forms or imagining that we touched on in chapter 4, considering several specific examples of this play between images. Further possibilities of the interplay between images then open up: we will discover how images associated with Hiroshima open into broader rememberings of human cultures, and explore an example in which images of Hiroshima and Vietnam speak to each other—and to us—with considerable power and immediacy. In response to the imaginal memory of nuclear images (our remembering and theirs), the soul's deepest work of individuation is stirred. The deep work of nuclear images will be echoed and amplified by a brief plunge into Jung's exploration of the psychology of alchemy, or the soul's elemental transmutations. Finally, we emerge to recall, in the light of this remembering of images, the world, for the love of which we "die" into shapes of memory.

Each place and image we visit will display the most basic or archetypal themes that have characterized the unfolding of the nuclear age. The following explorations are intended to suggest ways of commemorating these foundational patterns, evoking their presence, allowing them to speak. This work of commemoration will, like Father Kleinsorge's wounds, deepen and broaden. For it will be revealed as a commemoration of humanity, of the soul's suffering and its individuation, and, finally, of the great Common Place of humanity and soul: the world itself.

IMAGES OF PLACES

The inherent relation of memory and rhetoric which is given in the origin myth of the art of memory (see chapter 4 above) suggests a "rhetorical" perspective on the particular images of places we remember. For these are parts of a speech of the soul; with a metaphoric ear we may discern in what way they speak to us.

Listen to the rhetoric of the place of the Naval College hallway, how it speaks to the man, the Navy veteran, who is remembering it, and also to us all. Again, this hallway is about fifty yards long, well-lit, with the east-facing wall mostly glassed-in and the opposite wall featuring six recesses in which are placed three-dimensional copper facsimiles of war scenes. Here the rhetoric of memory and of War, of Mars, blend into one speech or way of speaking about our history and its remembered conflicts that gives particular and privileged place to War and military victory (hence the victory of Mars).

But listen hard with an imaginal ear to what the Navy veteran has to say about this place and the place of the Hiroshima man dying on a stretcher within it—or what this place itself has to say, through the amplifier of the veteran's voice. The Hiroshima man "would have been at the end" of the hallway, a granite wall in which is set an inscription: something to do with "excellence." Regarding the Naval College itself: it is "a continuance . . . of what's always been."

This is extraordinarily eloquent speaking! The Hiroshima man, who is dying, who is at *his* end, lies at the *end* of the hallway that displays "a continuance . . . of what's always been." This is the end of that continuance. Moreover, it is an end set in stone. The victim of Hiroshima is caught between a rock and a hard place. With the end of Hiroshima and Nagasaki, or thus we have been told ever since, we saw the end of The War—or the *end of war* itself, depending on how one hears it. With Hiroshima and Nagasaki, the *world itself*, as it had been known, ended. Yet, juxtaposed with this ending, the ensuing history of the nuclear age has seen "a continuance...of what's always been." Or, this end *itself* is somehow "a continuance . . . of what's always been," a form of revelation of the rock-hard, monumental reality of Death: our fate, set in granite: a gravestone, petrified life, what remains after Medusa's stare. How well all this is illuminated for us in this place!

Despite all the loss and horror implied here, this place has something to do with excellence. "Excellence" in this imaginal remembrance may have many connotations other than that intended by the architect of the Naval College: not only is there a way of excelling in War, but there is also an excellence in the end of war and in the way we may die. Excellence may pertain to the envisioning of Strong-Armed Ego who wars, wrestling with Death; it may pertain to the more classical Greek sense of the hero: the *arete* or excellence of Akhilleus that lay precisely in the way he died. More, there is somehow an excellence *within* death itself. And it would be excellent if the nuclear age did finally see an end to war (e.g., through disarmament not extinction); but this would require our willingness to suffer in a very hard place.

In trying to amplify the rhetoric of this place, to make its speech audible to the imaginal ear, I have been focusing on the ways it addresses us as a collectivity, as members of a world community. There may be a more personal dimension to this place as well: there usually is in remembrances we imagine. Remembered by a man who has rather recently left the Navy, this place may speak too of an end to an era in his individual life, of a certain kind of striving for excellence or way of continuing "what's always been" (this place's phrase for what Lifton calls "symbolic immortality"). There is (whether taken on an individual or collective level or both) an edge of sadness here: of mourning and identification with the mourned: of commemoration of ancestral selves. Granite-like, the old dies hard.

It is evident here that much of the work of imaginal memory involves a close *listening to the rhetoric of places*, which in themselves are treasure-houses harboring a wealth of metaphors whose speech, remembered, goes right to the heart.

There is a different kind of rhetoric inherent in the Night and Day rooms remembered (together with the hallway leading to them) by the woman who has recently become interested in the nuclear dilemma. In the Night room, as described in the previous chapter, she sees on the ceiling all the stars and constellations. There is no air or movement in this room; on the walls are black shadows: the remains of people who, dying in a nuclear holocaust, walked through the wall into blackness. After taking only one step into this room, the woman draws back in fear; then, still curious, she steps into the adjacent Day room. Here it is "hot, hot"; there is a burning orange and yellow sun radiating its heat. There are white outlines of people on the floor, which remind the woman of the shadow-outlines painted on city streets one year by antinuclear protestors marking the anniversary of Hiroshima. In this room there is a metal garbage container or dumpster, filled with garbage and "melted, deformed, dripping" people. After viewing this place, the woman steps back into the hallway and discovers, to her horror, that all the other doors have disappeared. There is no way out; only the doors to the Night and Day rooms remain.

Here we are in more ghostly, terrifying—yet also fascinatingly suggestive—terrain. We notice immediate parallels to two of the Renaissance cosmic images cited in chapter 4. Remember Ficino's advice: "Why not make a universal image, that is, an image of universe itself?" "Deep inside your house you might set up a little room . . . " And remember Robert Fludd's "Day" and "Night" Theatres, each to be placed within the Great Common Place, and each holding activities and images particular to Day and Night.

This image reveals the nuclear world as a *house* of the cosmos: through horror the Mysterious is remembered. The stars and constellations in the Night-room sky evoke awe and dread, together with the black shadows—remaining memories—of those who walked through a wall of holocaust into fathomless, airless black. Evoked by the nuclear threat here is a spectre of a final walk, a black-shadowed procession. At the same time, room is made for a particular kind of fear, *cosmic* fear: a fear in which the forbidding power of the final Surround, the encompassing place of World, is made evident. We are reminded that the House of the World is not necessarily a cozy home; it is also a place of dread, of the *mysterium tremendum et fascinans*, of the finality of Night. The remembering of this room recalls Night in its archaic essence; in a time of ever-dawning technological "promises," it is through primary nuclear dread that the archaic, prenuclear Night Side finds once more a place within which it can dwell.[2]

After this forbidding remembering of Night, one might imagine finding some relief in the Day room. But there are frightening shadows, outlines or tracings of memory here as well, no less discomfiting because the black has turned to white and the sun has appeared. This room presents itself with a particular fascination. Could it embody a white-hot shadow within the "dawn" of the nuclear era, an intensely destructive light such as the youth Phaethon (see chapter 2 above) brought too close to earth?

The *white shadow*, or *shadow of white* is a phenomenon all its own. There is a curiously exact echoing of the rhetoric of this room in an essay by James Hillman, titled "Notes on White Supremacy," which explores the many "shades" of white in the archetypal imagination. Hillman asserts *"that white casts its own white shadow,"* and can lead to a variety of deadly historical phenomena (e.g., "black-and-white" thinking by which an individual or group, believing itself to be whitely innocent, inflicts black death and terror on those assumed to be the "opposite" color).[3] The white-shadowed outlines here foreshadow the third place-image in which the woman finds herself: "white solid walls" leaving no way out except through the two rooms of nuclear death. This white is horrifying indeed: an impenetrable wall of the white imagination. Remember the forbidding whiteness of Moby Dick with which Ahab struggled. Another, more overtly ghostly, remembering of white is found in one woman *hibakusha's* recollections:

> When I was evacuated at the time of the bomb, people had white medicine on their faces, and these white faces have sometimes appeared in my dreams. . . . The other day my child had a skin rash, so I put white medicine on his face. In the middle of the night I woke up, and seeking his face, I felt frightened. . . . I remembered the white faces I have seen in the dreams. . . .
>
> (quoted in *DL*, p. 173)

There will be more to say about certain images and themes within this constellation of places below. These could be amplified with a considerable amount of anthropological and historical-religious data, but it seems best to let the remembering of these tremendous rooms linger as further illustrations of the hugely powerful psychic realities made present through this remembering of nuclear realities.

The last place-image to be looked at seems, by contrast, to be rather straightforwardly biographical: the dark elementary-school hallway remembered by the woman peace activist, into which the terrified Vietnamese girl will come running. But there is nonetheless an elemental aspect to this place; images of elementary schools in dreams often suggest places where basic elements of life are learned and remembered, the elemental emotions and other realities of childhood given place. In this case, there is an elemental fear (which, in association with the Vietnamese girl, we will consider more closely below), a panic, an accompaniment of the God Pan—himself an elemental pursuer—that breaks through. The placing on the wall of Munch's painting, *The Scream*, suggests a connection between this elementary panic and imagination's art made possible when the terrified girl comes into contact with the school nurse. There is another way of stating what this place-image seems to say: the place of elemental fear is also an elementary learning-place, and a place where a frightened child can be nursed. The nuclear reality becomes a "school" in which children (actual and/or imaginal) can learn. (There may be associations here to childhood memories of school as also the first place of collective attempts to avoid learning about the realities of the nuclear age: the place of illusions of civil defense, of "duck-and-cover" drills of the 1950s through which children were encouraged to deny and suppress nuclear terror.) And *images of children*, in ways to be sketched below, arise very frequently in association with the place of Hiroshima, where the world received its first schooling in nuclear reality.

"Fascinating" Images

Reflecting on her feelings about the Day room described above, with its container filled with "melted, deformed, dripping" people and garbage, the woman who envisioned the place recalls uneasily that "the Christian part of me said" not to look at those things, for that would be almost "perverse." But, referring to one figure, she acknowledges that "I wanted to see how the face looked."

An undertone of fascination with hideously deformed and injured figures colors much remembering and imagining of Hiroshima, Nagasaki and potential nuclear holocaust. Mrs. Hatsuyo Nakamura, one of the survivors chronicled in *Hiroshima*, returns to the city four days after the bombing, though quite ill. For "All week, at the Novitiate [where she and Father Kleinsorge were staying at the time], she had worried about her mother, brother, and older sister, who had lived in the part of the town called Fukuro, and besides, she felt drawn by some fascination, just as Father Kleinsorge had been."[4] Dr. Hachiya tells, in his *Hiroshima Diary*, of how one man repeatedly described grotesque scenes he had witnessed. "It seemed to give [the man] some relief to pour out his terrifying experiences on us; and there was no one who would have stopped him, so fascinating was his tale of horror."[5] Yasuko, the young woman protagonist of Masuji Ibuse's novel, *Black Rain*, is—despite herself—fascinated with the horror of Hiroshima, and at one point cannot stop herself from looking at three dead women in a water tank.[6]

What is going on within this immemorial fascination with woundedness, death and pain that the images of Hiroshima force us to remember? Lifton observes that "Much of the survivor's fascination with these horrors has to do with his inner contrast between those experiencing them and himself—in the unconscious reassurance that 'they, not I, are being brutalized,'" and adds that "aggressive and perverse" fantasies may be evoked by these scenes (*DL*, p. 51). Part of the value within the imagination of Hiroshima is precisely that we are confronted with or must *face*—as the woman in the Day room feels compelled to see a deformed face—these darkly disturbing fantasies that we all can remember experiencing in some form. Such fantasies we usually consign to the place of refuse or garbage container within, as the above image aptly puts it.

More psychological precision is needed as we face the depths of what we ordinarily refuse to look at. Returning to the opening pages of this book, to Dante's fascination with a demon and Ziegler's evocation of the "bottomless" fascination with hell, we might ask again: *who* within us, or what demon, is fascinated with the horror? Could a clue be found in "the Christian part" of our culture with its fantasies of white innocence? Remember Bruno burning at the stake. What is the place of sadism within the religious spirit? Or, to turn this on its head and elaborate: does our late twentieth century "love of the grotesque" disclose hidden possibilities of religious imagination, of a different kind of love, of devotion to what is painful, than is evidenced by the sadistic literalism of Bruno's inquisitors? To try and answer this question at present would be premature; more concentration on the memorably painful images of nuclear reality is needed first. What is apparent now, however, is that *the place of Hiroshima is a place of religious cruelty*; and it is a religious cruelty that we remember in granting Hiroshima its place.

Keeping this fascinating power of the imaginal in mind, let us consider more closely the deformed realities of the place of Hiroshima, focusing now on three particular images that are relatively familiar to the world's imagination. The first image is from the inside cover of the pamphlet, *Days to Remember*: the face of a child as "He stands, riceball in hand, wondering" at the ruins of Nagasaki on the morning of August 10, 1945.[7] The second image is that of the Reverend Mr. Kyoshi Tanimoto, the Methodist pastor of Hersey's *Hiroshima*. "He wears his black hair parted in the middle and rather long: the prominence of his mustache, mouth and chin give him a strange, old-young look, boyish and yet wise, weak and yet fiery."[8] We are going to be most interested in Mr. Tanimoto's rescue activity after the bomb (he himself received virtually no physical injuries): ferrying people in a boat across a branch of the Ota River to a safer place in Hiroshima's Asano Park. The third image is related to Dr. Hachiya by a visitor: "Well, I saw a man whose eye had been torn out by an injury, and there he stood with the eye resting in the palm of his hand. What made by blood run cold was that it looked like the eye was staring at me. Doctor, the pupil looked right at me. Do you think the eye could see me?"[9] We will pay close attention not only to this image itself but also the way it is rewrought and amplified in a subsequent nightmare of Dr. Hachiya's. This gives a disturbing example of the complex interplay between remembering images and the dreaming psyche, one which helps us to better see the changed vision of nuclear images.

Nagasaki Child

The first image of *Days to Remember* is that of a child. With a spotted hood over his head, the boy stares blankly. There are a few blotches of wounds or burns on parts of his face; aside from that his skin is smooth. The image presents a picture of blotched innocence; the wounds we see on the child's face suggest the wounds opened in his heart by the horrors he is seeing. The message added by the authors to the lower part of the picture evokes this seeing: "We wish you,/ And children/And fellow human beings of the world/To know/What happened/ That day/As seen by the eyes of this child." Remember the Child. See the world of nuclear devastation through the vision of the Child's presence; sense the wounded, dying innocence.

The *Child*, from the first, has been an important dominant of the nuclear (particularly, the antinuclear) imagination. In 1951 *Children of Hiroshima* was published, and the editor of the (1982) English edition says that talk about its translation began in 1979, "the International Year of the Child."[10] Prominent in the Hiroshima Peace Park is the Children's Monument, erected in honor of Sadako Sasaki, the girl who died at twelve years old from bomb-induced leukemia after just failing, according to the story, to fold a thousand cranes, which, according to Japanese legend, would have saved her life.[11] The "children" of Hiroshima are not only actual girls and boys, but also all who suffered the bombing and struggled to be reborn after the death of the city: this is the message implicit in Robert Jungk's *Children of the Ashes*. But the spectres of wounded and dying children have figured the ultimate horrors of nuclear devastation. After the bombing of Nagasaki, Harry Truman is said to have refused to order any more bombings "because he could not bear the thought of killing 'all those kids.'"[12] The horrors suffered by the Children of Hiroshima and Nagasaki have appeared in the nuclear imagination to prefigure the even greater horror of millions of young lives brutally ended in a global holocaust. And with the resurgence of strong concerns about nuclear weapons in the 1980s, a principal focus of pain and research is the effects of the nuclear threat on children. As of this writing an emotional controversy over the extent of such effects engages researchers, educators and parents.[13] In all these ways, the numinous power of the child archetype asserts itself.[14] For the Child is the carrier of the imagination's futurity—its remembering of the future—and also its freshness, vulnerability, innocent sensitivity and relative defenselessness. From this perspective of the Child, we ask: What about the children? what about the future?[15]

The Child also evokes the remembering of the past, and the forever present archetypal world; and thus is a powerful carrier of memory. Thus, *Ad Herennium* observes that "incidents of our childhood we often remember best" (III. xxi. 35), and Jung initiates his "confrontation with the unconscious" by reenacting his childhood games (*MDR*, pp. 173–4). The Child, as picture of Innocence, comes into imagination trailing clouds of glory. The face of the Nagasaki Child evokes this innocence and its devastation. It seems to say: Become as a child and enter the Kingdom of Nuclear Horror.

It is well to remember that here is one of many possible perspectives of, and on, the Child: a rather idealized picture constellated in part by the total horror of nuclear devastation. There is another side to the Child's innocence defenselessness: this can serve defensive purposes. Mary Watkins, exploring characters in the nuclear imagination, speaks of the "imaginal child" who, immersed in playful innocence, blocks emotional awareness and active concern regarding the nuclear threat. And she adds:

> Besides the imaginal child's self-centeredness, absorption into the world of play and pleasures, besides her innocence and naive belief in the continuation, the eternity of life, we confront the child's feelings of impotence, inability and inadequacy within ourselves; the voice that stops our potential activism by saying "this problem is too complex, too big for me."[16]

This voice of the Child fuels an evasion of moral responsibility, and its attendant anxiety, and is thus, observes Watkins, "potentially lethal."

There are also darker, less innocent facets of the Child. There is childishness and infantilism that can be as nonmoral as Freud's id. There is something titanic in the Child's imagination. Said Jung at the outset of the nuclear age, "The situation is about the same as if a small boy of six had been given a bag of dynamite for a birthday present" (*CW* 10, par. 485). It was, after all, a "Little Boy" that destroyed Hiroshima. Recently, psychological research on the relation between children and the nuclear threat has been focusing on the childhood roots of the development of images of the enemy.[17] While this research is addressing psychological dilemmas faced by actual children, it also reflects a fundamental ambivalence or ambiguity of the Child as archetypal reality.

Remembering the Nagasaki Child, we initially remember the innocence of the childlike, and its threatened futurity. But this place of memory inevitably implicates a disturbing ambiguity in the imagination of the Child, which in the nuclear age can become its own worst enemy.

The Ferryman

The next image is that of Mr. Tanimoto, with his longish black hair and mustache. He is old-young, boyish-wise, weak-fiery: these paradoxically present qualities suggest that he is a liminal figure, moving in more than one world. There are echoes of this in the figure of Lao-tzu, whose name may mean "Old Boy" and who is said to have written the Tao-Te-Ching before vanishing from this world. And he reminds as well of Hermes/Mercurius, who also moves between worlds and is a paradoxical combination of opposites.[18]

Mr. Tanimoto's activities on the day Hiroshima became another world reveal his liminal character. As the firestorm following the bombing spread, he

> walked to the river and began to look for a boat in which he might carry some of the most severely injured across the river from Asano Park and away from the spreading fire. Soon he found a good-sized pleasure punt drawn up on the bank, but in and around it was an awful tableau—five dead men, nearly naked, badly burned, who must have been working together to push the boat down into the river. Mr. Tanimoto lifted them away from the boat, and as he did so, he experienced such horror at disturbing the dead—preventing them, he momemtarily felt, from launching their craft and going on their ghostly way—that he said out loud, "Please forgive me for taking this boat. I must use it for others, who are alive."[19]

For the remainder of "that day," Mr. Tanimoto ferries boatloads of wounded people, ten to twelve at a time (using for propulsion a bamboo pole he finds) across the river to the park. In the evening, continuing his work, the "ferryman" transports a pair of wounded priests upstream to where they can get to the Jesuit Novitiate outside of Hiroshima.[20]

This activity defines the character of Mr. Tanimoto more precisely. In his guise we meet the Ferryman who takes and pilots the vessel of the dead who are about to go "on their ghostly way." And the living whom this Ferryman brings to the other shore are themselves Walking Ghosts in the Land of Death-in-Life. This Ferryman and the topography of his world are familiar figures of the world's myth, folklore and the soul's ecstatic journeys.[21] Alcestis, Aeneas and Dante all see Charon in his "ancient ferry" (*Inf.* III. 79) as he takes souls across the Acheron, and we remember as well the *yana* or "raft" of Buddhism, which vehicle provides for that extinguishment of desire that is a journey to the Other Shore and *nirvana*. To take one more of the numberless instances of this underworld vessel and topography, recall the prelude to Bruno's *Italian Dialogues*, considered in chapter 4 as an example of a confluence of the art of memory and active imagination. The difficult journey alluded to in that context involves Bruno and his companions deciding to take a boat on the river Thames and finally managing to hail an ancient, leaky craft with two ancient boatmen. There are difficulties over the fare, but finally they are on their way. However, they are dropped off in a dark, dirty and unfamiliar place that turns out to be near their starting-point. Only after further adventures do they make it to their destination. In this instance, Bruno's art of memory relies directly on an underworld topography for its places and images. The mercurial figure of Mr. Tanimoto, the Ferryman of *Hiroshima*, discloses an underworld topography of that place, which may be remembered by the figurative art of imagining.

The structure of the archetypal irrupts into Hersey's reconstruction of *Hiroshima* in the form of a constellation including the Ferryman, the ghostly craft or vessel of death, the river, the dead and the dead-in-life, who are taken from the City of Death to the Other Shore. As this topography of myth is re-membered, so too is the archetypal reality of nuclear horror. This is the world's *rite de passage* into the era of Death-in-Life, a conjunction of "timeless" reality and unique historical predicament.[22] Asano Park, the safer place, may be in empirical terms the place of rescue, but in mythic terms is the safe place of death. Mr. Tanimoto's transports are at once strenuous efforts at ensuring survival and movements toward, and within, a topography of death.

As the first, or initiatory[23] revelation of nuclear horror, *Hiroshima's* portrayal of the movements of the Ferryman suggests that subsequent efforts to deal with nuclear reality will somehow follow the same pattern—including the present work.

It becomes apparent that any figure arising from the place of Hiroshima is not only a single image but also bears within itself multiple realities. Thus, the figure of Mr. Tanimoto stirs the memory of a whole topography of soul in the nuclear world, so that the features of the *site* of devastation and its "inform chaos" become *places* of memory. The image of this Ferryman discloses another order of places and images, the rhetoric of which speaks precisely to our condition.

Eyeball-Man

The third image—the man holding his severed eyeball in the palm of his hand as the eye looks right at Dr. Hachiya's visitor—likewise constellates its own imaginal order. This figure is more difficult to work with, not just because of its particularly striking horror, but because it engages one of the more haunting themes in the survivor psychology of Hiroshima: the persistent sense that one is being stared at accusingly by the eyes of the wounded and dead. This both echoes and provokes self-condemnation and death guilt. For instance, a history professor describes walking through the ruins of Hiroshima looking for his family, "looking carefully at everyone I met . . . the eyes—the emptiness—the helpless expression—were something I will never forget. . . . There were hundreds of people who had seen me. . . . They looked at me with great expectation, staring right through me. It was very hard to be stared at by those eyes" (quoted in *DL*, p. 36) . . .[24] Memory and guilt are kept vividly alive—along with the images of the dying and dead themselves—by these eyes "through" which one is seen.

The visitor's image soon becomes a visitation, a presence within Dr. Hachiya's psychological vision. In his entry of 23 August, he records a discussion with another doctor who ran the Eye Clinic at the Communications Hospital, concerning the blinding burns to the eyes received by many who had looked at the nuclear flash. The following night, says Dr. Hachiya, "I slept poorly and had a frightful dream."[25]

> It seems I was in Tokyo after the great earthquake and around me were decomposing bodies heaped in piles, all of whom were looking right at me. I saw an eye sitting on the palm of a girl's hand. Suddenly it turned and leaped into the sky and then came flying back towards me, so that, looking up, I could see a great bare eyeball, bigger than life, hovering over my head, staring point blank at me. I was powerless to move.

Awakening from this nightmare, Dr. Hachiya, thinking that the visitor's story had been "too much" for him, lies in bed and worries about an inability to remember names of acquaintances and friends "since the *pika* [flash]." This "blindness for names" leads in turn to worries about whether his own eyes may not somehow have been indirectly damaged by the *pika*. "Maybe my eye nerves were weakened by the *pika*. I could not believe I had retrograde amnesia. Can one get an optic amnesia?"

Before and after the nightmare, Dr. Hachiya's thoughts and ruminations revolve around blindness and forgetfulness. The nightmare, by startling contrast, presents a horrible vision of total and unforgettable seeing: it is not only the dead, but the *dreamer*, who is seen and remembered. All the dead look right at the dreamer (note the implied psychological identification of dreamer and the waking visitor); the dreamer looks as an eye, "bigger than life," leaps up and stares down at him, rendering him "powerless to move." The dreamer is thus fixed in memory by the Eye(s) of the Dead, rendered as a static memory image. He will not be forgotten.

Dr. Hachiya's ruminations surely express his individual psychic struggles, his contradictory impulses to be blind to the horror of his world, to forget what he has seen (also his sense as a survivor that he has in fact been blinded to and forgotten the dead), and his need to see and remember—all of which impulses express and provoke death guilt.

But the dream, as the nightmare of *Hiroshima Diary*, is also a primary nightmare of the world's nuclear imagination. As Richard Rhodes puts it in his recent chronicle of *The Making of the Atomic Bomb*, "the dream of this Japanese doctor who was wounded in the world's first atomic bombing and who ministered to hundreds of victims must be counted one of the millenial visions of mankind . . . "[26]

Let us probe the *vision* of this dream more closely. The unforgettable image of the man holding his eyeball having penetrated the consciousness of Dr. Hachiya, the dreamer is placed, "It seems . . . in Tokyo after the great earthquake [of September 1, 1923] . . ." That disaster and the one in Hiroshima are condensed, so that Hiroshima becomes a kind of Tokyo or capital of the country after the earth-shaking horror of the atomic bombing. There are probable allusions to the entire Pacific War and the great upheaval of Japan and its heart or capital city that began (though with much earlier roots)[27] with the rising militarism and nationalism of the earlier twentieth century. And because Hiroshima is an end-of-the-world time, and the capital city of a country in nationalistic or tribalistic cosmology connotes the center of the world, the dream can also be seen to imagine the earthquake at the heart of the larger nuclear world. By speaking in the image of Tokyo after the great earthquake, the dream seems to stress these cultural and cosmic or world-motifs.

The images of the multitudinous eyes of the dead and of the "great bare eyeball" that flies up to look down upon the dreamer, are worth close attention. Both are variants of the "eye-motif" that Jung explores in his alchemical work. He cites a number of alchemical and religious images of *scintillae* or "sparks," stars and eyes that are relevant to our nightmare. The *scintillae* are sparks of consciousness, or soul, scattered throughout the world. One symbol "shows eyes in the stars, in the clouds, in the water and in the earth" (*CW* 14, par. 45). As a parallel to this Jung cites Zech. 4:10, which portrays "the seven eyes of the Lord that run to and fro through the whole earth." Ficino likens the stars to eyes[28]; and one alchemist says of heaven that: "It is like an eye and a seeing of the soul, whereby the state of the soul and her intentions are made known to us" (quoted in *CW* 14, par. 46). The eye-motif in memories of Hiroshima is epitomized by the dream of *Hiroshima Diary* which too is "like an eye and a seeing of the soul . . ."

Remember as well that cosmic Night room into which we briefly stepped earlier in this chapter. In that room the world's nightmare is dreamed onward; eye-like shine the stars in this post-holocaust vision.

Jung's work on the eye-motif is involved with his important revisioning of his psychology in which the "unconscious" is viewed as a "multiple consciousness," or "ego-consciousness as being surrounded by a multitude of little luminosities" (*CW* 8, pars. 388, 387). The luminosities are the psychic complexes that as autonomous "splinter psyches" each have their own psychic vision or consciousness (*CW* 8, pars. 202ff; *CW* 14, pars. 47, 270–1). In this vision the ego is being seen by figures of soul; this seeing is made present by the "eyes" of images. This would seem to be the predicament of ego after the Great Earthquake of Hiroshima and Nagasaki. We are being seen, remembered, by "splinter psyches," one of which is imaged as the severed eye of the Hiroshima victim.

This "seeing of the soul" evokes guilt and, finally, terror in the felt presence of the daimonic. In the dream, this is accentuated by the one eye in whose presence the dreamer is powerless. We recall here the imaginal eye of memory, the "eye of the soul" or *oculus imaginationis* pictured by Fludd's memory treatise. Now the detachment of the eye from its socket becomes a movement through horror to a nonordinary kind of vision; the detached eye is a kind of "third eye," an eye of the nuclear imagination and its memories, an intensifying of the sight of the eyes of the decomposing dead. "Bigger than life," it has a life of its own, having been torn from the human context; flying up from the dreamgirl's hand—as though in shamanistic ecstasy—it stares down from above (the motif of the eye[s] of heaven). It is now a *higher* eye.

Eyeball-Man (as we may call him), in the dream-context of *Hiroshima Diary*, appears then as a terrifying presence of soul in the world of "after-the-bomb." *Hiroshima Diary*, written by a doctor and early medical researcher of the effects of nuclear weapons, records the world's beginning awareness of nuclear realities. In remembering eye-images we focus on the imaginal background not only of guilty self-scrutiny, but more generally of research and in-sight into the nuclear world. In a number of ways, Eyeball-Man and Dr. Hachiya's dream embody self-examination. We are given a vision of consciousness in the nuclear world: *the images of this world as eyes of the soul*. The images are eyes as they decompose themselves and reveal the decomposure of our selves in this house of dying and remembering. This nuclear consciousness is multiple, torn and scattered in inhuman death, and unnerving in the intensity of its presence. By these images that are eyes we are seen and remembered.

Interplays of Imaginal Memory

Nagasaki Child, Ferryman and Eyeball-Man are relatively well-known images or familiars of our collective memories of Hiroshima and Nagasaki (though they are hardly known at all as imaginal *characters* or *presences* of memory). In meeting them the value of imaginal memory as a way of exploring the psychological power of such images is made apparent. This exploration further deepens and extends its range when the possibilities of interplay between forms of imagining and between differing images are considered. In this section I shall elaborate on several forms of such imaginal interplay. First to be considered will be the interplay and movement between active, inactive and archetypal imaginings (see discussion of these in chapter 4, pp. 72–74). This will lead into a consideration of how images develop into imaginal characters in the context of particular placings or configurations of these characters in memory. Exploring such possibilities of configuration opens in turn into a widening range of images: images from a variety of cultures and images pertaining overtly to places other than Hiroshima. We will discover unexpected ways in which images from the place of Vietnam, and from the place of Hiroshima amplify each other's power.

Interplays between Active, Inactive, and Archetypal Imagining

The most basic theme in the interplay between active, inactive and archetypal forms of imagination is that of the movement and stasis of the imaginal. We have witnessed how the work of memory engages both moving and unmoving aspects of psychic images. Active imagination involves a concentrated focus upon an image that notices when and how the image changes. We are equally concerned with noticing how the image does not change, even as it may move within the field of (ego's) consciousness.

Edward S. Casey further observes that active imagination, while engaging figures of archetypal, hence transindividual, import, nonetheless remains in practice largely an individual and personal mode of psychological work, in general keeping "the scene of imaginative action confined to the immediate vicinity of the imaginer's personal sphere of concern."[29] It is important to see how the places and images of a memory house are also figures that quite precisely embody aspects of one's individual psyche and to become aware of potential values in working with these figures from this perspective. The work of active imagination involves here a movement between personal and collective concerns; within memory, a deep and enduring impression of the intricate ways in which images embody both of these dimensions can form. The practice of imaginal memory, however, extends beyond the specifically personal sphere of concern both further and more frequently than most active imaginations, becoming—as we saw with reference to Ferryman—a way of exploring the underworld topography of the place of Hiroshima. In active imagination, one always begins with an individual image. Imaginal memory, in part following the lead of the Renaissance, may involve beginning with such collective images as those encountered in the previous section (though even here some aspects of the individual psyche inevitably come into play.) Imagining "placescapes" of memory involves a differentiation of images that is less an unfolding in the developmental sense and more a holding, carrying and placing of eternal and unmoving qualities of images.

Active imagination may both arise from, and form a prelude to, such "inactive" or archetypal imaginings. One way in which active imagination can serve as a helpful prelude to this latter work involves an encounter with individual psychic conflicts and resistances regarding realities of the imaginal in general and the place of Hiroshima in particular. Janet Dallet describes an instance in which her resistance to active imagination itself became personified as a woman, "another 'me,'"[30] who sat to her left and talked "about how absurd this whole business of active imagination was." This imaginal person, while expressing the rationalistic resistance to work with psychic figures, at the same time provided Dallet with a way of entering into that "most nonrational" work: a first experience of genuine dialogue with an imaginal other. One can work with resistance to nuclear imaginings by asking *who* might be opposed to the work and in some way listening to what they have to say (also responding actively to this).

At one point a woman—an image of someone I had actually known—appeared in front of me to the right, in a rather formal dress, and voiced objections to my work. Through meeting her I became more aware of concerns that this work with images of death might be somehow illicit; she voiced what I later saw as death guilt and a fear of violating the "sacred" suffering and death of others. At the same time, the woman became aware of a fascination with the horror and multiplicity of images then emerging in the work. She might even wish to see these for herself. While our meeting did not resolve the conflicts and ambiguities, these were given a deeper imaginal sense; and the recognition emerged that the resistance to and fascination with the nuclear underworld are powers extending beyond the individual self.

Such meetings show an entry into imaginal work through the *personifying* of initial conflicts constellated by it, or realizing these conflicts as experiences not of oneself alone, but also of an imaginal character. This realization, brought about by the tension of initial conflict, becomes an initiation into the realities of the imaginal world.

Forms of active imagination directly involving nuclear images can prove helpful, deepening one's sense of the subjectivity and values embodied by an image. Often, a good way of beginning active imagination is to draw or paint an image. This is a form of devoting oneself to the reality of the image, engaging it in a care-ful way through precise attention to the "art" of imagination. The image responds by disclosing more of itself, though often in a manner contrary to the habitual self's expectations. In one instance, the Navy veteran who had placed the Hiroshima man on a stretcher at the end of the Naval College exhibition hallway, took a pencil and began sketching this man on his stretcher. As the sketch emerged, other workshop participants commented on the strength apparent in the contours of the victim's body. The veteran was surprised when he noticed this himself: here was an image of a man in deep pain—in fact, "in a pretty much hopeless condition," yet with an unexpected strength. There was a kind of "excellence" (as the granite inscription discussed previously puts it) within this suffering, a strength in a hopeless condition at the "end" of the "continuance . . . of what's always been." In the memorial place of the Naval College, this image is particularly *strong*.

Various further possibilities of active imagination that follow upon the remembering of nuclear images and their memory places may present themselves. Here the complexity of simultaneous movement and stasis becomes apparent. There can be a simultaneous awareness, as suggested in chapter 4, of an image fixed in its locus and of the image moving overtly in a field of visual imaging as one observes or faces it. The static memory image is the psychic essence, that which remains still within movement. Caution is needed so that one does not flee the impression of this static essence, making the movement manic, an escape. Imaginal memory requires an ego that is hermetically present at the borderline of active, inactive and archetypal imaginations. For instance, in one imaginal place (not visually present in consciousness) the old-young figure of Mr. Tanimoto may stand still—his face animated yet motionless—while in another place, one carries on a dialogue with him (let us say he is visually imagined here, but this is not necessary). He speaks, and then one speaks in turn, and later may write down the dialogue. One may move in imagination between the still and moving images. Again, the back-and-forth moving of Ferryman's vessel across the River of Death may be present in the background (let us say, as a *thought* or intimation combined with a faint feel of water and memories of the bodily rhythm and sounds of rowing, but not as a visual image), as one faces Mr. Tanimoto and/or speaks with him. And the movement of the boat of the dead behind the imaginal scene is itself a form of stasis, by which one is moved toward Death-in-Life.

Let us consider, this time more closely, another instance of imaginal memory, this one involving the man, trained as a scientist, who imagined the House of Desire mentioned previously. He now remembers a scene he imagines to be from Hersey's *Hiroshima*, of a streetcar filled with people literally bursting into flames in the heat of the blast.[32] Somehow he cannot feel the horror of this as (he thinks) he ought to; instead he finds himself wondering about the physics and chemistry of the ignition. This has numerous connections to themes in the man's individual life: his feeling that he has "weak" imagery, is unable to feel and act as he wishes to. He remembers instances when he observed others getting involved in dramatic rescue activities requiring agile strength and courage, which he contrasts to his assumed lack of competence. Further discussion brings up the man's struggles with a crippling illness and of feeling deprived of his individuality, initiative and manhood by an overbearing father. Working with the streetcar image will have direct and indirect connections with these individual dilemmas. The people bursting into flames begin to figure as a *psychological* horror, an interior (though not only private) hell. The man's experienced failure to feel, his weakness of imagery, is the strength of his feelings of weakness, failure and inferiority. This is the finally mysterious hell that consumes him at times and keeps him from getting around in life as he wishes.

In the hell of this weakness and the man's self-condemnation we also recognize collective themes of psychic deadening and consequent guilt over the inability to feel sensitively: dilemmas too of actual *hibakusha*, whose deadening combined with a burning condemnation of their actions or lack thereof. Lifton sees this as part of the "living hell" of Hiroshima (*DL*, p. 491). And the fire fuels the weakness; in the presence of the flames of death the man stands at the intersection of his individual hellfire and the living nuclear hell. Through his felt weakness, he—far from being literally unable to *feel* the imagery—in fact participates in its constellation. And in this fatal, burning weakness the man ends up contemplating the scientific aspects of the streetcar's ignition. This echoes collective and cultural dilemmas around scientism, technicism and nuclearism, which fuel, and are fueled by, psychic deadening. He is in a position to feel the weakness of this position as he sees the burning of its inward hell. Thus, one image of memory constellates a range of possibilities for the work and reflection of soul that relate simultaneously to individual and collective nuclear dilemmas.

This becomes a starting-place of active imagination. As the man concentrates on the image—the first move in the process of active imagination—he begins to notice its features, making out shapes of individuals in the flaming streetcar, and also its interior upholstery. As the image becomes more differentiated, its texture, the warp and woof of its *interior*, become more apparent. The man now notices a desire on his part to enter the scene and go help the victims. This is a definite change in the image, since (as we have observed) the man's response is itself part of the constellation. At this point the man might imagine himself entering the image and running toward the burning streetcar, his imagined self remaining with its habitual body and ego yet engaged in (what from this persepctive is) an unaccustomed heroic activity. A variant of this would be for the witnessing self to remain on the periphery of the scene, watching himself in his usual, or another, body, as he runs toward the streetcar; and observing what then takes place.

But the desire to rescue that guides these possibilities of imaginal action requires a careful look: may these rescues not represent attempts to flee the position of weakness, its consuming hell, that is, to rescue the image of the self as well as the burning others? (It could be worth considering also the extent to which such psychic rescue attempts guide the man's life activities.) There can be value in the implicit attempt to strengthen the ego, but we have also noticed the value of the position of weakness. Another way would be to remain in the latter, unheroic position, the man noticing his impulse to get involved as part of the image, as already a new form of involvement, and then noticing what else may happen within the scene. Also he may feel shifts in mood or sensations and movements in his physical body—these too being part of the imaginal scene. Do the figures appearing in the flames notice and/or recognize him, or call him in some manner? Does he recognize any of them? Where might the passengers of this hell-car have been headed when it caught fire, and from where do they come? Perhaps these figures remember a time before the torment and dying, about which they may wish to speak. The man may move toward the interior of the streetcar while aware of his desire to rescue, but not acting on this in the imagination. Instead he now notices more closely the upholstery, the inwardness, of this horror, how the flames feel from the perspective of the victims. Near or in the car, various forms of dialogue (verbal and nonverbal) may become possible or necessary as the man (either as himself or another figure of the imaginal) enters the texture of this peculiar burning.

These modes of engagement suggest the possibilities of active imagination that might arise from this remembering of nuclear hell, its active power to strike the soul. What of the *in*activity of this moving, flaming image, or its unmoving essence upon which the art of memory itself would focus? How is it placed in memory as a fixed focus of imaginal movement? After his initial engagement with and reflections on the image, the man imagines it as a painting on the wall above the bed in the master bedroom of his friend's old house, the House of Desire. He is now imagining in accordance with the tradition of the "art" of memory. This presents a further possibility of imagining through actually painting the picture. Here, however, we will stay with reflections on its place in a configuration of memory. Connections between the burning painting and its place in the House of Desire are evident in the immediate and ancient relation between fire and the burning of desire: the fire is placed in its rightful house. But this is also a way of giving the flames of weakness, guilt and torment a place in the memory of this house and its desirous qualities. Here, as in traditional images, hell and desire are remembered together. The burning streetcar of Hiroshima pictured within the House of Desire becomes a place of essence, of essential connections between the pathologizings and the desires of soul. We arrive then at the aspect of the image that does not change, at the static and frozen quality of these flames of hell.

As our sense of how images go together develops, we work toward apprehension of possible archetypal configurations within the place of Hiroshima. According to Casey, such archetypal placescapes as Camillo's Theatre involve

> delineating and denominating mini-systems of archetypes. Each such system will contain a finite (but not necessarily specified) number of members, each of which derives its symbolic meaning from two factors: (1) its own intrinsic, auto-iconic (i.e., self-resembling, non-repeatable) nuclear signification; (2) its relationship with the other members of the mini-system in question (which is how its locus in imaginal space is determined).[32]

The "delineation" of configurations of images requires a sense at some level of their inherent qualities and relational tendencies, even if these are not entirely conscious to one's imagining ego. Thus, the man places the painting of burning in the House of Desire while unconscious of the myriad relations between fire and desire in myth and religion worldwide (though he would on reflection remember some of these connections). While the imagining ego has an active and deliberate role here, it becomes equally apparent that *the images places themselves in configurations*, suggesting a consciousness and intentionality not necessarily apparent to the ego. The *images remember or recognize each other*.

The "denomination" of images, their *naming*, is an important part of the archetypal attunement involved in this work. Hillman, in working with dream-images, sees much value in the imagining of their names (*DU*, pp. 62–3). If names are given in a dream or imaginal remembrance, these may carry unexpected significance as transhuman figures in human guise. Recall Father Kleinsorge from *Hiroshima*, with his "apparently negligible" cuts. As a mythic figure (quite distinct from the actual person) we saw him as portraying our collective tendencies to minimize or leave unacknowledged the depth of the psychic wounds of Hiroshima and Nagasaki. His name, "Kleinsorge" or *Little-Care* becomes itself part of this pattern. To reiterate the pattern traced in the previous chapter: Little-Care, with seemingly minor, superficial wounds, returns to the place of Hiroshima. Then Little-Care's wounds swell and open wider, and a deeper caring and concern emerges. In this case, the name given in the actual text becomes itself an emotionally striking, powerful, and active image.

In most cases, no such significance is apparent or accessible (e.g., if we do not know the translations of Japanese names), but the names of figures may have other resonances, or simply deepen one's sense of the other as personified, a reality of the psyche, a remembering image. If names are not given or known (in dreams and/or imaginal rememberings), then one need not arbitrarily assign them. Instead, as Hillman observes, the roles and actions of figures within the imaginal frame suggest epithetic names. The cults of mythic figures are in fact "*cults of epithets* that image the divine figures in concrete terms: . . . Protector-from-Evil Hercules, Warlike Hercules, Victor Hercules—the name gives an image and suggests a mytheme" (italics in original). Often names themselves are descriptive epithets, as with Pentheus (He-Who-Suffers) and Phaethon (The Brilliant), or—to name two examples from Japanese mythology—Izanami, "Female-Who-Invites" and Iaznagi, "Male-Who-Invites."[33] Mt. Tanimoto, in our earlier discussion of his role in *Hiroshima*, gained an epithetic or mythic name: Ferryman. Proper names of Nagasaki Child and Eyeball-Man were not given, but their characteristics suggest epithetic names, in which we sense the power of these characters. In name-images we find much of the power of the archetypal imagination (though certain characters may appear who are at once powerful and not to be named).

The work of configuration may involve the imagining(s) of several distinct but related images in adjacent memory places. The images may have been present previously, with their relations not yet apparent. Or one image may, with its inherently polycentric nature, turn out to disclose its own cluster of places and images, so that images dwelling within the initial images may become part of a psychic topography. Thus, we found that Mr. Tanimoto the Ferryman bears in memory, or is the dwelling place of, the images and places of the land of the dead.

As a further instance of archetypal configuring, let us recall the image of the woman whose burnt face resembles a comic mask, as recorded by Dr. Hachiya in *Hiroshima Diary*. Here is certainly a tortured contradiction: disfiguring pain transfigured into a comic mask. We do not know what other images Dr. Hachiya had in mind, but two assumptions seem likely. First is that Dr. Hachiya's figure reflects Japanese culture in the form of the Noh plays in which certain of the actors wear masks. The second assumption is that some character within Dr. Hachiya actually found the disfigured face somehow funny, that her presence stirred some urge to laugh. In each case, the remembering of her human face unmasks deeper, prenuclear psychological realities.

The Noh plays of Japan present—partly through "the unreal reality of the wooden masks worn by the participants"[34]—the images of the Gods and other figures of Japanese myth and culture. The Noh plays embody the special love of nature that distinguishes the traditions of Zen and Shintoism, but their use of masks, as Donald Keene observes, resembles that of Greek drama.[35] "Mask carving has," he continues, "been considered an important art in Japan, and together with the gorgeous costumes, the masks add much to the visual beauty of the No[h]." Comic masks would appear in farcical pieces performed as interludes between the more serious pieces of the Noh performance, and the beauty of the masks does not exclude certain horrifying or frightening visages, such as those of demons or witches. The woman's face, now burned into a comic mask, suggests the "unreal reality" of the drama that began with the dropping of the Hiroshima bomb, and Dr. Hachiya's sense of the attendant "unreal" horror.

A mask, more generally, is known in cultural imaginations world-wide as a talismanic image of myth, drama, ritual and religion. In the guise of masks, we face not only human realities but those of larger or archetypal powers enacting their drama upon the world's "stages" of ritual and history. Through masks, the presence of these powers makes itself felt, so that one sees the human drama more deeply, as itself a "mask" expressing fundamental realities of existence.

But what's so funny about this "comic mask?" How is unimaginable pain transfigured into a comic image? How is such an image a fitting expression of the painful realities faced by us all after Hiroshima? Now other, more recent, cultural memories expressive of the sheer absurdity and tortured contradictions of the nuclear drama begin to emerge: here comes Dr. Strangelove into this play-house of memory, still with his black-gloved right hand going for his own throat. Next appears the singer and songwriter, Tom Lehrer, whom we remember for such songs (from the fifties and sixties) as the one he is now singing: "We will all go together when we go." These two have joined Mask Woman (as she may be named) in this little theatre of memory. Dr. Strangelove looks just like he is in the movie. I do not know what Tom Lehrer actually looks like; here he appears as a young man. His name is We-All-Go-Together-Man and he is playing his guitar.

Try and listen to his song as we continue to reflect. Each of these characters is in his or her own way twisted and funny, giving the spectre of nuclear death a comic face. But theirs is a "gallows," or one might say, *grave* humor through which we face the gravity of our situation, and its ludicrous possibilities. Who would ever have imagined a species that could destroy itself (and not only itself) by accident? *We will all go together when we go*. Perhaps some character in us is bowled over with laughter, laughing himself to death, his laughter joining in memory the echoes of We-All-Go-Together-Man's song.

Laughter echoes in memory: remember that there are various occasions for laughter as Dante moves deeper into Hell, and that the ancient Athenians heard obscene jokes as they mimicked, in initiatory ritual, Persephone's journey to the underworld. Remember too Freud's early work on jokes and their relation to the unconscious. Laughter can be a way of remembering, of evoking the underworlds of memory, soul and death as we move in their direction.

Yet this configuration of characters: Mask Woman, Dr. Strangelove and We-All-Go-Together-Man remind us too that our situation is no joke; they expose its tortured contradictions. In the psychic interludes they create, we see the farcical character of what we are doing and this strangely revivifies our appreciation of the seriousness of the drama. These characters mean business: with great precision each figures a different face of the nuclear world. We-All-Go-Together-Man mocks the disfigurement of our togetherness that is yet our fate. Dr. Strangelove shows us the right hand by which the world, desiring, strangles itself. Mask Woman makes us aware of a laughing at the world's deformity and pain, or reveals that there is a form of laughing through which this deformity and pain can be remembered.

Mask Woman, Dr. Strangelove and We-All-Go-Together-Man, "carried, held and digested" in memory, work inactively to make space so that the place of comedy in nuclear pain is discerned. Imagine that, after a number of months, another character appears in the scene, a Russian man. He springs from a Russian joke about civil defense in which one character says to another: "What do we do when the alarm sounds?" "Wrap yourself in a white sheet and walk slowly to the cemetery." "Why slowly?" "You wouldn't want to start a panic, would you?"[36] There appears a figure, a middle-aged man, hunched and wrapped in a white sheet, walking slowly to the cemetery. He is the spirit of the joke, its melancholy, slow-walking-toward-death humor. His name is Grave-Man.

Now Mask Woman, Dr. Strangelove, We-All-Go-Together-Man and Grave-Man are all together in memory. Dr. Strangelove strangles himself. We-

All-Go-Together-Man sings his song of ourselves. Grave-Man wouldn't want to start a panic. Mask Woman makes us face the world this is.

We have noticed that this configuration, with its relation to the masks of drama, evokes the "theatre of memory." In chapter 4 we witnessed the dramaturgical aspect of the art of memory as present in *Ad Herennium*, with its image of the actors, Aesopus and Cimber, being dressed for the parts of the sons of Atreus; in Cicero's use of the word "persona"; and in the Memory Theatres of Camillo and Fludd (these latter being also "world" theatres). We then noticed that Jung frames the work of active imagination in histrionic terms, as taking place on an inward "stage" of the soul. All this suggests many possibilities for the practice of imaginal memory. Memory figures might play their parts in a drama set in the Theatre of Hiroshima, for instance, or a Globe Theatre of the nuclear world. Different scenes might take place in theatres echoing in their structure Fludd's Night and Day Theatres placed in the signs of the Great Common Place—as does the imagination of the above-discussed Night and Day rooms of the nuclear cosmos. The tragedies and comedies of the nuclear world would then be enacted "as in a public theatre."

The masks of theatre reveal the Gods and other mythic characters; another question relevant to the imagining of a nuclear memory theatre is: Who will play the parts of the memory images? A wealth of possibilities present themselves. The art of memory recommends that familiar of well-known individuals be incorporated as memory images. Who would like to be Mask Woman or Grave-Man? Who will be Walking-Ghost-With-No-Hair, and who will be Eyeball-Man? Perhaps one imagines national leaders or other prominent figures cast in these roles; these actors could be past as well as present personages. Behind the mask of Walking-Ghost-With-No-Hair may be the Chairman of the Joint Chiefs of Staff, while Socrates plays the part of Grave-Man, embarking on his practice of death. Perhaps the actors and actresses are people who (for most of us) are closer to home. But even the most familiar faces play transhuman or archetypal roles in the dreaming of memory. The theatre is not literally and actually the world, and—precisely for that reason—reveals the world in its aesthetic, moral and psychological essentials. Its personifying—epitomized by classical masks—is simultaneously a depersonalizing.

The theatre of memory need not, of course, be seen in the literal shape of state and play-house. Any imaginal scene in any place can appear within a theatrical or dramatic *perspective*. Then whatever is going on is imagined *as-if* it were taking place within a theatre, and the figures seen *as-if* they were dramatic characters. (This perspective is already implicit in the world's imagination of the "theatre" of nuclear [and/or conventional] warfare, the unreal reality of which is literalized, taken for granted.) However imagined, the dramatic perspective is an opening into forms of active imagination, or the enactment of scenes, in which characters are defined and revealed, speaking and otherwise acting vis-a-vis one's imaginal ego and each imaginal other. Thus may be imagined, for instance, the discourse of Walking-Ghost-With-No-Hair (the Chairman of the Joint Chiefs of Staff) and Grave-Man (Socrates).

Intercultural Interplays

Another possible feature of the work (play) of imaginal memory is also suggested by Mask Woman and the other people of her configuration. Since "We will all go together when we go," the deepening of appreciation and awareness of other nations and cultures is an important part of our work (and play). In this is an echo of Bruno's concern with universal love and brotherhood to be realized through the harmonies of memory. While such ideas of the spirit need to be approached with caution and seen as images (not literally realizable monolithic utopias), imaginal memory can bring together the play of contrasting cultures in quite powerful ways.

Mask Woman led me to an introduction to the spirit of the Noh plays of Japan. Now, even as I remember her tortured face I remember too something of the sharp wonder captured by one play about Komachi, an old woman who when young cruelly spurned her lovers. Komachi remembers when

> Crowned with nodding tresses, halcyon locks,
> I walked like a young willow delicately wafted
> By the winds of Spring,
> I spoke with the voice of a nightingale that has sipped the dew.[37]

One feels in these lines of something of that precise attunement to the natural world and its almost "unbearable" beauty (*mono no aware*, the "sad beauty of existence")[38]; the realization of which is sought by the practice of Zen. Dr. Strangelove—based on a familiar figure, Edward Teller, "father" of the American H-bomb—evokes cultural memories and fears of the predicament of advanced technological societies in general, epitomized by the image of the mad scientist. As Dr. Strangelove is strangled by his own autonomous hand, I am reminded of a statement of Jung's, that "mankind, because of its scientific and technological development, has in increasing measure delivered itself over to the danger of possession" (*CW* 9, 1, par. 455) by the archetypal spirit.[39] While a worldwide dilemma, this spectre is rooted in the Western scientific imagination. We-All-Go-Together-Man evokes specifically American cultural memories. I am reminded by his singing of Walt Whitman's exuberant embrace of the world in the latter's poem, "Song of Myself," with its open, rebellious spirit. The adventuresome puer-spirit of We-All-Go-Together-Man's satire somehow recalls as well the journey of Huck Finn. Grave-Man expresses a stout spirit of Russian humor and the sense of tragedy, melancholy and depth found, for instance, in Tolstoy's story, "The Death of Ivan Ilyich." In this story, the protagonist, Ilyich, discovers the values of his individual soul through suffering his dying by an obscure disease. There is a sad stoicism here, an ironic vision of vitality attained through an awareness of one's approaching death.

Such cultural memories evoked by an image are, to use Casey's phrase, an aspect of its "nuclear signification." These diverse cultures of images are related, bound together, by common archetypal themes: here, by a movement toward death seen through the comic. Yet the images are precisely bounded and distinguished—their boundaries given by their shapes and by their placing within variegated memory loci. Their very plurality, conjoined with their archetypal "togetherness," gives added depth to each figure and the configuration as a whole, suggesting possibilities of reflection across cultures. What, for instance, does the puer-spirit of We-All-Go-Together-Man have to say to Grave-Man in his melancholy? What might Mask Woman wish to say to Dr. Strangelove? Would Dr. Strangelove's fitful self-strangling be given pause by her tortured yet comical visage? Each character adds something distinct to the physiognomy of the configuration, a particular way of stirring the comedy of nuclear terror through memory which can help us remember ways in which different actual cultures can speak quite powerfully to one another. Between these characters are imaginal—not literalized and nationalistic—boundaries: boundaries that yet acknowledge, and even commemorate, the way each image is inextricably bound to the others. A love among images can develop, and the imagining ego find the hidden, or forgotten, eros among and between the actual peoples whose humanity the images can help us remember.

In images and configurations, one may thus remember and differentiate cultural values, and in imagination find compassion for actual peoples and cultures. For memory, even as it moves in the direction of the grave, keeps things alive; it is a "saving" awareness. It is in memory that the faces of human culture must first be saved.

Hiroshima, Vietnam, and the Interplay of Memory

Just as images arising from or evoking different cultures may speak powerfully to each other, so may images arising from places and events other than the atomic bombings. Because Hiroshima is the place of the most concentrated act of violence in history thus far, echoing images from numberless places and times may find a place there. Here I will reflect on one character from Vietnam as an example of this larger dimension of the interplay of images in memory.

Remember the Vietnamese girl, recalled by the woman who would place her in the elementary school hallway, and by a man in association with images of lines of *hibakusha* wandering in and out of Hiroshima. Why does Fleeing Girl, as she may be called, appear so often in connection with the place of

Hiroshima? She presents for many of us an active, emotionally striking image of modern war's indiscriminate brutality, in particular the savagery of the Vietnam conflict and the unresolved conflict in the U.S. about Vietnam. Her grieving, panicked face helped bring the reality of the war home for many in this country. Ranging in memory, we find similar young-girl victims of the Nazi Holocaust and Hiroshima: Anne Frank and Sadako Sasaki. These images seem particularly striking, suggesting the ultimate violations given with war. They stir to consciousness the reality of young girl's lives—a reality forgotten in the largely male activities of war.

Fleeing Girl's appearance, as she runs in naked panic, suggests an ultimate vulnerability. All the masculine armor, nuclear "defenses" and space-weapon fantasies of nations notwithstanding, we are totally vulnerable—as if naked and defenseless—in the nuclear world. This girl brings to the fore, with the horror of Vietnam, the largely-forgotten sense of terror and unsafety that many felt in the years immediately after Hiroshima. Something, or someone, within us, is yet in panic, fleeing. Lifton, with reference to images of dead and dying women and children in Hiroshima, observes that women and children in general are "universal symbols of purity and vulnerability" . . . (DL, p. 49). Powerless, Fleeing Girl yet embodies an archetypal power, an image of innocence as well as vulnerability. But she, in her naked fleeing, "uncovers" the "fleeing" innocence of our culture (Vietnam is often taken as signifying the end of imagined American innocence, and there may be indirect associations to unconscious guilt over the bombings of Hiroshima and Nagasaki). In the background is war's explosive, deadly, poisoned rape (this girl is often thought to be fleeing a napalm attack). The rapist is the death-terror to which we all may be prey in the nuclear world. In myth, images of innocence often constellate a dark violating pursuer: remember Death, who rapes Persephone; and Pan, the goat-God of terror who pursues fleeing nymphs. Both Gods, we have witnessed, are associated with the place of Hiroshima: Death-Terror. We remember these as we remember Fleeing Girl.

NUCLEAR WOUNDS AND THE ALCHEMY OF HORROR

Writing on the fortieth anniversary of the first nuclear explosion at Alamagordo, physicist Glenn Seaborg said of the initial synthesis of the element plutonium in early 1941 that: "It was the first realization of the alchemist's dream of large-scale transmutation, the first synthetic element seen by man."[40] In his *Alchemical Studies* (CW 13, par. 163), Jung observes that alchemy reverses the Christian myth of redemption, making man the Redeemer in God's stead:

Man takes the place of the Creator. Medieval alchemy prepared the way for the greatest intervention in the divine world order that man has

> ever attempted: alchemy was the dawn of the scientific age, when the
> daemon of the scientific spirit compelled the forces of nature to serve
> man to an extent that had never been known before . . . Here we find
> the true roots, the preparatory processes deep in the psyche, which un-
> leashed the forces at work in the world today.

Alchemy is often enough cited as a foundation myth of the scientific imagination.[41] And the un-healing images we have been remembering have precise
parallels to certain images of alchemical psychology, especially its phrase of
the *nigredo* or blackening, melancholy, mortification, separation, dissolution,
pulverizing, putrefaction and stench, dismemberment and other such "unendurable torments" as those undergone by the priest in the visions of Zosimos. In the
memorial psyche, the night of nuclear wounding and death appears very much
like an alchemical hell. A look at this *alchemy of nuclear horror* is essential precisely because alchemy's pathologizing operations are forgotten in the more
common assertions relating the spirit of science to the medieval quest for elixirs
of immortality or the means to transmute "base" metals into gold.

The alchemists themselves not only insisted that *aurum nostra non est
aurum vulgi*, "our gold is not the common gold," but also stressed the necessity
of the darker phases of the work. Because alchemy cannot do without the blackening, we can expect this to appear together with the drawing of the nuclear
sun from matter. This we see, in Dr. Strangelove's black-gloved hand.[42]

An alchemical perspective on nuclear images means the remembering of
the leaden heaviness of the gold, the blackness within the sun; the remembering
of the dark psychic base of scientific imagination; and the freeing of "soul and
spirit from the black body of the literal bomb and our anguish over the chance
of its use"[43] and—as I forgot to acknowledge in that statement—its use at
Hiroshima and Nagasaki, together with the larger history of violence there
evoked. (Our forgetting of the horror of alchemy and of Hiroshima and Nagasaki are in psychic sympathy.) In the following, nuclear wounds in general
are seen as images of the "black sun" of the nuclear age. I will focus particularly
on how the concentration of memory upon these images involves, re-lives, the
emotional and psychological experience of alchemy. The implications of this
alchemical perspective—in particular, its relation with dismembering imagery
and the "work of melancholy"—will re-emerge in the next chapter.

First, let us review some particular instances of parallels between nuclear
and alchemical images. In the previous chapter the unhealing effects of radiation on Father Kleinsorge's wounds echoed the wounded and dismembering visions of Zosimos and of Dionysian consciousness. The vision of Eyeball-Man
and the staring eyes of Dr. Hachiya's dream evoked an alchemical vision of *scintillae*, eyes of the soul, sparks in the nuclear dark. The Night room we visited
earlier in this chapter evokes this same vision. Moving from there into the Day
room, we found no relief. The whitening (in alchemical terms, the *albedo* or

illumination) and the burning (calcination) only revealed the horror in more detail. The metal garbage container that aroused the curiosity of the woman imagining the room (and our own), with its "melted, deformed, dripping" people and garbage, has close parallels in alchemical imagining. The alchemists found their *aurum non vulgi* in medieval Christian places of refuse, hidden within what is rejected. There are comparable alchemical visions of the vessel in which the *prima materia*—original, crude material—is "tormented," dissolved, burnt, melted down, deformed. The image of the people burning within the Hiroshima streetcar also reminds us of the alchemical burning and container, witnessed by Zosimos (the burning "upon the fire of the art"). The paradoxical, old-young, boyish-wise, weak-fiery Ferryman evoked a number of figures, one of whom, Hermes/Mercurius, is the guiding spirit of the alchemical *opus* and the journey to Death.

More parallels could be cited, but the intention here is less the direct alchemical amplification of nuclear images than the differentiation of an alchemical perspective on their memory. For this, reflection upon some alchemical images, in the manner of the restating or *iteratio* that is part of the *opus* and with the nuclear images kept in the background, will prove to be of much value. This may be unfamiliar territory for many readers. It may help to pause frequently, allowing one image at a time to work on one's awareness, become active, more deeply impress the memory. This is again a way of practicing imaginal memory; as the impression of the image deepens, its metaphoric speech can be heard. Associated nuclear and other memory images begin to surface, and alchemy is rendered an immediate psychological experience rather than an obscure relic.

Two illustrations in *Psychology and Alchemy (CW* 12, figs. 34, 48) show the putrefaction in the form of a skeleton. In one, this *nigredo* stands atop a black sun (*sol niger*) with flames circling its perimeter; upon its right hand is perched a raven. The ring of flames around the black globe suggests a fierce burning within and behind this eclipse of spirit and its flights of melancholy. The original body of the *prima materia* has wasted away, rotted and burned by a blackening sun: all that is left standing is a skeletal structure. In the next figure the skeleton lies in a foreground by an open grave in which a man (perhaps the adept witnessing this horror) stands, while to the left and right two seated men shoot arrows at a target. The target-shooting, or aiming for the goal of the work, cannot be reached, observes Jung, without the putrefaction. The shooting on target and the decay of death must coincide. The skull reclines on a bundle of sticks, perhaps intended as fuel for the fire underneath the alchemical vessel, which is often shown as a death's head (*CW* 14, pars. 626ff).

One verse in George Ripley's *Cantilena,* an alchemical parable (see *CW* 14, pars. 368ff), describes a time just before the birth of the renewed king from the chamber of the Queen Mother, "when the Child's Limbs there had putrefy'd" (quoted in *CW* 14, par. 434) . . . Jung notes that the *nigredo* or "dark initial state . . .is often regarded as the product of a previous operation" analogous to therapeutic reflection that constellates the unconscious (or encounter with one's shadow) (*CW* 16, par. 376). In Ripley's parable, the *nigredo* of the king's death has already occurred when the putrefaction has to be reiterated as part of the alchemical circulation. The new innocence, or "whiteness" of the Child must rot before a profounder illumination may become apparent (this second whitening is different from the "first white" of naive or unpsychological innocence)[44]. Even the Child must die. Says the alchemist, John Pordage:

> the delicate Tincture, this tender child of life, must descend into the forms and qualities of nature, that it may suffer and endure temptation and overcome it; it must needs descend into the Divine Darkness, into the darkness of Saturn, wherein no light of life is to be seen: there it must be held captive . . . It must enter into the fierce wrathful Mars, by whom (as happened to Jonah in the belly of hell) it is swallowed, and must experience the cure of God's wrath; also it must be tempted by Lucifer and the million devils who dwell in the quality of the wrathful fire.
>
> (quoted in *CW* 16, par. 510)

The "tender child" must suffer as prisoner of Mars and Saturn, the two pagan dominants of the *nigredo*; it must be disfigured by Mars's war-fire and be stuck in the lonely dark of Saturn.

The Old King, or ruling way of life, must also die; as he does so, earth's streams become "foul and stinking . . . "[45] The alchemists often mention the "stench of the graves" which as Jung says pertains to "the underworld and to the sphere of moral corruption" (*CW*14, par. 254). In one "deplorable but picturesque poem" Mercurius, "A weakling babe, a greybeard old," describes his own death:

> A fiery sword makes me to smart,
> Death gnaws my flesh and bones apart.
> My soul and spirit fast are sinking,
> And leave a poison, black and stinking.
>
> To a black crow I am akin,
> Such be the wages of all sin.
>
> (quoted in *CW* 13, par. 276)

Mercurius, as the "transformative substance" of alchemy, is both agent and sufferer of the stinking blackness. He is rent by a fire that is a sword of dismemberment; his flesh and bones are picked apart by death. The decomposure of his death is a stinking of soul and spirit that leaves only poison, a black stinking and foul air which takes wings as a crow, as "all sin." Yet this burning dismemberment, decay and death-smell show not only the blackness of "moral corruption," but its attendant "blackness of guilt" (*CW* 14, par. 607) in his poisonous substance. Guilt too is an underworld poison, a blackening stink.

The alchemical properties of sulphur and salt may appear in our work. Sulphur contains the qualities of compulsive, "burning" desire, the excess of which has a blackening and corrosive effect (*CW* 14, pars. 138ff). In its torment of passion, sulphur—the active spirit of the sun—is associated with hell and the devil, indeed "is the true black devil of hell . . . "[46] There is a "vulgar" sort of sulphur that is bound in the "infernal prison house . . ."[47] Sulphuric passion has an imprisoning quality that binds one to the repetitive compulsions of affects. This vulgar sulphur at the same time may bind one to the emotional currents of mass consciousness, so that individual qualities remain unconscious (*CW* 14, pars. 191-3). Yet, as active agent of Sol, sulphur has as well a "true" variety, in the heat of which the interior mystery of the soul is discerned (*CW* 14, par. 196). Then the blackening and corrosive effects of sulphur work homeopathically, corroding this element's imprisoning (or literalizing) aspect until desire is recognized as image and metaphor. Sulphur is active in the penetrating emotional power of the *imagines agentes*.

According to Gerardus Dorn, sulphur, "when sublimated, changes into the 'highly esteemed salt of four colours'" (quoted in *CW* 14, par. 143). According to the author who calls sulphur the "black devil of hell," this element can only be conquered by salt. Salt reflects the *albedo*, the illumination of a whitening, and is the reflection of the moon's cooler nature—or the moon herself—in the earth. It conflicts with sulphuric heat for this reason, wounding it. Yet there is a hidden likeness: "In the sharp or burning taste of salt the alchemists detected the fire burning within it. . . . " (*CW* 14, par. 319). The complex qualities of salt (as well as sulphur) belie any simple opposition, say, of desire and reflection. The affective qualities of salt's reflections must be remembered.

The burning of salt is a sharp bitterness (*CW* 14, par. 245ff) akin to seawater and vinegar. Memories often have the bitter quality of salt, as illustrated by, for instance, the Seder dinner on Passover during which the participants taste of bitter herbs to remind of the Israelites' bitter and tearful bondage in Egypt. But this bitter whiteness or realization is "colored": salt is "of four colours" according to Dorn, and regarding the bitterness two alchemists dialogue thus:" [He:] This is the stone that hath in it glory and colour. And She: Whence cometh its bitterness and intensity? He answered: from the impurity of its metal" (quoted in *CW* 14, par. 245). There are a variety of hues in the bitterness of salt. And its *albedo* also brings insight and wisdom and adds tang to the experience of spirit (*CW* 14, par. 324-5). According to Jung, the many-hued bitterness of salt, and of one's realization of the shadow's black sun, disclose the varieties of feeling and affect. Bitterness and wisdom coincide,[48] and allow the discerning of the glory and colours within the stone. And this stone or *lapis* is the matter of the world while salt is its soul, the *anima mundi* (*CW* 14, par. 321). The bitter realities of the world, brought into the vessel of alchemical reflection, disclose the hues of soul and its wisdom.

The salt of alchemy is quite valuable in work with *imagines agentes* associated with the place of Hiroshima, wounding their sulphuric activity after they have burned their way into memory. Alchemical insight provides a way of seeing these images and their mortifying injuries. One's occasional return to them in memory becomes an *iteratio* in which their particular sufferings gain patient regard. What are the elemental and affective qualities that emerge from these woundings and dyings? In alchemical language, what are their hues of color? Before some figures one feels and reflects upon the "blackness" of the sun, or the fire that is a sword of dismemberment (the sense of falling apart); or the fury of Mars as the image of a child putrefies, devoured by war. One may feel moves toward impassioned activity as sulphuric desire, or this may be conjoined with the cool embittered wisdom of salt that reflects the soul of the world.

One way of apprehending the "colors" of wounds is to notice with an alchemical eye their "exact pathological details" and imaginal location. Nagasaki Child and Mask Woman, for instance, disclose ways in which nuclear horror is *faced*. The smooth face of Nagasaki Child, with its several wounds or blotches and blank look, we saw to evoke the blotching of the Child's innocence and future, leaving only benumbed blankness. In the ruins of the nuclear psyche the Child is, as it were, devoured by Saturn and Mars in Hell's belly. Here, imagined with precision, is one of the faces of the nuclear world, or one of the ways the world has been *faced* by collective cynicism, deadness and what Lifton calls a sense of "futurelessness." In the place of Hiroshima, an image of a child suffers a psychic death. Mask Woman's face tells of a different way of facing the world—a physiognomy of comedy that reveals tortured contradictions. But the features of this comedy, while they can also reflect cynicism, open us as well to a burning of pain and a variety of other affective qualities. Again, we reflected upon the picture-image of an atomic-bomb victim with burnt skin hanging from his or her fingertips. Instead of facing, this evokes "touching" qualities of images. With "hands of fantasy" the art of imagination makes contact with the horror suffered by *hibakusha* and psychic images of the nuclear world in general. One may at the same time remember with new sensitiveness the activities of actual hands and fingers, such as caressing, playing the piano, pointing in anger or pushing a button, holding or "lending a hand."

In such ways as these, the House of Memory becomes an alchemical vessel, a way of letting a fire build with contained effect that is also a way of working within a foundational frame of scientific culture. Working closely with the varieties of feeling that arise with different images associated with the place of Hiroshima fuels a slow, fierce burning in which sulphur and salt are again conjoined. In part, what appears pictures one's own responses, just as "the alchemist's operations upon things like salt, sulphur, and lead were also upon his own bitterness, his sulphuric combustion, his depressive slowness" (*RP*, p. 90). And, as Hillman adds, this work engages also the soul in the materials themselves: the raw materials and the "stench of the graves" hidden or forgotten in our culture's alchemy. Jung, who carefully placed medieval alchemy in its cultural and historical context, observes that the alchemist worked "In the blackness of a despair which was not his own, and of which he was merely the witness. . . . (*CW* 14, par. 493). Thus, also is our witnessing, in memory, of the alchemy of nuclear horror.

REMEMBERING WORLD

Recall again Augustine's discovery of the world in memory, and whatever images of "heaven, earth [and] sea" were present as we began this practice of imaginal memory. Remember the "renaissance" of world-memory in the systems of Camillo, Bruno and Fludd. There is Camillo's Theatre, from within which one may view the divine activities of creation, ranging from the Gods' original banquet to the Promethean culture of human being. There are the encyclopedic memory systems of Bruno, who loved the world too much: images of minerals, plants, animals, qualities of existence and creators of culture ranged within the frames of the Gods. There are the Night and Day Theatres of Fludd, each with its place in the Great Round with its houses of planets, and by which Yates remembers the cosmological nature of the Shakespearian Globe Theatre. All these worlds of memory we saw as reflections of Ficino's talismanic suggestion that one make an "image of the universe" and set this up as "a little room," "Deep inside your house." Thus, the world will again be *housed*, and the house of soul remembered as world.

For memory images are inherently "worlded," inhabiting a world. Images are themselves worlds or, as Hillman says, "Each image coordinates within itself qualities of consciousness and qualities of world . . ."[49] Whatever images that arise from the place of Hiroshima inhabit their particular worlds; with them, we are able to remember these realms. Remember the worlds of Mask Woman, Dr. Strangelove, We-All-Go-Together-Man and Grave-Man; and before them, the worlds of Nagasaki Child, Ferryman and Eyeball-Man. Each distinct place is also its own world and at the same time embodies and intimates a much larger and encompassing world: the Naval College hallway, the Night and Day rooms and the elementary school hallway. We can remember all the places and images of *memoria* as "parts" of speech: the world speaking to us of its pain, its hidden treasures, its forgettings, it beauties and dyings. The place of Hiroshima, remembered, is housed "deep inside" the larger world, persuading, even exhorting us to remember that world with care.

We follow Bruno. We love the world so much that we end up "dying" in a place of religious cruelty: The place of Hiroshima, where we remember disfigured images that figure the profound pain of our being.

As the remembering eyes of the dead in Dr. Hachiya's dream remind us, though, it is not only we who remember. Nagasaki Child, Ferryman, Eyeball-Man, Grave-Man, Walking-Ghost-With-No-Hair and the rest will, through our practice of memory with its strange love, walk with us as we go into the world; walk as they stand in the House of Memory; commemorate with us the world.

7

Final Openings

"Essentially," says James Hillman, the art of memory was "a moral activity of the soul. Learning and remembering served psyche" (*MA*, p. 179). The art of memory links the powers of imagination with moral activity and concern. In different ways, the medieval and Renaissance practitioners of the art sought increased vitality and vision in their moral activities and concerns through their careful, devoted attention to the soul's essential images. Rememberings of the place of Hiroshima require a similar devotion to essential images of the nuclear world. Itself a form of moral activity and concern, this work helps sustain and deepen the vitality of our concerns and activities more directly aimed at the development of a sustained cultural commitment to peace.

Yet the devotion of memory to images arising from the place of Hiroshima opens deep and enduring wounds; these must be cared for and attended to. In the course of our rememberings—and those of the images—we have discovered values intrinsic to the open, and opening, wounds remembered. To care for the intrinsic values embodied in these wounds may be the deepest dimension of the "moral activity" of imaginal memory. We will need to remember the place of Hiroshima if we are to sustain long-term efforts to avoid nuclear holocaust, and to attenuate the more general tendency toward mass violence as a way of strongarming Death. But this statement must also be turned on its head: we need to prevent nuclear holocaust in order to go on remembering the place of Hiroshima.

The practice of imaginal memory, and the wounds remembered, are none-theless relevant in various and precise ways to our witnessing and concern for the world. Like Bruno's "figurative art," the form of imaginal memory we have elaborated embraces intense moral concern, and the ego's awareness of the au-tonomous activities of psychic images. This awareness is at once crucial to our moral concern, and itself a way of serving the powers of soul: a therapy of psyche (*psychēs therapeia*) in the original sense. Moral concern is seen here as always involved with psychic images, an activity of the soul. As we witnessed with regard to the medieval art, the practice of memory is a holding-together of the soul's moral activities and images in deepest pain.

It is well to pause and reflect on this *holding-together of moral activity and suffering images*, for it bears crucially upon the all-too-often forgotten side of the moral imagination—the place of religious cruelty. In explicitly and deliber-ately entertaining images arising from Hiroshima, we are forced to remain aware, to remember, that what Hillman calls "pathologizing" can involve moral activity and that moral activity can involve (and often conceal) pathologizing. We must attend to the pathologizing within our moral activities, or—having forgotten these psychic realities—risk becoming moralistic, literalizing our moral concerns after the fashion of Strong-Armed Ego. Then we end up oppos-ing literalized moral adversaries in a cold war of the spirit.

In openly and simultaneously engaging moral concern and images of ex-treme pain, the practice of imaginal memory shows a certain masochistic qual-ity. Echoing the medieval devotional art, it is a devotion, in the fullest sense, to the pains and deaths of soul in the nuclear world: a "discipline" and a submis-sion to the powers of Fate that the figures of Strong-Armed Ego (e.g., Apollo and Herakles) attempt to beat back. (More reflections on the relations of masochism, sadism and moral activity will follow. The former two terms are taken here to signify the way in which desire and pain are inevitably drawn to each other in the soul's deeper movements—in ultimate terms, the inevitable intimacy between love and death or the soul's endings that we have often wit-nessed in this book.)[1] Here we can extend Hillman's statement: imaginal mem-ory serves the suffering of soul, and that is its moral activity.

With these initial reflections in mind, I will sketch and explore five areas in which imaginal memory—as a practice of death—can contribute to "deaths" to which our culture must open itself if we are to witness its continuation and the attenuation of Strong-Armed Ego's massive violence. There is first the fate of Strong-Armed Ego himself. This primary figure of our culture suffers and dies in the practice of imaginal memory. A look at how this takes place will reflect possibilities of the death of his habitual violence. Second, I will reconsider the theme—with which this book opened—of remembering nuclear hell, or the place of religious cruelty since Hiroshima. It will become apparent that *hell it-self dies* when images of torment are placed in memory as metaphors or talismans of the soul. This involves a look at the relation of Hell and Hades to which I alluded in chapter 5, and a remembering of a disturbing shadow of the moral imagination that is reflected in the dilemma of nuclear "deterrence." Implicit in these first two topics is our third, "the work of melancholy." This again speaks to the death of Strong-Armed Ego, but now in a manner that acknowledges continuing values of this figure. And melancholy leads us back to another topic whose importance we have witnessed—the power of remembered place. There are interesting connections between the "love of place" and the forgetting of literalized nationalistic boundaries. The forgetting, or *opening* of such boundaries, speaks to our fifth topic—the relation of psychological commemoration, and the ability to identify and empathize with members of other, including adversary, groups as actual human beings. This points toward a final opening to the place of the imagination of otherness in the time of "after Hiroshima."

"Inviting" Death

We gain a basic perspective on the death of Strong-Armed Ego by returning to Freud's positing—after World War I and the development of his cancer of the jaw—of an instinctive movement in the psyche toward death. In this context Freud reflects on sadism, masochism and aggression, stating in the *New Introductory Lectures* that: "We are led to the view that masochism is older than sadism, and that sadism is the destructive instinct directed ourwards, thus acquiring the characteristic of aggressiveness."[2] For masochism has the more primary relation with the instinctive desire for death. Freud continues:

> And now we are struck by the significance of the possibility that the aggressiveness may not be able to find satisfaction in the external world because it comes up against real obstacles. If this happens, it will perhaps retreat and increase the amount of self-destructiveness holding sway in the interior. . . . Impeded aggressiveness seems to involve a grave injury. It really seems as though it is necessary for us to destroy some other thing or person in order not to destroy ourselves, in order to guard against the impulsion of self-destruction. A sad disclosure indeed for the moralist!

We need not remain within Freud's instinctualist frame to appreciate the acuteness and relevance of his remarks. For there are strong parallels to the predicament of Strong-Armed Ego that we discribed in chapter 2. Lifton's observations about the relation of violence and the "murdering" of death echo here, as does Hillman's assertion, made with reference to Herakles, that: "Rather than die to metaphor, we kill literally; refusing the need to die, we attack death itself" (*DU*,

p. 110). In the egoism and literalism of victimization it becomes necessary to destroy others in order to ward off images of death and annihilation—including the death of habitual individual or cultural ego-styles.

The relevance of Freud's remarks is striking in the nuclear context, in which much traditional international aggressiveness "comes up against real obstacles" that inhibit its "satisfaction in the external world." Again, Freud's insight transcends its mechanistic paradigm: the violence of Strong-Armed Ego against others is inhibited even as it is fueled by the existence of nuclear bombs. The power of self-destructiveness both retreats and increases, "holding sway in the interior." And it is precisely the *interiority* of death that Strong-Armed Ego would deny. The sense of this interiority of death, or an entering *into* death, is conversely what the practice of remembering nuclear images seeks to cultivate. There is in the nuclear reality "a grave injury" to the human propensity to violence. This injury is our collective fate, whether it be acted out in nuclear hostilities or remembered as a profoundly necessary wound opened in Strong-Armed Ego's murderous tendencies.

But at this point the logic of Freud's assertions breaks down. For if it is necessary to destroy an external (read: literal) other in order to avoid destroying the self, we are now embroiled in a tortured contradiction. For literal nuclear destruction of one's national adversary would be simultaneously a mode of self-destruction. Sadism and masochism would rejoin in this collective movement toward—in Freud's phrase—"an earlier state of things."[3] Now it is necessary *not* to destroy the literalized other if we are "to guard against the impulsion to self-destruction." Yet (and here the logic of conventional arguments in support of nuclear deterrence breaks down too) self-destruction must follow the inhibition of literal violence.

Let us distinguish, however, between two modes of self-destructiveness. One would be the destruction of Strong-Armed-Ego (and all within his reach) through his acting-out of violence. The other would consist in an acknowledgement of and submission to the "self-destructiveness holding sway in the interior," or—to use Herakles's own phrase from the *Alcestis*—"Death, who rules the world of spirits." Because Stong-Armed Ego is driven to literalize and attack Death, the first way of self-destruction leads in the present world toward literal nuclear (and/or other mass-) death. The second way of self-destruction realizes nuclear death as metaphor, as modern mask of an archetypal power, the ruler of Hades. Death would thus again be known as a ruler. This implicates a cultural shift regarding the sado-masochistic tendencies of the soul. For as Hillman notes with regard to the classically-defined "shadow" qualities of our culture—"aggression, violence, power, sadism"—these "aren't shadow at all; that's the whole Western ego!"[4] In the first form of the self-destruction of Strong-Armed Ego, the sadistic tendency is dominant in the sense that the destructiveness appears to be directed outward. But the shadow of this ego—the masochistic attraction to death—is at the same time acted out as literal fate. Has not this shadow taken shape in the world's submission (thus far)—buttressed by Strong-Armed Ego's belligerence—to instruments of nuclear terror and torture? It would be well to remember the irony of the *Alcestis*, which might be seen as a Hermetic trick played by Death on Strong-Armed Ego, who unconsciously accedes to the former's "hospitality." The deeper reality is that Death "rules the world of spirits" *in* which the characters of the drama operate. Thus, the second way of self-destruction involves the ego's sensing of the masochistic undercurrents of soul, and acknowledging of the sadistic rule of Death. But Death's sadism is not tied, like Strong-Armed Ego's, to literal victimization, aggression and violence; in fact, it is quite inviting. In Death's house the soul's destructiveness has already "taken place," and so need not be fended off. This deeper sadism involves a subtler, more disciplined and psychological, fascination with the soul's dying movements: a fascination that recognizes reality as the theatre of the imaginal, a "world of spirits" or shades. And it involves Death's hospitality to images of memory and their torment: there is shelter here, and a place for that love that exists between Death and his bride.

In this way, the practice of imaginal memory is a kind of *house* and *invites* the death of Strong-Armed Ego's violent literalism. And this can be seen as a contribution to "deterrence," though not of the sort that relies on the strength of literal weapons.

MEMORY, MORALITY, AND THE DEATHS OF HELL

There is more to say about the soul's fascination with pain, torment and dying, which we witnessed at the beginning with da Signa's exhortation to "remember the eternal torments of Hell." Ours has been a work of remembering Hell as well as Hades, and we have hinted at a crucial relation between the two. Thus far we have distinguished the two realms only loosely, mirroring a cultural tendency to equate them. But they are distinctly different places (notice, however, the complete obliteration of any such distinctions at the site of nuclear destruction). Let us consider what it is that transforms Hades into Hell—into the place of religious cruelty—so that we may better grasp the reverse movement of our practice, or how Hell, the place of religious cruelty, *suffers* death in memory. Reflecting on the "deaths" of Hell, we also face painful realities of memory and morality. And we will again find ourselves speaking about "deterrence," in this case the remembering of Hell as a part of Prudence.

Hillman, in *The Dream and the Underworld*, discusses the effect of "Christianism" on the cultural imagination of Hades. Christ, be observes, outdoes Herakles in his harrowing battle with Hades, "actually wip[ing] out the entire kingdom, including death itself" (p. 87). The Herculean victory of Christ has a crucial effect on our way of imagining Death:

> the Satanizing of Thanatos. The black figure with wings, indistinct, and even at times gentle in pagan descriptions, became "the last enemy" (I Cor. 15:26) and the personification of the principle of evil. The underworld became thoroughly moralized; death became equated with sin.

Here is the cultural background of the moralistic tendencies whose danger we cited previously. The victory of Christ's everlasting life over death places Hades in Hell, at once intensifying and moralizing the soul's torment and anguish. The sado-masochistic tendencies we have already discussed are given a more specific focus; their cruelty becomes more systematic. As the woman who remembers with uneasy fascination the nuclear cruelty in the Day room—in a place of garbage, of "refuse"—inadvertently acknowledges, these tendencies appear in tandem with "the Christian part" of our cultural life. The fascinated demons and sufferers, now imprisoned for eternity in Hell, coexist with pagan figures placed there too. Thus, the way toward the latter will for our culture be through hellish torment.

Here we must qualify Hillman's critique of Christianity's "hellish image." In our culture the way toward the remembering of Hades is *necessarily* through Hell. The Christian influence is important (whatever our particular faiths), but in the following I will consider a somewhat larger theme: the place within the moral imagination of particularly intense anguish, or cruelty, "religiously" remembered. Of this the traditional Christian imagination of Hell is one instance, as problematic as it is relevant for our work.[5]

The "moralizing" of Hades means that the cruelties of Hell become a basic place of the moral imagination. As Alfred Ziegler, who pointed the way toward our initial recognition of the psychological fascination of hell, asserts:

> One should bear in mind that neither Heaven nor Hell is limited in its significance to the moral/theological, but both are also areas of pathology. Hell is not merely a place defined by various religions as penance, hell-fire, or eternal damnation but also one of the purest images of human illness.[6]

Ziegler nicely emphasizes the demonic "purity" of Hell's pathologizing, and particularly its sadism. (Heaven and Hell are an archetypal tandem, which can be taken to suggest a "heavenly" quality inherent in visions of Hell.) What is missing, however, is an exploration of the hellish suffering *within* the "moral/

theological," or the cruelty of morality. This, again, is what the practice of re-membering *nuclear* hell seeks to recall.

There are many ways of perceiving visions of Hell and their functions. One traditional view, noted by D. P. Walker in his reflections on why the doctrine of the literal eternity of Hell persisted so long (into the seventeenth century), is that visions of hell are a necessary deterrent to immoral and (particularly) anarchic behavior.[7] Certainly these visions have sanctioned various forms of (social, political, religious and psychological) authority (hence the authority of the Freudian superego and the authoritarian personality of Strong-Armed Ego). A traditional psychological view elaborated by Ziegler with reference to hell-fires is that these also portray collectively-repressed "asocial or antisocial burn-ings."[8] Images of hell reveal too the concrete existential situation of a people, as Joseph Kitagawa reminds us with regard to popular depictions of Buddhist hells in medieval Japan.[9] There is also the anguish of *hibakusha*, the guilt-ridden tor-ment of whom Lifton recognizes in the "living hell" of Hiroshima.

Particularly important here—and not only because of its obvious nuclear relevance—is this last, the relation of hell and death guilt: the "hell" of Death and the "death" of Hell, and their relation to struggles of the moral imagination. Recall Freud's "sad disclosure for the moralist." In the passage quoted above, Freud's reference is to the psychic situation of melancholia or depression. The "work" of this involves self-deprecating fantasies of the ego that express guilt over repressed hostile impulses. As Freud puts it in *The Ego and the Id*, a judg-ing and punishing superego subjects the ego to the aggressivity of the id turned inward, its sadism having reverted to masochistic torment. This "interminable self-torment" is the appearance in psychoanalytic guise of Hell and its eter-nity.[10] Freud's further remarks are equally revealing. The harsh superego of melancholia is "a kind of gathering-place for the death instincts" involving "a systematic torturing of the object, in so far as it is within reach." And "From the point of view of instinctual control, or morality, it may be said of the id that it is totally non-moral, of the ego that it strives to be moral, and of the superego that it can be supermoral and then become as cruel as only the id can be."

The superego is thus the Gathering-Place of Death; Hades is housed in im-ages of torment. And it is through suffering bound up with morality that the soul's impulsion toward death enters into life. Once again, our culture's victory over Death turns out to be pyrrhic: the movement toward Hades reappears in the very moralizing that renders Death a Hell, a punishment for the guilty. The Gathering-Place of Death is inherent in the moral imagination.

Thus our movement will be from moralizing, which places a literalized other (external opponent or the guilty self) in a hell, toward the place of Hades. This implies the death of literalized visions of hell, while hell remains a ghost of the imagination, of the tormented moral activity of the soul. Here is the place of nuclear hell in the practice of imaginal memory.

This death that moves hell into the place of shades is a way of getting at our culture's troubled relationship to moral imaginings. History reveals the long shadow cast by morality. Along with compassion and the desire for humane justice, there have often enough appeared desires to hurt and be hurt, desires for vengeance and retribution. The soul's hells, when literalized in totalistic moral visions, are often acted out in inhuman violence. An ominous contemporary illustration of this literalizing tendency—with its exultation of one exclusive path of "symbolic immortality"—is the violence of some religious fundamentalist movements. Another is the very notion of nuclear deterrence, which rests on a rarely acknowledged desire, in the event, to wreak vengeance on a truly God-like scale (this shadow of nuclear deterrence or nuclear winter of hate being rationalized as purely pragmatic and prudential in nature).

There is a need for other, more psychological, ways of remembering the cruelty, the hell, that claims a place in religious and moral imagining. The intent here is not to reduce morality to something outside of itself. Acknowledging this suffering within the soul's moral activities in no way denies what Jung saw as the soul's inherent and archetypal involvement with moral concerns.[11] Rather, our moral anguish and ethical reflections gain psychological resonance when remembered together with the cruelly precise suffering of the nuclear *imagines agentes*. And this contributes to the discernment of individual conscience, which Jung saw as essential to the development of the moral imagination. For suffering, hurt and anguish are crucial to one's discovery of the power within moral concern; without the witnessing of some hell, morality remains an abstraction—perhaps a categorical, but finally empty, imperative.

And we need to allow Death to gather in our moral anguish. This deeper death of the pains of Hell allows the dying of the need to inflict actual and literal hells upon others as part of an aberrant quest for a sense of immortality. Yet Hell has its place. In this we return to the archaic House of Hades, in which (e.g., *Od*. XI. 368ff) a place of punishment and torment is imagined *within* Death's larger house, rather than Hades being relegated to Hell. It is with a view to this death of the need to inflict hellish justice on others that we have stressed, in previous chapters, the alchemical visions of hell which keep the metaphoric depths of images of "unendurable torment" in the fore, portraying the inevitable unhealing of the memorial psyche. Jung hints at the replacing of Hell in Hades when, with reference to certain medieval Christian meditations whose initial phases focus on hellish images, he notes that "the alchemical parallel is to be found in Hades or Chaos, the nigredo or tenebrositas. Pain and torture rule in this condition, which is a dead, unawakened state; the scintilla, the spark of the soul, is enclosed in a dark, suffering condition, in melancholia."[12]

As a counter to the moral literalism that denies Hades and thus condemns itself to the eternal damnation of others in hells, the practice of imaginal mem-

ory evokes strikingly painful images that remind us that the hell of moral anguish is also a place of shades. And struggles with death guilt are seen through
as remembrances of the debt owed to Hades. In evoking images of nuclear hell
in this manner, imaginal memory is prudential and has a deterrent value. But
this, like the deterrence we found in the death of Strong-Armed Ego, is not of a
conventional sort. For even as the cruel morality in images of nuclear horror is
openly entertained in this house, there is movement away from reliance upon
the *justice* of threatened nuclear vengeance.

A MELANCHOLY CURE

The theme of melancholy we find woven through the above discussions, as
it is woven in the fates of Strong-Armed Ego and of Hell. Previously, we have
witnessed the importance of melancholy in memory, and the melancholic inspiration or "heat"—a special sensitivity to fantasy-images—that Albertus considered favorable to the art of "reminiscence." The art of memory—from its foundation in the horrible deaths in Scopas's collapsed banquet hall and in *Ad
Herennium's* evoking of the lonely rhetoric student—has been a work of melancholy. So too the current practice, which seeks to remember the profound and
fatal sadness at the heart of the nuclear world, in the stubborn and unhealing
wounds of Hiroshima and Nagasaki. These open both toward a feared future destiny and the pain of what-we-have been as a species: the pain of our being. For
us, the melancholy aspect of imaginal memory turns out to be felicitous.

To remember the nuclear *nigredo* plunges the Heraklean ego into melancholy—an un-healing which for this character has a profound healing value. To
apprehend this value let us consider a rarely-remembered tradition about a
melancholy Herakles.

In *Saturn and Melancholy*, Klibansky, et al., discuss the mythological
background of the motif of the "drooping head" in Durer's portrait of *Melen-
colia I*, noting that: "The primary significance of this age-old gesture . . . is
grief, but it may also mean fatigue or creative thought."[13] They cite a variety of
figures represented in this position, observing that: "In fact, the veiled head of
the classical Kronos rests as sadly and as thoughtfully on his hand as does the
head of the melancholy Hercules on his in some ancient representations."[14]
Herakles as sad and thoughtful, resting his head on his hand: this is an interesting contract to his usual heroic ego. Klibansky, et al., refer to two Etruscan
gems reproduced in Roscher's *Lexicon* of Greek and Roman mythology, in
which Herakles holds his drooping head in his right hand, and his club—as a
support—in his left. In the first of these he is seated and faces a spring. Roscher
captures the fascination of Herakles's unexpected pose in the first gem, which

presents he who "is always doing something, ever striving: the undefatigable hero exhausted, the restless one resting, musing (*sinnend*) over his tormented and mournful destiny . . . "[15]

Here Herakles has been tormented into contemplating and musing, tortured into submission by Fate. He is presented beardless (in typical Italian fashion, says Roscher). This emphasis on his youthfulness, together with his likeness to Kronos-Saturn who discloses the contemplative wisdom of age, suggests an appearance of the puer-senex tandem within this death of Herakles's acting-out. His club is now a means of support (again, an association with age: remember the Sphinx's riddle), not an instrument of violence. His melancholy musing is at the same time a source of renewal and healing: he faces a spring, "the water of life"—and of his death. It is also the "welling-up" water of remembering and forgetting, this melancholy cure of Herakles's ego-mania.

This last remark is a reference to the likely mythic history of Herakles's melancholy position. This history is discussed in Pseudo-Aristotle's *Problemata* that is reproduced at the beginning of *Saturn and Melancholy* and taken by Klibansky, et al., as a source of the concept of "melancholic frenzy," or "inspired" melancholy.[16] The *Problemata* takes the "madness" of Herakles as its first example of the madness of melancholy, referring to two fatal episodes. The first occurs after one of Herakles's heroic trips to Hades. This time he had chained the mad-dog Kerberos and brought him up to the world of life (he also rescued Theseus, who had been stuck to a rock in Hades). Herakles has, in addition, just dispatched a man named Wolf (Lykos) who was menacing his family, when Madness, at the behest of Hera, possesses him so that he kills his wife, Megara, and their three boys. The theme of remembering and forgetting is implicated here; Euripides, in his play, *Herakles*, implicitly names this mad fit as a forgetting and a sleep.[17]

In a way, this book has been concerned throughout with countering what is revealed here as a form of *manic forgetfulness*. It is interesting that this example of a "melancholic" symptom bears more resemblance to what we would call psychotic mania. But the author of the *Problemata* is of course not wrong in relating this to melancholy. Herakles's first fatal madness is a precise style of manic depression in which the ego is "dogged" by the underworld of melancholy it seeks to fend off, and finally becomes possessed by the madness it would chain and destroy. And this is a sleep, a death, a forgetting of the human family. It is well that we seek to remember the children who may fall victim to the Heraklean madness of the nuclear world.

In the second episode of Heraklean madness referred to here, the hero is driven to immolate himself on a pyre. (He had put on a poisoned cloak, stained with the blood of the centaur—and underworld ferryman—Nessos, who Herakles had shot with an arrow tipped with the Hydra's blood for molesting his second wife, Deianeira.[18] Nessos had persuaded Deianeira to give Herakles this cloak—thus again an underworld animal takes revenge on the hero. The cloak, when Herakles donned it, caused his skin to break out in burning pain and could not be removed.) Relating this fate to the warlike tendencies associated with Herakles, Hillman comments sardonically: "In the end, Hercules goes up in fire. . . . Will ego psychology lead us into war and fire?" (*DU*, p. 111).

Profound melancholy, mourning and guilt result when Herakles awakens to his fate, his killing of his wife and children. This death guilt is also an irremovable burning wound, a torture that we would name a living hell—but one which makes place for contemplation, mournfulness, rest and the musing of memory. Herakles now ponders over his fate, and the violence of his life; the action of his club is stilled.

In this "rest" and remembering, there is yet a deeper sleep and a deeper forgetting than in the ego's mania. It is the death and for-getting of Strong-Armed Ego's getting, striving and doing. Thus, also with our melancholy work of remembering and contemplating with, nuclear images. It is not Strong-Armed Ego's violence alone that is at issue, but his role as *rescuer*—a leifmotif of Euripides' *Alcestis* and *Herakles*—and his incessant activity to which Roscher alludes.

Consider the reflection of this cultural complex in the example, discussed in the previous chapter, of the Hiroshima streetcar with its burning occupants. The man's imagining ego felt a desire to enter the scene and try and rescue the people, thus giving life to a heroic ideal that he felt he had not lived up to in his actual life. We considered this urge with some caution, reflecting upon the various values of remaining in the "position of weakness" and impotence in the face of tormenting fate. To attempt a rescue in this context could mean a more subtle form of avoidance, of Heraklean acting-out and literalizing of death—a "rescue" of ego itself. The alternative ways of entering into the burning pain of this hell and remembering its tortured destiny that were suggested in the previous chapter involve a quieting and a "resting" of ego's heroic activity, a stilling of the club and drooping of the head, a heaviness of pondering, mourning and musing—a quite definite work of melancholy.

Yet it takes a certain strength to remain in a position of weakness, of submission to the *daimones* of fate. Remember the strong image, sketched by the Navy veteran, of a man on a stretcher in Hiroshima, "in a pretty much hopeless condition." The strength of ego is not entirely forgotten, but is no longer opposed to literalized images of "weakness" against which manic defenses are necessary. Seen as an inevitable condition of human being in the face of the ill-fated powers of soul, the position of weakness is greatly strengthened, and ego's openness to weakness rests on deeper strength: the strong powers of imagination. And in the death that is melancholy there remains some of the mad inspiration the author of the *Problemata* finds in Herakles; let us remember this foundation of the tradition of melancholic inspiration. Herakles lives on even in that inspirational sensitivity to imaginal powers, that intellectual contemplation governed by Saturn, but usually opposed to Herculean muscle-power. And in the death of ego's frenzied activity, we discern more acutely the activities of images that inform the moral actions we take in the nuclear world. In this too, we cannot avoid encountering the daimonic power of the hero *as image and quality of the imaginal*, distinct from even as he informs the ego or habitual self.[19]

Thus we recognize, remember and revalue aspects of Strong-Armed Ego. Caution is needed, since it is so hard to see as image this habitual style of our culture. This is why our stress on moral *activity* must not forget the essential *in*activity of soul displayed by imaginal memory.

For the work of melancholy is Herakles' last labor.

REMEMBERING PLACE, FORGETTING NATIONALISM

The imagination of place is, we have seen, essential in a variety of ways to memory and soul. In the *Phaedrus* we saw the power of a particular place at work in the evoking of mythic memories. We witnessed too the place of memory in time—or memory as the way place is "timed" and time is "placed." Again, places and images (and images of places) are crucial to the art of memory. In our exploration of this treasure-house of invention, it became apparent that place is the house of memory and its treasures. And memory in turn houses, or treasures, images of places in the soul. This rich interrelation of place-house-memory gained a place in the *house* of the heart as we looked directly at the place of Hiroshima in relation to the place of memory. There the urgency of remembering the power of place became apparent. There is a direct connection between the memory of place and the place of memory, the forgetting of which is reflected in the historical obliteration of Hiroshima and Nagasaki, and in the obliteration of place basic to nuclear scenarios. The work of imaginal remembering of the place of Hiroshima, as we have witnessed, reconstructs the *place* of place in memory and imagination. The examples of place-images explored in the previous chapter revealed this reconstructive power of imaginal memory, and spoke to us very strongly through what we heard as their rhetoric.

The imagination of place has yet more to tell us, however. This becomes evident through a reconsideration of melancholy, and the place of its work in the art of memory. We discovered Saturn, governor of melancholy, at work in what Casey describes as the boundary-making power of place, and hence in the remembering of places for images. We have seen too that Saturn—or the senex—with his single vision, oppressiveness, defensiveness and paranoia—is an important character in the authoritarian personality of Strong-Armed Ego. Saturn, as God of boundaries, is thus closely bound up with the psychological power of nationalism's often paranoid borders, which function, ironically, to keep "out" (in the guise of external and literal enemies) what is really an "inner" death and sadness.

Though I alluded in chapter 2 to the need recover values in senex-consciousness, as has been done in the section above with regard to the ego of Herakles, this book has had nothing good to say about nationalism. It has often enough been said that, in the nuclear world, it is nationalism (at least in its more extreme forms), and not any given nation that is the enemy. Of the malignant influence of nationalism when this gets bound up with collective images of revitalization through violence, there is no doubt. Yet it is not enough to call for the elimination of nationalism and national boundary-making—or even their attenuation—for they are bound up with individual and collective identities and memories, and governed by an archetypal power. The weakening of Strong-Armed Ego's nationalism *is* essential, but there is an essential value in nationalistic imagery that we must remember, and whose claim we must honor.

Recall that the *Phaedrus* reveals an erotic sensitivity toward, or love of, place (chapter 3, p.40). The forms of *topophilia* are many, but love of place is usually taken in terms of collective or national place-images, or "love of country" (for which one may be called to die in war). We less often remember the love *inherent* in more particular places, like the sacred grove by the Ilissos River, or the houses of memory explored by Bachelard.

Having listened to the rhetoric of several place-images of the nuclear world, let us give an ear to "the rhetoric of place itself."[20] This can be heard in John Mack's exploration of "Nationalism and the Self" (on which we have already drawn for the idea of the "egoism of victimization"). Speaking of the "subjectivity" of the self, Mack observes that the latter "may be conceived of metaphorically as a kind of place, or the locus of experience."[21] The "place" of self becomes intimately bound up with group and national places. And the motif of the "house" of memory then reappears, this time in the image of one's communal or national "homeland." Mack quotes a Palestinian who said, during a 1980 meeting with Israelis, Americans and other Arabs, that if his people had a state, "we would have a place to go back to if in a plight."[22] In another meeting, an Israeli conversely spoke of Jerusalem, "about which my feelings are stronger than about any other place in the world."[23] The Palestinian's desire for a homeland gives a distinct image of the yearning for the house of place. There is a suggestion of or a return to the "house" of the maternal, or the "motherland." The Israeli's passion for Jerusalem bespeaks the erotic and spiritual power of place. There is also the image of the Holy City, which—like the house and like Kyoto for the Japanese—is an *imago mundi*, as Eliade has shown.[24] We remember in these images the fearful power of the love of place, speaking in the rhetoric of intensely nationalistic and religious passion. It is well that we the recover rhetoric of place from that of nationalism.

With this rhetoric in memory, let us return to our previous reflections (chapter 5) on the devastating and forgetting of place in the nuclear age.

The obliteration of place—or its reduction into "site"—has its cultural history. In part, this is related to our culture's technological advances. James Oglivy addresses a general loss of the sense of place in his discussion of "the demise of the story-teller," a carrier of shared—and precisely "localized"—as well as private experience.[25] For postindustrial culture is characterized by a

> disintegration of the near/far structure of human experience. As travel becomes trivial the odyssey is no longer suitable subject matter for a story. The equalization of the near and the far accomplished by high-speed transportation—which is not to be reduced to a species of communication—renders the entire phenonemon of *locality* less significant and hence less a source of sharing than it once was. When local lore gives way to the abstract grid [or map of sites] of the real-estate developer the loss includes more than the land. The very vocabulary of intersubjective experience is semantically grounded in a sense of *place* which, once destroyed, leaves the language of intersubjectivity impoverished.

Oglivy is speaking, I believe, of the *bounded* character of place, upon which the distinction between "near" and "far," this world and that, is based. It is not necessarily travel that becomes trivial, but the making and crossing of boundaries of imagination and story. Flying from place to place, we tend to forget the primordial numinous quality of border-crossing, the archetypal quality of the crossing of the threshold or ford. These imaginal phenomena are given with what we identified (in chapter 5) as the senex-quality of place, which, together with place's (puer-like) "vertical" connections, discloses its power.

Casey further explores the destruction of the sense of place in Western thought, singling out first the Cartesian and post-Cartesian reduction of particularized place to generalized three-dimensional space which, because it abstracts from and lacks all qualities of unique places, "means no place at all."[26] He then observes that the "internal" sense of time (not the "placed" time of memory elaborated in the present work) has been considered, by Kant and others, as more fundamental in human experience than amorphous space. Thus, "place has been doubly displaced since Descartes—first by 'space' of a universal sort that has no place for local place, and then by time, which since Kant and the Romantics has overtaken space itself as having the privileged position."

The nuclear world discloses something terrifying about this development which "means no place at all." The most revealing comment by Descartes in this regard is quoted by Joel Kovel in an examination of the contribution of the Cartesian division of self and nature to the nuclear terror. Descartes concludes during his *Discourse on Method* that: "I was a substance whose whole essence or nature consists only in thinking, and which, that it may exist, has need of no place."[27] That within our culture which "has need of no place" comes to final flowering in preparations for nuclear annihilation.

Now the value of what we have remembered in nationalism—the rhetoric of place—becomes evident. Menaced by the nuclear thinking of the Cartesian ego, we my see the resurgence of nationalistic concerns in present history as also an attempt, if blinkered, at "self"-healing by Strong-Armed Ego. Yes, boundaries are necessary—no boundary, no place. The paranoid boundary-making power of nationalism expresses, if in narrow and literalized form, a fear all too real: that all boundaries, and all distinct places, may be obliterated—indeed, *are* being obliterated by our culture's ego-structure which "has need of no place."

This fear speaks too of the archetypal power of Saturn, which seeks, like the rhetoric student of *Ad Herennium* (a student also of the "rhetoric of place"), distinctly bounded precincts, places in which images and memories can be housed, which soul can inhabit. The psychology of nationalism (in particular, its more extreme varities) and its pathologies—paranoid defensiveness, egoistic victimization of others and the repression of the collective shadow—in sum, the forgetfulness we spoke of in chapter 1—appears now as the ill epiphany of this power of bounded places.

The practice of imaginal memory, through its engagement with the powers of places and images, speaks quite precisely to this predicament. By providing a place for senex-consciousness, and its melancholy ruler as it realizes place as metaphoric locus, it counters the dangerous literalism and totalism that so often accompany nationalistic visions. And the lonely, melancholy state which, as tradition advises, is best for the art of memory is a way of placing the soul's deep separations, sadnesses and deaths. For the movement toward death (and death's stasis) is the "inner" life of senex-consciousness, even as the Old King defends against his own dying at all costs. Thus, our practice of death works to weaken or attenuate the paranoid defenses against death that translate politically into militarism, repression and victimization of opponents of the state. And we remember how deep the need for place is in the soul, apprehending the former's boundary-making power in a deeper place than the need for national boundaries.

Lifton quotes the remarks of a Japanese writer (a non*hibakusha*, but originally from Hiroshima) that capture the present dilemma and its possibilities:

> I have been traveling widely, and I feel strongly that there should be no separate nations—no demarcation of borders between countries. I felt, while traveling in Europe, that in many places these barries became very low—very small—and this is one way to peace . . .

Nowadays people begin to talk again of patriotism. Let patriotism be tied up with love for a particular place. Those who come from Texas can love Texas. If one loves Texas, one can also love California—there is no war between Texas and California—or between Hiroshima and Shiga Prefecture. This is what I mean when I say that patriotism should be love for one's native place.

(In *DL*, p. 391)

Counter to the writer's antinationalist sentiment is "Senex-conscious, [which] by maintaining the wall and law against something which does not like a wall and a law, makes possible the psychological region of the borderline and a host of symbols whose existence requires boundaries."[28] But the soul's need for boundaries is implicitly answered by his plea: "Let patriotism be tied up with love for a particular place." For places must be bounded and separated. Like ourselves, this man is groping for a way that allows for the claims of the boundaries of soul while countering the dangers of nationalism. Imaginal memory shows us one way.

And yet the memorial psyche, with its love of places (for one place implies a multiplicity of others), allows for a variety of places of love, of care for the particular image. In this sense the practice of imaginal memory is precisely *not* "one way" only. Nationalism tends to narrow and harden into what may be called a "monotheistic idolatry," a most uncivil religion in which only one "god" and one sort of identity is permissible. The practice of memory imagines boundaries in a polycentric context; its eros is polytheistic, like Plato's description of memory in the *Phaedrus* and like Camillo's Theatre. Differences are essential to the memory; memory "loves" differences: different places and weird *imagines agentes*. As eros deepens in memory, empathy and compassion extend: hence the love and power of a particular place that saved Kyoto. Thus, the forgetting of nationalism—carried more by generalizations and stereotypes than aesthetic appreciations of the particular—finds a counter too. Remembering the claims and place of Saturn is a movement toward the for-getting, the "death," of nationalism's monotheism, its literalizing and victimizing ego and its cold war of hate. (This does not imply the equally monotheistic and simplistic opposing of Love to Hate. Rather, the soul's hatreds which are literalized in national "images of the enemy" have their place too: the halls of nuclear hell may provide a most suitable place for Hate, and the love of hating.)

The practice of imaginal memory thus works in an area of crucial cultural need: that of the re-construction of the memory and imagination of place, the *de*-struction of which we have seen to be fundamental to the nuclear terror. This remembering of place is revealed to us through the forgetting of national egoism, and itself reveals a deep resistance to the nuclear (or any form of) obliteration of places treasured, loved and inhabited by soul. And though we are focusing on places of hell in our practice, this contributes to an aesthetic sensitivity to place in general, or to what E. V. Walter calls "making, keeping and dwelling in good places."[29] This is why the "speaking" of place is a primary moral activity of soul: it is a form of rhetoric that argues most strongly against that which would leave no place to remember. And we may argue in turn that nationalism itself must die for the love of place.

COMMEMORATING THE OTHER

There is a unique value in remembrances of Hiroshima and Nagasaki that again bears upon the necessary attenuation of literalized boundaries between national and other groups. The soul, "wounded" by the remembering of nuclear images, opens in empathy and compassion to those beyond "our" borders. This is partly because, as Lifton suggests, we are all survivors, in imagination, of Hiroshima and feared future holocaust; thus empathy—and compassionate identification—come more readily in the context of that place. This points toward the possibility of moving beyond the boundaries of "pseudospeciation," the imagining of foreign groups as not-quite-human.

The nature of the identification experienced with these others in the psychological place of Hiroshima is more precisely revealed through the commemorative nature of imaginal memory. In "intrapsychic memorialization," as discussed in chapter 5, one "incorporates" the presence of another *within* the place of one's individual psyche; *place is made for the other*. This prepares the way for identification with the other, for the dwelling of the other within the place of oneself, the house of memory. Because the place of Hiroshima evokes imagery of humanity as a whole, its psychological commemoration involves a movement beyond the egoism of national and/or group memory against which I argued in chapter 1.

Moreover—and like intrapsychic memorialization in general—the present form of commemoration is akin to the work of mourning. Psychic identification implies a memory of connection; mourning also involves the work of separation between ego or self and other. Pain, grieving, sadness and loss are intrinsic to psychological commemoration as they are to the work of mourning; separation is made possible through a hidden remembering of the other. Separation takes place within the precincts of Saturn's melancholy aloneness (chapter 4). It is a form of death, in Lifton's phrase a "death equivalent," paired with connection. Separation (*separatio*) is also an aspect of the alchemical blackening or *nigredo*, the necessary rending apart of images of world and soul. The form of death that is psychological commemoration is the precondition to a deeper re-membering of the other *as other*, as apart from oneself. Separation is how connection takes place.

Throughout this book, we have focused on images of death, separation, disintegration (or dismemberment) and stasis as sources of psychological and moral reflection. There are deaths of cultural habits that are necessary to the attenuation of the tendency toward mass violence in general and the nuclear threat in particular. Thus, Strong-Armed Ego dies into the soul's instinctive movement toward Hades, and Herakles's frenzied activity is stilled in melancholy, mournful rest; and disintegrates into a variety of active images. The single vision of national chauvinism disintegrates, leaving us with the love of particular places. This disintegrative process echoes the torment and alchemy of hell. And it is through this disintegration of psychic structures within which mass violence is organized, that psychic integrity (paired by Lifton with the death-equivalent "disintegration") is deepened, placed, remembered.

Necessary too is the essential stasis at the core of imaginal memory and its manner of commemoration, which stopping is a basis for movement away from the action of literal violence. In the psychological commemoration of what is other in the place of Hiroshima, new wounds are opened, and old ones renewed, so that the "grave injury" cited by Freud may be done to the structures of ultimate, or nuclear, violence that imply the final forgetting of the other. To realize this fatal injury it is necessary to remember intensely the Ancestors of the nuclear world: their wounds are still new, still beginnings.

Psychological commemoration involves a deep opening in memory to the actual woundings and deaths of historical persons; and an identification with their sufferings, a com-passion, that connects the death of separation and the remembering of the lives of others. But, as the ancestral characters—Eyeball-Man, Grave-Man, Mask Woman, Fleeing Girl, Walking-Ghost-With-No-Hair, We-All-Go-Together-Man, and others—remind us, this is also a commemorating of *imaginal* others—the *imagines agentes* of the soul and world in pain. And we commemorate, honoring with a gift of imagination, the *place* of Hiroshima itself in the terrain of our memories, thus remembering the power of place, the power of world, together with the place of memory.

The impressions of this commemoration are made more lasting and forceful by Hiroshima's "universality," its imagination of obliterated boundaries, its utter inclusiveness. We are all within the bounds of the place of Hiroshima.

Part IV

Appendixes

Appendix A:
Mnemosyne and Lethe

A closer consideration of how the springs of Mnemosyne and Lethe separate in late classical, Pythagorean imagery yields more nuanced insight into certain aspects of memory and forgetfulness. By comparing and contrasting this late separation of the two springs to the archaic Hesiodic imagination, we deepen our outstanding of relations between memory and the ego, and then hit upon a theme of great relevance for contemporary debates about "national security."

Kerenyi reflects upon the separating of Mnemosyne and Lethe (or Lesmosyne) in Plato's myth of the Ameles and the "Orphic" gold foils found at several grave sites dating from the fourth and third centuries B.C.E.[1] We have already noted Plato's valuation of Lethe; let us consider the imagery of the gold foils, which constitute a "Greek book of the dead" ("ML," p. 127).

There are several fragmentary versions of the group of foils we are concerned with here; they differ in certain details, but correspond in general themes, particularly on the newly dead man's need for the water of Mnemosyne. The longest fragment tells the initiate that he will find two springs by "the houses of Hades." He should not drink from the one on the left (not named, but it is evident that this is Lethe), but rather approach the fountain of Mnemosyne, on the right, before which guards are standing. The soul should say to the guards that: "I am a child of Earth and Starry Heaven," and that he is perishing, parched with thirst; then he should ask for a drink of the cold water of Mnemosyne. This he will receive, and then will dwell as a lord (*anax*) among other heroes.

As in Hesiod, there is an encounter with death which leaves one needing replenishment from the primary or archetypal source of memory. But in this picture one's survival takes place *after* one's own death, and one partakes of a memory without forgetfulness. Forgetfulness (of one's former lives in Pythagorean belief, and of the Platonic Forms)[2] is necessary and characteristic of the living, but if the dead drink Lethe's water, they will not be "immortalized": not remembered. In the reincarnational cycle posited by Plato and the Pythagoreans, one re-enters this life by drinking from Lethe's water of Un-Care, and exits by drinking from Memory, the water of wisdom. The streams of Mnemosyne and Lethe, though still adjacent to each other, have been split apart by the bipolar or dualistic distinctions of the Apollonic spirit with its disdain for the immediate desires of the body.[3]

This splitting-apart of Mnemosyne and Lethe is a matrix for the identification, discussed in chapter 3, of memory as mainly under the control of the ego. Present here is the *idealization* with which the heroic ego, in particular, remembers itself. In the initiation-schema depicted by the gold foil tablets, Memory discloses, instead of the Immortals and heroes of the past, a future prospect in which the initiate, himself immortalized, lives a heroic life as a "lord" in the next world.

In fact, as Kerenyi says, "The 'thirst' of the dead is nothing other than the 'will' of the living" ("ML," p. 126). The heroic will "dies" into a psychic image of thirstiness; this is its underworld counterpart. The ego, with its heroic will, its acquisitive thirst for life, becomes immortalized, and idealized, in these remembered images. This theme is echoed in one of Freud's more curious passages:

> The experiences of the ego seem at first to be lost for inheritance; but, when they have been repeated often enough and with sufficient strength in many individuals in successive generations, they transform themselves, so to say, into experiences of the id [underworld], the impressions of which are preserved by heredity. Thus in the id, which is capable of being inherited, are harboured residues of the existences of countless egos; and, when the ego forms its super-ego [including the ego-ideal] out of the id, it may perhaps only be reviving shapes of former egos and bringing them to resurrection.[4]

In the Hesiodic imagination, the sense of the paradoxical interplay of remembering and forgetting—which we have also found in depth psychology—is richly present. But it is largely forgotten by the ensuing stress on memory in those strains of Platonic and Pythagorean thought informed by the perspectives of Apollo and the heroic ego with its will. Imagined from these perspectives, memory can become a servant of the (heroic) ego's quest for immortality. In this light, forgetting cannot but appear inferior. Here too is the archetypal background for the premise questioned previously: that memory is, for the most part, under control of the ego.

There is a close connection between this basic premise and the idealizations of nationalistic memory with their forgetting and their egoism of victimization. The latter involves a repression of memory when this is taken in the sense intended by Broughton and Zahayevich (see chapter 1), but there is equally a repression of Lethe's for-getting. And, as always, the inferior or repressed powers insinuate themselves—in this case, in the unconscious forgettings and lacunae of nationalistic memory. Because Mnemosyne and Lethe are an archetypal tandem, the presence of one implies the presence of the other; thus, we also find the profoundly memorable engagement of Aeneas and Anchises by the River Lethe.

Yet to refuse entirely the separation of Mnemosyne and Lethe or the necessary relation between ego and memory is also untenable; for the separating and distincing perspective of Apollo aids our more precise reflection on the nuances of remembering and forgetting. And our work with memory necessarily engages the ego as well (though this comes to find strength more in imaginal others and less in its own literalized will-power).

The separation of the two springs or rivers in the imagination of antiquity reveals something highly germaine to psychological currents of the present. We have seen how Plato, in qualifying Lethe as the current of Un-Care, illuminates for us the current of heedless forgetfulness within nationalistic remembering. We can qualify this further by returning to the scene in Hades in which Anchises speaks to Aeneas, saying that souls to be reborn drink from the River Lethe (*Aen.* 940–7). He then alludes, as Kerenyi points out, to the Ameles with the phrase *securos latices,* "careless drafts" of this water of oblivion ("ML," p. 124).[5] Thus, he brings out the element of "'security,' which is present in the original meaning of Lethe as hiddenness." This further amplifies the theme of Un-Care in the nuclear age. Lifton, speaking of psychic dilemmas around "national security" in the nuclear era, also points to the root significance of security, saying this "means safety or freedom from danger or risk. More specifically it refers to 'feeling no care or apprehension' (the word secure being derived from the Latin *se* [without] *cura* [care])" (*BC*, p. 352). What are the connections between the thirst for security, national forgetfulness and the drink of oblivion in the nuclear world? What appears from one perspective to be the most safe, most prudent, most secure way of proceeding (staying "strong" in the belief that the real enemies are external) is from the perspective of later antiquity's imaginings a form of deadly carelessness by the edge of the River Oblivion. Carelessness is revealed as the shadow of security; in much recent discourse about how to attain more "national security", it would be more accurate to speak of "national carelessness." By considering the undercurrent of Lethe concealed by blinkered notions about security, we may remember life's deathbound currents and acknowledge their place, instead of being heedlessly carried toward oblivion by them.

Appendix B:
The Rhetoric of Memory

The story of Simonides, discussed in chapter 4, reflects the mythic foundation of the rhetoric tradition. An exploration of the inherent relatedness of myth, rhetoric and memory can help us listen more closely to the speaking of images.

Myth is in the "memory" of rhetoric—and myth *is* the rhetoric of memory, its persuasive power. Thus, Socrates, after relating the myth of (the man) Er and of the Ameles, says that we will be saved "if through it we would be persuaded [*peithometha*]" to avoid staining our souls (*Rep.* 621B–C). This persuasiveness of myth is the speech of soul, and for this reason rhetoric as well as memory is of key importance to archetypal psychology as

> a style attempting to be precise in distinguishing among the faces of the soul, all the while appealing to that many-sided soul by speaking in figurative language to the emotions, senses, and fantasy, working its persuasion through artfulness, even if at times becoming bombastic, contrived, even piously woolly. . . . In Renaissance rhetoric anima appears once more, this time as Aphrodite Peitho, the persuasive Venus who turns our head with a well-turned phrase.
>
> (*RP*, p. 213)

Hillman is speaking here of the need for psychological rhetoric that voices the different manners of speaking specific to the variety of archetypal images, each of which persuades after its own fashion. For example, when Bruno speaks of radical religious and political reform, of a religion based on tolerance and love for the animate world based on direct connections with celestial and superceles-tial realities, we can hear the rhetoric of the puer, who in his idealism seeks rad-ical change and immediate relation with spirit. Yet the senex, who always ap-pears in tandem with the puer, can also be heard in Bruno, speaking in images of grand circular systems precisely ordered and numbered. In this connection Yates observes "a pathological element in the compulsion for system-forming which is one of Bruno's leading characteristics" (*AM*, p. 306). And the relig-ious reform is predicated on a return to the "pristine" theology of Hermes Tris-megistus: here the puer's longing for the original or "pure" religion and the senex appeal to ancient traditions merge and reveal a hidden identity (just as the ultimate conflict of puer and senex is reflected in Bruno's imprisonment and execution by Inquisition authorities).

Jung remembers the rhetorical power of archetypes from his "confronta-tion with the unconscious," when in writing down his fantasies he used "high-flown 'language,' for that corresponds to the style of the archetypes. Ar-chetypes speak the language of high rhetoric, even of bombast" (*MDR,* pp. 177–8). In the *Phaedrus*, Socrates speaks of the orator's need to cultivate "high-flown speculation [*meteorologia*]," (270A) and then says that the orator must have exact knowledge not only of his subject or of rhetoric itself, but of the different types of soul (272Aff). Only on the basis of this precise knowledge of soul can the speaker know how different people can be persuaded by different styles of rhetoric. The orator must be a psychologist and know how to speak the variegated language (*logos*) of psyche, just as Plato persuades through myth. Remembering that another main subject of the *Phaedrus* is memory, we see that rhetoric and memory are mutually constellated, and require an archetypally pre-cise knowledge of soul.

For a further development of the psychology Socrates says is necessary, we can turn to the art of memory and its places and images. We can picture the orator delivering his speech, while "behind the scenes" he moves through im-aginal halls from one locus and image to the next, remembering in order the parts of his speech. This information is placed with images such as Ricci's war-riors locked in combat in a palace reception hall, or on *Ad Herennium's* figures with crown or purple cloaks, disfigured or stained with blood or red paint and set in archways and houses of ancient Rome. Let us see these places and active images of memory as themselves parts of a speech, its imaginal structures and persons. They are themselves ways of speaking: each place and image has its own eloquence and rhetoric, its own mythos, and stirs the memory through its persuasive and affective power. Consider the eloquence with which the figures of Dante's *Inferno* speak to us through their disfigurement and suffering.

The rhetoric of memory is myth, and places and images the particular mythos of the art of memory. This suggests a reconsideration of the relation of word and image, language and the sensual imagination. Places of memory are likened to wax tablets, and images become the written characters impressed upon them. Images are letters and letters are images: we can *hear* the speech of visual, tactile, intellective or other images just as we *see* images in words. Ricci's memory easily exploited Chinese ideograms to compose striking images. Bruno lauds the efficacy of Egyptian characters:

> the sacred letters used among the Egyptians were called hieroglyphs . . . which were images . . . taken from the things of nature, or their parts. By using such writing and voices (*voces*), the Egyptians used to capture with marvelous skill the language of the gods.
>
> Afterwards when letters of the kind which we use now with another kind of industry were invented by Theuth or some other, this brought about a great rift in memory and in the divine and magical sciences.[1]

Bruno here refers to and transforms Plato's criticism of writing in the *Phaedrus*, stressing images in a way Plato did not intend. We need not take literally Bruno's criticism of non-pictorial letters and words; it is rather a matter of re-capturing the imaginal background of speech, as does the art of memory. The "language of the gods" is myth; through the art of memory, rhetoric keeps touch with its mythic foundation and we remember the speaking of images, the language of the Gods.

The Renaissance memory tradition saw this and sought to recapture the divine speech in magic images. One of the main concerns of the Venetian Renaissance was oratory, and the images of Camillo's Memory Theatre, imagined in perfect proportions, were probably intended to capture celestial harmonies for the purposes of rhetorical persuasion. Thus, "the Theatre . . . magically activated the speeches which the orator remembered by it, infusing them with planetary virtue through which they would have magical effects on the hearers. . . . Thus, the perfect proportion of, let us say, the magical Apollo image, would produce the perfectly proportioned, and therefore magical, speech about the sun" (*AM*, p. 168). Camillo with his "planetary oratory" is carrying forward the suggestions of Socrates that the orator know the types of soul (here the planetary images) so that, through the correspondence between the speech and its audience, the latter would be persuaded. And this work of persuasion would be done not mainly for utilitarian purposes, but in the service of divine realities: one should speak "what is pleasing to the Gods" (*Phdr*. 273E; see *RP*, p. 216).

The art of memory, then, gives us a rhetorical perspective on memory, a way of seeing and of hearing images as voices of the soul and, finally, as the language of the Gods. And it is pleasing to the Gods when we remember their own rhetorical art.

Notes

PREFACE

1. On the elaboration of archetypal psychology, see the following works by James Hillman: (*Archetypal Psychology* (Dallas, TX: Spring Publications, Inc., 1985 [1983]), for a concise account of the field; *Re-Visioning Psychology* (New York: Harper & Row, 1975) for a more detailed account of archetypal psychology and its basic premises; *The Myth of Analysis* (New York: Harper & Row, 1978 [1972]), which presents a critical re-working of some major themes and premises in the practice of analysis; and *The Dream and the Underworld* (New York: Harper & Row, 1979), which reimagines dreams and images of death against the backdrop of the ancient imagination of Hades. The reader seeking further background in archetypal thought will find the following additional works helpful: David L. Miller, *The New Polytheism* (Dallas, TX: Spring Publications, Inc., 1981 [1974]), which explores and amplifies the key notion of psyche as structured by a multiplicity of archetypal dominants or powers expressed in a polytheistic pantheon; Rafael Lopez Pedraza, *Hermes and His Children* (Irving, TX: Spring Publications, 1977), which looks at myths of Hermes—together with their psychopathological necessities—in an exploration of archetypal psychotherapy; and the following two works by Mary Watkins: *Waking Dreams* (New York: Harper & Row, 1977 [1976]), which explores in detail various ways of working with images while stressing their value and depth as independent of the desires and preconceptions of the habitual ego; and *Invisible Guests: The Development of Imaginal Dialogues* (New York: The Analytic Press, 1986), which carefully demonstrates how dialogues between the habitual ego, and a multiplicity of imaginal figures can be developed and articulated, while providing a critical survey of mainstream developmental psychology's bias against the image.

2. The use here of the term "imaginal" follows that of Henry Corbin (*"Mundus Imaginalis* or the Imaginary and the Imaginal," *Spring 1972*). The latter term denotes imagination as a primary formative reality of the psyche, as distinct from the connotation of "imaginary" as "made-up" or "unreal."

3. For discussions of "soul" from the standpoint of archetypal psychology see James Hillman, *RP*, pp. x-xi; *DU*, ch. 3 and pp. 212–3, n. 48; and *"Anima Mundi*: The Return of Soul to the World," *Spring 1982*: 71–93.

4. See Hillman, *DU*, pp. 45–6 and R. B. Onians, *The Origins of European Thought About the Body, the Mind, the Soul, the World, Time, and Fate*, 2d ed. (Cambridge: At the University Press, 1953).

CHAPTER 1

1. Boncompagno da Signa, *Rhetorica Novissima*, ed. A. Gaudentio, *Bibliotheca Iuridica Medii Aevi II* (Bologna, 1981), p. 278; quoted in *AM*, p. 59.

2. *The Challenge of Peace: God's Promise and Our Response*, par. 302; in *Catholics and Nuclear War*, ed. Philip J. Murnion (New York: Crossroad Publishing Co., 1983), p. 329.

3. *Inferno* (New York: The New American Library, Inc., 1954). Here and throughout this work I follow John Ciardi's translation.

4. Alfred Z. Ziegler, *Archetypal Medicine*, trans. Gary V. Hartmann (Dallas, Texas: Spring Publications, Inc., 1983), pp. 137, 138.

5. See the classic work by A. R. Luria, *The Mind of a Mnemonist*, trans. Lynn Solotaroff (Chicago: Regnery, 1976).

6. In Cicero, *De inventione. De optimo genera oratorium*. Facing trans. by H. M. Hubbell, (Cambridge: Harvard University Press, 1949), II. liii. 160.

7. See David L. Miller, *Christs* (New York: The Seabury Press, 1981), pp. 151–2 for a critique of the usual "oppositional fantasy" about remembering and forgetting; see chapter 3 below for further discussion of the relation between the two.

8. John E. Mack, "Nationalism and the Self," *The Psychohistory Review*, 11, 2–3 (1983): 60.

9. John M. Broughton and Marta Zahayevich, "The Peace Movement Threat" in *Education for a Living World*, ed. Douglas Sloan (New York: Teachers College Press, 1983), pp. 153, 152 for this and subsequent quote, respectively.

10. See C. T. Onions, ed., *The Oxford Dictionary of English Etymology* (Oxford: Oxford University Press, 1966), p. 194. I am indebted to Edward Casey, whose exploration of commemoration (*R*, ch. 10) led me to realize that the practice of memory proposed in this book is a way of commemorating images associated with the place of Hiroshima.

11. Mircea Eliade, *Myth and Reality*, trans. Willard R. Trask (New York: Harper & Row, 1963), p. 91.

12. Ibid., p. 134.

13. A few remarks on how the terms "archetype" and "archetypal" are used in the present context, and how these bear on our method, may be helpful. Concerning the re-membering of images in the nuclear world, what David Miller says in another context (reflecting on images within theological ideas) has precise relevance: "The perspective here . . . is to view such images as *archetypal*. By this is meant just what the world orig-inally implied. *Typos* denoted the imprint made by a sculpted ring when it was pressed on warm wax. It has to do with the forms of pressure and suggests noting where a preson is im-pressed or de-pressed. It has to do with what strikes one. To add the prefix, *arche*, deepens the idea. It is not just any striking or impression, but rather the most fundamen-tal, archaic, deepest, most original one. . . . there is [here] an attempt to deal with images . . . where they press on the life of the self or *psyche* ('soul') most profoundly" (*Christs*, p. x.). It is striking that the wax figure is one of the main traditional images used as a metaphor or simile for memory. This archetypal image echoes in still-current figures of speech, for example, "striking impression," or that which is most deeply "imprinted" or "impressed upon" the memory. Of importance too is the notion of the archetypal and of archetypes as perspectives upon—and given by—*images*. An archetypal perspective re-fers to the apprehension of autonomous, perhaps uncanny powers of the imaginal. This requires a certain attunement to imagination, a poetic engagement (whether or not this involves actual poetry) or *mythopoesis* that enacts Jung's view of archetypes as "'myth-forming' structural elements" of the psyche (*CW* 9, 1, par. 259). This *mythopoetic method* that realizes archetypal sense in the present image will be our way of working with memorial figures in the nuclear world. And myth, from the perspective of this method, is experienced as the speaking-in-images of the Gods, of the most fundamental powers and structures of a world ensouled. In our later work with nuclear images we will become aware that "Archetypes were, and still are, living psychic forces that demand to be taken seriously, and . . . have a strange way of making sure of their effect" (ibid., par. 266).

The "myth-making" method of archetypal psychology is, stresses Hillman, given with and by the imagination: "(a) . . . the fundamental nature of the archetype is acces-sible to imagination first and first presents itself as image, so that (b) the entire procedure of archetypal psychology as a method is imaginative. Its exposition must be rhetorical and poetic, its reasoning not logical" (*Archetypal Psychology: A Brief Account* [Dallas, Texas, Spring Publications, Inc., 1985], p. 4) . . . Of course much depends on the im-ages governing one's understanding of logic. The present work will at times appear non-logical if logic connotes only linear, abstract, clear, unified, orderly, systematic and syl-logistic. But the soul's images each have their own logic (*logos*, language, "psychol-ogy") and we must seek to speak their *mythoi*. This exposition is thus in a way scattered (as in a re-membering of Dionysian dismemberment), unsystematic (as in the puer's [spirit of youth's] counter to the encompassing systems of the senex, that old man of in-tellect), and tied to the concrete sensuousness of particular images (each of which de-serves the loving, sensual feel of Aphrodite). Its method of speaking in terms of metaphoric myth echoes the primary processes of Freud and the intuitive or fantasy-thinking of Jung. It is circular not linear (though not tautological, not saying the same thing [*tauto*] only), but restating, echoing, returning ever from another perspective to glimpse a new facet of the imaginal, of things unchanged yet never quite the same. Mary Watkins speaks of holding together dream images rather than taking the dream ego as "symbol" for waking reality. Thus, "the relating of the day and the dream world does not lead always in the direction of the dayworld, but circles back and forth, never getting far from the experience of the imaginal" (*Waking Dreams*, p. 130). What is required is a dreamlike logic that sticks with an image so its archetypal value begins to stir and it becomes striking, memorable.

14. Printed in The *Amicus Journal* (Spring 1985): 40. Reprinted with permission from Albert Goldbarth and the Natural Resources Defense Council.

CHAPTER 2

1. Cited in William E. Lawrence, *Men and Atoms* (New York: Simon & Schuster, 1959), p. 250.

2. See Robert Jay Lifton's meticulous exploration of this latter horror in *The Nazi Doctors* (New York: Basic Books, 1986).

3. Subsequent quotations from the *Alcestis* are taken from *Alcestis/Hippolytus/Iphegenia in Taurus*, trans. Philip Vellacott (New York: Penguin Books, 1974), with page numbers to be indicated in the text. Here and throughout this book I generally follow the original, rather than the Latinized, forms of Greek names.

4. Hillman refers to Carl Kerenyi's remarks on Herakles's last labor: descending to Hades to capture and drag to the surface the underworld dog Kerberos (*The Heroes of the Greeks*, trans. H. J. Rose [London: Thames & Hudson, 1981], p. 177): "this task . . . involved the violation of a sacred realm. The House of Hades behind its firmly fixed boundaries had been such a realm ever since the division of the universe between the highest gods. Its violation was an unheard-of exploit, which not even a hero could venture upon, least of all an ordinary hero. The heroes were tragically connected with death, save only the divine hero, the victorious fighter against death." See also the more recent observations of Walter Burkert (*Greek Religion*, trans. John Raffan [Cambridge: Harvard University Press, 1985 [1977]), pp. 208–11; and Gregory Nagy (*The Best of the Achaeans* [Baltimore: The John Hopkins University Press, 1979]), p. 9. Burkert notes that: "Heracles has broken the terrors of death; as early as the fifth century it was said that his initiation at Eleusis protected him from the dangers of the underworld" (p. 211), while Nagy insists (with reference to Akhilleus [Achilles], who knowingly lives out his fated death in loyalty to his friend, Patroklos) "that the hero must experience death. The hero's death is the theme that gives him his power—not only in cult but also in poetry."

This does not mean, however, that Herakles lacks *any* connection with death; we shall witness the fruits of his last labor and his way of dying (as well as of killing) in chapter 7 below.

5. Speaking of the myth of the hero in general, Wolfgang Giegerich notes its "aim-

ing for separation and violence" and wonders about "the question of to what extent this vision (of fundamental separateness) is responsible for the problems of the modern West (alienation, fragmentation, pollution, etc.) and specifically shapes the scientific mind." He adds that: "Our fate . . . may well depend on whether we are able to move out from our confinement in the ultimately deadly hero myth" ("Ontogeny = Phylogeny? A Fundamental Critique of Erich Neumann's Analytical Psychology," *Spring 1975*: 125).

6. Hillman, however, stresses the value of the imagination of Mars and the contrast between the martial and nuclear imaginations ("Wars, Arms, Rams, Mars" in *Facing Apocalypse*, ed. Valerie Andrews, Robert Bosnak and Karen W. Goodwin [Dallas, Texas: Spring Publications, Inc., 1987], esp. pp. 126–30).

7. Mike Perlman, "Phaethon and the Thermonuclear Chariot," *Spring 1983*: 87–108 and "Phaethon's Vision of Enlightenment: The 'Success' of the Nuclear Bomb," *Nuclear Reactions* (Albuquerque, NM: Image Seminars, Inc., 1984), pp. 107–22.

8. A particularly sensitive work on this subject is A. G. Mojtabai's *Blessed Assurance: At Home with the Bomb in Amarillo, Texas* (Boston: Houghton Mifflin Company, 1986). Mojtabai, with adroit yet tactful persistence, interviewed a variety of citizens of Amarillo, which is adjacent to Pantex, the plant where all U.S. nuclear bombs undergo final assembly. She describes in plain detail the ways in which fundamentalist Christian belief helps most of those whom she interviewed to maintain a sense of meaning and order in a chaotic, nuclear-imperiled world, in the creation of which many of these same people participate in a particularly direct manner. In a conversation with one man, the latter remembers early movies in which "there was no question about who the good guys were. Roy Rogers was clean living—good guy. Dale Evans, Gene Autry—all of them without exception said: The good always wins. . . . there was always killing, but the good always wins. *Always*" (p. 162). Therefore, he now anticipates, Jesus will be victorious over Satan. One must keep in mind this man's sincerity and human concerns; it is the archetypal pattern here displayed that is "inhuman": if "the good always wins," there will be killing, *always*. In the imagination of Christian fundamentalism, Christ must perform truly Herculean tasks so the Old King of the Christian spirit may maintain his power.

9. On the psychology of nationalism see Jerome Frank, *Sanity and Survival* (New York: Random House, 1982 [1967]), ch. 6 and John E. Mack, "Nationalism and the Self," *The Psychohistory Review*, 11, 2–3 (1983): 47–69. On paranoid processes in group psychology, Mack cites the work of Charles A. Pinderhughes, who speaks of a physiologically-conditioned tendency to dichotomize the world of human groups into opposites: In Group and Out Group. There are opposing tendencies toward "affiliative-affectionate" and "differentiative-aggressive" ways of relating to others, with the former leading to in-group bonding and the latter to out-group stereotyping and scapegoating, or "group-related nonpathological paranoias." See Pinderhughes, "Differential Bonding: Toward a Psychophysiological Theory of Stereotyping," *American Journal of Psychiatry*, 136 (1979): 33–7. Whatever the empirical validity of Pinderhughes's concepts, we note a stress on the fantasy of opposites, the phenomenology of which, as discussed below in the text, characterizes the hero and senex archetypes. On the paranoid

structure of the nuclear state, see Joel Kovel, *Against the State of Nuclear Terror* (Boston: South End Press, 1984), ch. 3. Kovel stresses the interplay between "elements of our psyche that are always available for being drawn into paranoid responses," the Cold War world with its all too real adversarial structure, and the existence of nuclear weapons. "Psychologically," he observes, "we understand paranoia as a condition marked by two features: grandiosity, or a heightened sense one's own importance, and a marked suspiciousness, while the presence of nuclear weapons gave free reign to the grandiosity of those empowered with them" (pp. 78–9). The pathology of this response is evident in the systematic cultivation, in various ways by the U.S., Soviet Union and other nations, of exaggerated images of enemies which pave the way for victimization and violence.

10. On the phenomenology of the *senex* figure see James Hillman, "On Senex Consciousness," *Spring 1970*: 146–65 and "The 'Negative' Senex and a Renaissance Solution," *Spring 1975*: 77–109. See also Murry Stein, "The Devouring Father" in *Fathers and Mothers*, ed. Patricia Berry (New York: Spring Publications, 1973). These papers elaborate the archetypal background of the above-cited paranoia. The use here and elsewhere of clinically-based terms such as "paranoia" does not imply a simple identity between individual and group or national psychological histories, but refers instead to powerful images *within* which both individuals and nations operate. These images or *active imaginal presences* in the actions of both individuals and national groups are, more precisely, where this study places the soul's deep disturbances.

11. T. W. Adorno, et. al, *The Authoritarian Personality* (New York: Harper & Bros., 1950); see also discussion in Lifton, *BC*, pp. 329–30n.

12. Giegerich discusses the opposition of the hero and the Great Mother as an archetypal background to the fantasy of opposition in "Ontogeny," pp. 123–6.

13. On the senex fantasy of opposites see Hillman, "Senex Destructiveness," pp. 77–8 and Raymond Klibansky, Erwin Panofsky and Fritz Saxl, *Saturn and Melancholy* (London: Nelson, 1964), pp. 134–5.

14. This is nicely described by Richard Falk, "Political Anatomy of Nuclearism" in Robert Jay Lifton and Richard Falk, *Indefensible Weapons* (New York: Basic Books, 1982), pp. 138–41. In the Soviet Union, the salutary coincidence of greater openness and much more serious efforts at disarmament that emerged after Mikhail Gorbachev assumed leadership is no accident; both reflect an attenuation of an archetypal power.

15. Erik H. Erickson, "Evolutionary and Developmental Considerations" in *The Long Darkness: Psychological and Moral Perspectives on Nuclear Winter* (New Haven: Yale University Press, 1986), pp. 65–72.

16. Wolfgang Giegerich, "The Nuclear Bomb and the Fate of God," *Spring 1985*: 12. Giegerich in this provocative article elucidates a quite different background for what I am calling "Strong-Armed Ego": the image of Moses as he, burning with anger, destroys the Golden Calf after descending from Mt. Sinai (Exod. 32). The elaboration of different archetypal images of ego is crucial, yet needs to be carried a step further to

facilitate a falling-apart of the monolithic vision we associate with ego. This step involves a differentiation of multiple styles of ego, each precisely qualified with reference to its behavior in fantasy. This book's evocation of "Strong-Armed Ego" is an effort in that direction.

17. "The category of *hibakusha*, according to official definition, includes four groups of people considered to have had possible exposure to significant amounts of radiation: those who at the time of the bomb were within the city limits of Hiroshima as then defined (. . .); those who came into the city within fourteen days and entered a designated area extending to about two thousand meters from the hypocenter; those who came into physical contact with bomb victims, through various forms of aid or disposal of bodies; and those who were *in utero* at the time, and whose mothers fit into any of the first three groups." Hibakusha means, literally, "explosion-affected person(s)." (*DL*, pp. 6–7).

18. Quoted in *DL*, p. 34, from Y. Ota, *Shikabane no Machi (Town of Corpses)* (Tokyo: Kawade Shobo, 1955), pp. 153–4.

19. See Kerenyi, *The Gods of the Greeks*, trans. Norman Cameron. (London: Thames & Hudson, 1979) pp. 230ff on Hades. The *Homeric Hymn to Demeter* (17, 31) refers to Hades as Polydegmon when he seizes Persephone, and drags her off to the underworld. Death's way of hospitably receiving the soul is to seize (*harpazein*) it.

CHAPTER 3

1. Carl Kerenyi, *The Gods of the Greeks*, trans. Norman Cameron (London: Thames & Hudson, 1979), p. 230.

2. Loren Eiseley, *The Invisible Pyramid* (New York: Charles Scribner's Sons, 1970), pp. 2–3.

3. See Mircea Eliade, *The Sacred and the Profane*, trans. Willard R. Trask (New York: Harcourt, Brace & World, 1959), pp. 43, 53).

4. In *The Homeric Hymns*, tr. Charles Boer (Chicago: The Swallow Press, Inc., 1970), p. 51. For the original Greek see "The Hymn to Hermes" in Hesiod, *The Homeric Hymns and Homerica*, ed. with accompanying trans. by H. G. Evelyn-White (Cambridge: Harvard University Press, 1982 [rpt. ed.]), 429–30 (p. 394).

5. Gregory Nagy, *The Best of the Achaens* (Baltimore: The Johns Hopkins University Press, 1979), p. 17. Nagy is referring specifically to the meaning of the verb *mimnēsko* (to remember) in the *Iliad*; see Marcel Detienne, *Les maitres de verite dans la Grece archaique* (Paris, 1973 [2d ed.]), pp. 9–16, 20.

6. Printed in *The Poems of Hesiod*, tr. R. M. Frazer (Norman , Oklahoma: University of Oklahoma Press, 1983). All further references to the *Theogony* are from this edition, and will be numbered by line in the text. In certain cases, I refer to the original text given in Hesiod, *Homeric Hymns*.

7. See discussion in Jacob Klein, *A Commentary on Plato's Meno* (Chapel Hill:

The University of North Carolina Press, 1965), pp. 158ff (regarding Plato's *Theaetetus* 187ff).

8. James Hillman, *Healing Fiction* (Barrytown, New York: Station Hill Press, 1983), p. 40. Of particular relevance here are the collective "screen memories" mentioned in chapter 1. Although much recent discussion has focused on the actual and literal occurrence of sexual abuse in childhood, psychological inquiry continues to show the deepgoing truth in Freud's insights.

9. As Hillman says (*Healing Fiction*, p. 46), "Back of history is Mnemosyne (Memoria), the imaginal, mother of historicizing, the soul's archetypal, *sui generis* process of musing in terms of history."

10. David Miller (*Christs* [New York: The Seabury Press, 1981], p. 152) speaks of a "Lethean fantasy" in which "forgetting is dislodged from the complex of ideas and feelings that we have about memory. These two are no longer seen in relation to each other at all." His assertion is somewhat hyperbolic, since he goes on—like other writers on the "religious" forgetting of ego-concerns—to speak of the memory within this forgetting (p. 153). Ineluctably, remembering and forgetting appear in relation to each other—however, not as simple opposites, as I attempt to show in chapter 1 and in the following discussion. I speak of an "archetypal tandem" to evoke the simultaneous presence and constellation of remembering and forgetting in the soul, but their mutuality and their differences do not imply the usual, conceptual opposition in terms of which our culture evaluates this tandem.

Other writers on the significance of remembering and forgetting in myth, religion and psychology who address the paradoxical relation of the two include (in addition to Kerenyi's article on "Mnemosyne-Lesmosyne"): Gerhard Adler, "Remembering and Forgetting" in *The Dynamics of the Self* (London: Coventure, Ltd., 1979), whose comparative survey includes a look at Biblical and Oriental (Hindu and Buddhist) traditions, but who nonetheless remains tied to a traditional oppositional schema; Nor Hall, *The Moon and the Virgin: Reflections on the Archetypal Feminine* (New York: Harper & Row, 1980), pp. 24–8; Russell Holmes, *Forgetting and Memory in the Writings of St. John of the Cross* (Diploma Thesis, Jung Institute-Zurich, 1978), who relates the Christian and Greek mystical traditions of "forgetting"; and James Hillman in *DU*, pp. 153–5, who attends especially to phenomena of forgetting and remembering in dream experience. Mircea Eliade has a valuable survey of "Mythologies of Memory and Forgetting" in his *Myth and Reality*, trans. Willard R. Trask (New York: Harper & Row, Inc., 1963), pp. 114–38, in which he places these myths in the context of his thinking about mythic or sacred time, or *illud tempus* (see chapter 1 above). However, he largely neglects the religious aspect of forgetting.

11. *Christs*, p. 154.

12. Augustine reflects on this paradox in his *Confessions* (X. xvi. 24–5), wondering that: "When . . . I remember memory, memory itself is, through itself, present with itself: but when I remember forgetfulness, there are present both memory and forgetfulness; memory whereby I remember, forgetfulness which I remember." But how can "forgetfulness" be remembered? Augustine first asserts "that forgetfulness, when we re-

member it, is not present to the memory itself, but by its image: because if it were present by itself, it would not cause us to remember, but to forget. Who now shall search out this? Who shall comprehend how it is?" But, he must ask, "How can I say this either, seeing that when the image of anything is impressed on the memory, the thing itself must needs first be present, whence that image may be impressed?" How, therefore, did forgetfulness "write its image in the memory, seeing that forgetfulness by its presence, effaces even what it finds already noted? And yet, in whatever way, although that way be past conceiving and explaining, yet certain am I that I remember forgetfulness itself also, whereby what we remember is effaced" (trans. E. B. Pusey [New York: E. P. Dutton & Co., Everyman's Library No. 200, 1932 (rpt.)]). (All further quotations from the *Confessions* in the text are from this edition, with chapter and section numbers given in the text.) Here the relation of remembering and forgetting becomes a mystical paradox, pointing to the God beyond both memory and forgetfulness. This paradox gives many later Christian mystics pause.

13. From *The Aeneid of Virgil*, trans. Allen Mandelbaum (New York: Bantam Books, Inc., 1971). All subsequent quotations from the *Aeneid* are from this edition; line numbers given here and subsequently in the text are from the numbering of this edition.

14. See also Miller, Christs. p. 152.

15. Edward Casey traces the "secularization" of memory in the ancient Greek imagination (*R*, pp. 11–15). In the Archaic Period (twelveth to eighth centuries B.C.E.; Hesiod's poems date from the last century of this period), remembrances of myth and poetry reflect the divinely powerful Goddess, Memory. In Plato "memory becomes a function of [pre-existent knowledge]" (*R*, p. 14) in the soul that the philosopher recollects through the dialectical process: there is no longer an inspiring Queen-Goddess beyond the individual's own remembering power. By Aristotle's time, memory (conceived as a cognitive-perceptual capacity to record, store and recall the "finitely rememberable" past [p. 15]) is completely secularized. This development leads to the later conflated identification of memory as a capacity of the ego largely within the domain of the conscious will.

In appendix A below, I discuss in more detail the parallel process of the separating of Memory and Forgetfulness with reference to certain images in Pythagorean thought (fourth and third centuries B.C.E.) that place the springs of these two at the initiatory threshold of Hades.

16. See the perceptive discussion of the ritual of Trophonios in Nor Hall, *Moon*, pp. 24–8.

17. Adler speaks of "remembering the future" as "the vision and recollection of the pre-existent pattern [of one's personality], the unconscious wholeness, and of the future possibility, direction, or goal" ("Remembering," *Dynamics*, p. 139). This view, valid as far as it goes, needs to be extended with a closer consideration of the imaginal "presence" of memory, including future anticipations.

18. In *Four Quartets* (London: Faber and Faber, 1974), p. 13.

19. See James Hillman, "Anima Mundi: the Return of the Soul to the World,"

Spring 1982: 71–93; and *The Thought of the Heart* (Dallas: Spring Publications, Inc. [Eranos Lectures, 2], 1981).

20. *Burnt Norton* in Eliot, op. cit., p. 13.

21. In "Anima," p. 80.

22. Here and in following passages from the *Phaedrus* I rely upon *Plato's Phaedrus*, trans. with commentary by R. Hackforth (Cambridge: At the University Press, 1972). Line and section numbers given in the text.

23. Bachelard renders topophilia as "love of space," but *topos* is more precisely rendered as *place*.

24. See James Hillman, "An Essay on Pan" in *Pan and the Nightmare*, W. H. Roscher and Hillman (Irving, Texas: Spring Publications, Inc., 1979 [rpt]).

25. We must imagine time precisely because, as Edward Casey says ("Time in the Soul," *Spring 1979*: 146), "imagination is very much part of our being in time: in fact, intrinsic to it."

26. Initially, Socrates describes three forms of "divine" madness (244A–245C). One of these is prophetic madness, through which the gift of oracular knowledge is received; the next is a form of possession occurring in rites of purification, through which one may gain release from present diseases (with which some are afflicted because of ancient blood-guilt); and the third form of madness is possession by the Muses. Later in the dialogue (265B), Socrates identifies the Gods from which the first two forms of madness come: prophetic madness is given by Apollo, and the "telestic" madness of rites of purification come from Dionysos. Socrates then adds a fourth form of madness which, in fact, is the best: possession by Aphrodite and Eros. This form or madness is the subject of his hymn to Love.

Counterposed to divine madness is that "resulting from human ailments" (265A). Socrates's distinction is important, especially for an archetypal psychotherapy (a form of which is proposed in Part III of this book) that must distinguish between diseased human conditions for which change should be sought, and the inhuman pathologies that are divine or archetypal necessities. Therapy seeks to change the former, but in relation to the latter reverts to an archaic sense of therapy as caring for or attending to the Gods.

27. Maurice Halbwachs, *The Collective Memory*, trans. Francis J. Ditter and Vida Yazdi Ditter (Harper & Row, Inc., 1980 [1950]), p. 23; italics added.

CHAPTER 4

1. Jonathan Spence, *The Memory Palace of Matteo Ricci* (New York: Viking Penguin, Inc., 1984), p. 10.

2. Ibid., p. 24.

3. Recall the observation cited in chapter 3 (p. 31): The Muses' power consists in the ability to allow the poet or storyteller to place himself in places and times of the (mythic)

past. From the beginning, to remember means to be in touch with the imagination of places and images.

4. Hillman's extended comments on the art of memory are to be found in *MA*, pp. 177–82 and 190ff; and *RP*, pp. 91–5. See also Edward Casey, "Toward an Archetypal Imagination," *Spring 1974*: 1–32 and Peter Bishop, "Archetypal Topography: The Karma-Kargyudpa Lineage Tree," *Spring 1981*: 67–76 for additional archetypal reflections on the art of memory.

5. Spence, *Memory Palace*, pp. 27ff.

6. See Cicero, *De oratore* II. lxxvi. 351–4. Further references to the *De oratore* follow the Loeb classics edition, trans. E. W. Sutton and H. Rackham (Cambridge: Harvard University Press, 1948), with book and section numbers indicated in the text. For further information on this story see Yates, *AM*, pp. 1–2 and 27–9; also Quintilian, *Institutio oratoria* XI. ii. 11–6, for a critical account of different versions of the story; and Spence, *Memory Palace*, pp. 2–3 for Ricci's version of it as told to his Chinese hosts.

7. Aristotle's notion of image—as a mental copy of an object of sense-perception—differs sharply from the implicit understanding of image in the *ars memorativa* tradition, as well as from a depth-psychological notion of the image. Common to both the art of memory and depth psychology is an apprehension of the *active power* of images, which are seen as capable of molding and transforming one's experience of the empirical world, not as passively-received impressions from this experience. This activity of remembered images is further discussed below and in Part III of this book.

8. The version of *Ad Herennium* followed here is translated by Harry Caplan (New York: Loeb Classical Library, 1968), modified in some instances following Yates. All further references to this title will be from this edition and indicated by book and section numbers in the text. For dating see translator's introduction.

9. Cicero defines the three parts of prudence (*memoria, intelligentia, providentia*) as follows: "Memory is the faculty by which the mind recalls what has happened. Intelligence is the faculty by which it ascertains what is. Foresight is the faculty by which it is seen that something is going to occur before it occurs" (*De inventione* II. liii. 160 in *De inventione. De optimo genere oratorium*, with trans. by H. M. Hubbell [Cambridge: Harvard University Press, 1949]).

10. Again, the Loeb classics edition is followed here: trans. H. E. Butler (Cambridge: Harvard University Press, 1961), with subsequent references indicated by book and section number in the text.

11. Spence, *Memory Palace*, p. 2.

12. This stress of the art of memory (and the present work) would seem to be contradicted by recent research on memory that indicates that bizzareness of images *per se* does not aid recall of material associated with such images. See Keith A. Wollen, Andrea Weber, and Douglas H. Lowry, "Bizzareness versus Interaction of Mental Images as Determinants of Learning," *Cognitive Psychology*, 3 (1972): 518–23. Within

their congitive-experimental frame, these researchers found that subjects were more likely to remember words associated with two *interacting* images (e.g., a piano with a cigar resting on it) than with non-interacting bizzare images (e.g., a dancing piano and a [separate] cigar lit at both ends).

However, these images have little to do with the *emotionally striking* strangeness of images in the art of memory. More, in this latter, memory images are either to be formed on one's own (hence embodying one's individual psychic life, with all of its implications) or they may be taken (especially in the medieval and Renaissance forms of the art) from artistic or religious figurings: images of collectively striking and weighty subjects, perhaps of considerable complexity and aesthetic value. These varieties of striking images embody profound individual and collective concerns, sufferings and joys of the soul—in sharp contrast to simple line-drawings imposed externally in an experiment on purely cognitive recall.

13. This needs qualification; as Edward Casey shows in *Remembering*, the great majority of our rememberings involve the ordinary and prosaic. In the context of the art of memory, however, what is ordinary in the sense of not being emotionally striking or active in the manner discussed below, is far less likely to stir the memory. Moreover, what may *seem* ordinary to most observers can be of great emotional significance, hence strikingly memorable, to a particular individual.

14. Gaston Bachelard, *On Poetic Imagination and Reverie*, trans. Colette Gaudin (New York: The Bobbs-Merrill Co., Inc., 1971), p. 19.

15. Albertus Magnus, *De bono* in *Opera omnia*, H. Kuhle, C. Feckes, B. Geyer, W. Kubel, *Monasterii Westfalorum in aedibus Aschendorff, XXVIII (1951), solution, point 18;* quoted by Yates, *AM*, p. 65.

16. Thomas Aquinas, *Summa Theologiae*, Question XLIX, article I; quoted in *AM*, p. 74.

17. On p. 174 of Ciardi's translation and edition of the *Inferno* (referenced in notes to chapter 1).

18. The primary source here is Ficino, *The Book of Life [De vita triplici]*, trans. Charles Boer (Irving, Texas: Spring Publications, Inc., 1980). See also Klibansky, Raymond; Panofsky, Erwin and Saxl, Fritz, *Saturn and Melancholy* (London: Thomas Nelson & Sons, Ltd., 1964), pp. 254–74; D. P. Walker, *Spiritual and Demonic Magic* (London: The Warbug Institute, 1958), Parts I and II; Yates, *AM*, s.v. index, "Ficino" and *Giordano Bruno and the Hermetic Tradition* (Chicago: University of Chicago Press, 1964) ch. 4; and Thomas Moore, *The Planets Within: Marsilio Ficino's Astrological Psychology* (Lewisburg, Pennsylvania: Bucknell University Press, 1982).

19. Ficino, *Book*, ch. 19.

20. Casey, "Archetypal Imagination," pp. 15–6.

21. For a more detailed account, see Yates, *AM*, chs. IX, XI-XIV; and *Giordano*, chs. 11–20.

22. Giordano Bruno, *The Expulsion of the Triumphant Beast*, trans. A. D. Imerti (Rutgers University Press, 1964), p. 70; cited in *AM*, p. 315.

23. Bishop, "Archetypal Topography," p. 74.

24. See "Asclepius III" in *Hermetica: The Ancient Greek and Latin Writings Which Contain Religious or Philosophic Teachings Ascribed to Hermes Trismegistus*, trans. and ed. Walter Scott (Boston: Shambhala, 1985), p. 339.

25. Fludd's memory treatise is embedded in a larger work, on which see *AM*, pp. 321ff.

26. Another connection to aesthetic sensitivity is through the recognition of rhetoric (after myth-making the historical foundation of the art of memory) as a voice of soul, anima (on this see appendix B). This recalls Jung's initial conversations with his anima-voice, which insisted that his fantasies were art (*MDR*, pp. 185–7). Jung saw a danger here of unpsychological literalism, a surface-focus on artistic form and creativity, and instead insisted on psychological and moral understanding of his active imaginations. Jung's stand is crucial to the development of depth-psychological perspective, but should not itself be taken only literally. It embodies a clash of rhetorical styles: Jung himself observed that the anima "did not have the speech centers I had." If the art of memory is the rhetoric of anima, we must take her way of speaking seriously.

In Jung's initial formulation of active imagination, written shortly after his own initial encounters with psychic figures (*CW* 8, "On the Transcendent Function"), he stresses the contribution of *both* the aesthetic and the intellectual tendencies arising from the imaginal encounters—the one focusing on the form of the images and the other on their meaning. Here we are attempting to reflect an aesthetic mode of psychological understanding. See also James Hillman, *The Thought of the Heart* (Dallas, Texas: Spring Publications, Inc. [Eranos Lectures: 2], 1981), pp. 34–6 on Jung's relation to his anima's aesthetic.

27. On the archetypal imagery of Priapus, see Lopez-Pedraza, *Hermes and His Children* (Irving, Texas: Spring Publications, 1977), ch. 6.

28. See Yates, *Giordano*, pp. 33–4 on the Hermetic principle of world-movement.

29. See *Great Dialogues of Plato*, trans. W. H. D. Rouse (New York: The New American Library, 1956), p. 65.

30. An interesting parallel to this is from a quite different cultural context: the destruction of the Oglala Sioux by encroaching white civilization as related by the Sioux shaman, Black Elk, who told John Niehardt: "You have noticed that everything an Indian does is in a circle, and that is because the Power of the World always works in circles, and everything tries to be round. . . . Our tepees were round like the nests of birds, and these were always set in a circle, the nation's hoop . . . But the [white men] have put us in these square boxes. Our power is gone and we are dying" (in John Neihardt, *Black Elk Speaks* [New York: Pocket Books, 1972], pp. 164–6) . . . Here the connection between the "circle" of life and the "square" of death is clear: the square cuts off the power of movement. This archetypal imagery in Black Elk refers to a tragic acting-out of the

pattern Fludd imagines in memory, in which the stasis becomes not an imaginal state but the literal and actual death of a culture.

31. Ficino, *Book*, ch. 1. Moore translates *rationes* also as "fantasies," since these are aspects of the World Soul (*Planets*, p. 176).

32. In Albertus's commentary on the *De memoria et reminiscentia* in *Opera Omnia*, quoted in *AM*, p. 68.

33. In "An Essay on Pan," *Pan and the Nightmare*, W. H. Roscher and James Hillman (New York/Zurich: Spring Publications, 1972), p. lxii.

34. Ficino, *Book*, ch. 19.

35. Quoted in Klibansky, et. al., *Saturn*, p. 258.

36. See ibid., pp. 18ff for a translation and commentary on the *Problemata*, and pp. 69–72 on Albertus's reading of it. See also *AM*, pp. 69–70.

37. In his article on "*Senex* Destruction and a Renaissance Solution," *Spring 1975*: 97–103, Hillman considers Ficino's therapy for the destructive influence of Saturn which involves moving *with* the God's melancholy. See also Moore, *Planets*, ch. 11, on Ficino's therapy. Another good account of Saturnine psychology that considers also the melancholy of the *puer eternus* is A. Vitale, "The Archetype of Saturn or Transformation of the Father" in *Fathers and Mothers*, ed. Patricia Berry (New York: Spring Publications, 1973).

38. Ficino, *Book*, ch. 22.

39. Edward S. Casey, "Getting Placed: Soul in Space," *Spring 1982*: 17. Also relevant is Hillman's description of the "archetypal repression" associated with the senex by which precise borders within imaginal regions—and thus the possiblity of psychological discernment—are recognized: "repression affirms the boundaries within the archetypal, so by repressing we affirm the boundaries of the patterns we live" (*Senex Destruction*," p. 94). More, "The imaginal realm calls for fixed boundaries, otherwise there can be no imaginal geography. It is not just inner *space* that matters, but inner *places*, a precision of *topoi*, each archetypal figure in the well-defined context of its landscape, its clime" (p. 95). (Here Hillman refers to Casey's article on archetypal imagination and topography [*Spring 1974*, op. cit.], and specifically to the art of memory with its "locus of the image" [p. 107, n. 42].)

40. See Sigmund Freud, "Mourning and Melancholia," trans. under the supervision of Joan Riviere, Collected Papers, vol. 4 (New York: Basic Books, 1969), p. 168.

41. *La cena de le ceneri*, ed. G. Aquilecchia (Turin, 1955); summarized and discussed in Yates, *AM*, pp. 309–13.

42. For more detailed accounts of active imagination see Jung, *Analytical Psychology: Its Theory & Practice* (New York: Vintage Books, 1970), pp. 190–204; Mary Watkins, *Waking Dreams* (New York: Harper & Row, 1977 [1976]), pp. 42–51; Janet Dallett, "Active Imagination in Practice" in *Jungian Analysis*, ed. Murray Stein

(La Salle, IL: Open Court Publishing Co., 1982), pp. 172–91 and references. Jung's account in *Analytical Psychology* is one of his clearest expositions of active imagination. See also Jung's account of his own "confrontation with the unconscious" (*MDR*, ch. VI) and his first theoretical paper on active imagination ("On the Transcendent Function," *CW* 8) which grew directly out of Jung's encounters.

43. See discussion in Edward Casey, "Archetypal Imagination," pp. 1–5.

44. C. G. Jung, "Psychological analysis of Nietzsche's *Zarathustra*" (Privately mimeographed seminar notes of Mary Foote, 1937); quoted in Mary Watkins, *Waking Dreams*, p. 43.

45. See Mary Watkins's careful articulation of the development of characters in imaginal dialogues: *Invisible Guests: The Development of Imaginal Dialogues* (New York: The Analytic Press, 1986), esp. chs. 7 and 9.

CHAPTER 5

1. In "Wars, Arms, Rams, Mars," *Facing Apocalypse*, ed. Valerie Andrews, Robert Bosnak and Karen W. Goodwin (Dallas, TX: Spring Publications, Inc., 1978), p. 128.

2. See Freud's Letter of December 1, 1896 [to Wilhelm Fliess] in *The Standard Edition of the Complete Psychological Works of Sigmund Freud* (London: Hogarth, 1953–74), 1: 233.

3. Giordano Bruno, *Opere latine*, ed. F. Fiorentino and others (Naples and Florence, 1879–91), II (i), pp. 51–2; quoted in *AM*, p. 248.

4. *Hiroshima and Nagasaki: The Physical, Medical and Social Effects of the Atomic Bombings*, ed. The Committee for the Compilation of Materials on Damage Caused by the Atomic Bombs in Hiroshima and Nagasaki, trans. Eisei Tshikawa and David L. Swain (New York: Basic Books, Inc., 1981), pp. 484–5. For this and the next chapter I have relied on the following sources, generally easily accessible, which the reader may find useful as resources in his or her exploration and practice of imaginal memory. Testimonies of *hibakusha* include: Arata Osada, Ph.D., comp., *Children of Hiroshima*, trans. not given (New York: Harper & Row, 1982 [1951])—a collection of short essays by *hibakusha* who were children at the time of the bombing; Michihiko Hachiya, M.D., *Hiroshima Diary*, ed. and trans. Warner Wells, M.D. (Chapel Hill: The University of North Carolina Press, 1955); Takashi Nagai, *We of Nagasaki* (New York: Duell, Sloan and Pearce, 1951); Hiroshima-Nagasaki Publishing Committee, *Days to Remember: An Account of the Bombings of Hiroshima and Nagasaki* (Tokyo: Hiroshima-Nagasaki Publishing Comm., 1981)—a photographic record of the bombings; and *Unforgettable Fire: Pictures Drawn by Atomic Bomb Survivors*, ed. Japan Broadcasting Corporation [NHK] (New York: Pantheon Books, 1977), with images that many find to be among the most powerful renderings of the atomic-bomb experience. The classic novelistic account of the bombing of Hiroshima (by a non*hibakusha*) is Masuji Ibuse's *Black Rain*, trans. John Bester (Tokyo and Palo Alto: Kodansha Interna-

tional, Ltd., 1969). A good collection of short stories, most of which are written by *hibakusha*, is in Kenzaburo Oe, ed., *The Crazy Iris and other Stories of the Atomic Aftermath* (New York: Grove Press, Inc., 1985). Robert Jay Lifton's *Death in Life: Survivors of Hiroshima* (indicated by *DL* in the present text) remains the primary source on the psychological effects of the Hiroshima bombing. See also Robert Jungk, *Children of the Ashes* (New York: Harcourt, Brace & World, 1961), for a sensitive account of the severe guilt and other sufferings of *hibakusha*, and of the struggles around the rebuilding of Hiroshima. John Hersey's *Hiroshima* (New York: Bantam Books, 1959 [1946]) remains a primary text of the nuclear world; it was republished in 1985 with a follow-up on the postwar lives of the survivors chronicled in the original edition. Millen Brand, in *Peace March: Nagasaki to Hiroshima* (Woodstock, VT: The Countryman Press, Inc., 1980) combines lyric and documentary elements in an account of his 1977 trip to Nagasaki and Hiroshima during which he joined with the Japanese for anniversary commemorations of the bombings. Jonathan Schell gives a good brief account of the Hiroshima bombing in *The Fate of the Earth* (New York: Alfred A. Knopf., Inc., 1982), pp. 36–45.

5. Ibuse, Black Rain, p. 92. Discussed by Lifton in *DL*, p. 545.

6. Jungk, *Children of the Ashes*, p. 184.

7. Osada, *Children of Hiroshima*, p. 166.

8. Ibid., p. 213.

9. NHK, *Unforgettable Fire*, pp. 52–3.

10. Ibid., p. 68.

11. In Osada, *Children of Hiroshima*, p. 167.

12. Elie Weisel, *Night*, trans. Stella Rodway (New York: Avon Books, 1960), p. 44.

13. Edward Casey, "Toward an Archetypal Imagination," *Spring 1974*: 15.

14. Mircea Eliade, *The Sacred and the Profane*, trans. Willard R. Trask (New York: Harcourt, Brace & World, 1959), ch. 2.

15. In archaic cultures, one or more past ends-of-the-world are often imagined as also the origin of the present condition of the world and humankind. See my article, "When Heaven and Earth Collapse: Myths of the End of the World" in *Facing Apocalypse*, op. cit.; and Robert Jay Lifton's article, "The Image of 'The End of the World': A Psychohistorical View" in the same volume. See also A. G. Mojtabai's account of Christian Fundamentalist end-time thinking in Amarillo: *Blessed Assurance: At Home with the Bomb in Amarillo* (Boston: Houghton Mifflin, 1986).

16. Jonathan Schell, *Fate of the Earth*, pp. 46–7.

17. James Hillman, *Inter Views*, with Laura Pozzo (New York: Harper & Row, 1983), pp. 137 & ff.

18. Nagai, *Nagasaki*, p. 189.

19. Hersey, *Hiroshima*, p. 87.

20. See also Jung, "Transformation Symbolism in the Mass" in *CW* 11, pars. 353ff and Mircea Eliade, *Shamanism: Archaic Techniques of Ecstasy*, tr. Willard R. Trask (New York: Bollingen Foundation, 1964), pp. 53ff.

21. James Hillman, "Dionysus in Jung's Writings," *Spring 1973*: 201; on the motif of dismemberment in Jung's alchemical psychology Hillman cites (in addition to references cited above from *CW* 13) *CW* 12, par. 530 and *CW* 14, par. 64.

22. In "Puer Wounds and Ulysses' Scar," *Puer Papers*, ed. Cynthia Giles (Irving, TX: Spring Publications, Inc., 1979), p. 104.

23. Edward Casey, "Getting Placed: Soul in Space," *Spring 1982*: 7.

24. Casey, "Getting Placed," pp. 9–10.

25. Floyd Hiatt Ross, *Shinto: The Way of Japan* (Boston: Beacon Press, 1965), p. 64.

26. As Peter Wyden (*Day One: Before Hiroshima and After* [New York: Warner Books, 1985]) notes, this decision entailed a good deal of conflict. For General Leslie Grover, military director of the Manhattan Project, made Kyoto his priority choice for the first atomic-bomb drop precisely because of its cultural, historical and psychological significance (pp. 191, 193). However, he was overriden by Secretary of War Stimson, who had visited Kyoto several times before the war and "was very much impressed by its ancient culture" (quoted on p. 198). While the power of place, as this example shows, does not always work in favor of a place's preservation, its potential to do so and to override nationalistic and wartime concerns is made evident here. So powerful was the place of Kyoto in imagination that it led to considerable conflict among American officials.

27. Casey, "Getting Placed," pp. 16–7.

28. Quoted by Robert Sardello in "City as Metaphor, City as Mystery," *Spring 1982*: 97.

29. Casey, "Getting Placed," p. 16.

30. Hersey, *Hiroshima*, p. 86.

31. Hachiya, *Hiroshima Diary*, p. 58.

32. Lifton discusses "anniversary reactions" of actual *hibakusha* in *DL*, pp. 282–7. Such reactions show how precisely soul keeps time in memory.

33. See Joanna Rogers Macy, *Despair and Personal Power in the Nuclear Age* (Philadelphia, PA: New Society Publishers, 1983) on the role of groups and group exercises in facilitating a greater connectedness with global dilemmas and possibilities of mass horror, and in developing a much deeper sense of interpersonal community than is usually found in our culture.

CHAPTER 6

1. Giordano Bruno, *Opera latine*, II (i), pp. 77–8; quoted in *AM*, p. 217.

2. Wolfgang Giegerich makes essentially this assertion in his essay, "Saving the Nuclear Bomb" *Facing Apocalypse,* ed. Valerie Andrews, Robert Bosnak and Karen W. Goodwin (Dallas, TX: Spring Publications, Inc., 1987). Ira Chernus discusses the numinous power given place by the Bomb with more detailed reference to the phenomenology of the Sacred as disclosed by the history of religions in his *Dr. Strangegod: On the Symbolic Meaning of Nuclear Weapons* (Columbia, SC: University of South Carolina Press, 1986), ch. 1, "A Limitless Power." He observes: "It may well be that nuclear weapons have become the Deus Otiosus of contemporary culture. The otiose god is the hidden god, the god who remains unrevealed to the living. It is often only through death that one can make contact with this god and bring him out of his hiddenness. Perhaps, then, the hidden Bomb beckons to us today as did the otiose god of an earlier age" (p. 18). The rhetoric of death, forgetfulness (hiddenness) and memory (revelation, beckoning, *recalling*) echoes here; in the Night room, the dead, who have walked into hiddenness, leave black-shadowed intimations of a forgotten God.

3. James Hillman, "Notes on White Supremacy: Essaying an Archetypal Account of Historical Events," *Spring 1986*: 38 and ff.

4. John Hersey, *Hiroshima* (New York: Bantam Books, 1959 [1946]), pp. 81–2.

5. Michihiko Hachiya, M.D., *Hiroshima Diary*, trans. and ed. Warner Wells, M.D. (Chapel Hill: The University of North Carolina press, 1955), pp. 15–6.

6. Masuji Ibuse, *Black Rain*, trans. John Bester (Tokyo and Palo Alto: Kodansha International, Ltd., 1969), p. 159.

7. Hiroshima-Nagasaki Publishing Committee, *Days to Remember: An Account of the Bombings of Hiroshima and Nagasaki* (Tokyo: Hiroshima-Nagasaki Pub. Comm., 1981), p. 1.

8. Hersey, *Hiroshima*, p. 3.

9. Hachiya, *Hiroshima Diary*, p. 101.

10. Yoichi Fukushima in Arata Osada, comp., Ph.D., *Children of Hiroshima* (New York: Harper & Row, 1982 [1951]), p. xi.

11. Observes Lifton (*DL*, p. 104): Sadako's story "has come to symbolize the bomb's recurrent desecration of the pure and vulnerable—of childhood itself."

12. Robert L. Messer, "New Evidence on Truman's Decision," *The Bulletin of the Atomic Scientists*, August, 1958: 56; Truman quote to Senator Richard Russell on August 9, 1945.

13. A valuable recent survey of this research and the questions it has stirred is provided by Petra Hesse in "Children's and Adolescents' Fears of Nuclear War: Is Our

Sense of the Future Disappearing?" *International Journal of Mental Health*, 15, 1–3 (1986): 93-113.

14. The classic essay on this subject remains Jung's "The Psychology of the Child Archetype" in *CW* 9, 1. See also James Hillman, "Abandoning the Child" in *Loose Ends: Primary Papers in Archetypal Psychology* (New York/Zurich: Spring Publications, 1975).

15. Concurrently with the concern about the effects of the nuclear threat on children, there has arisen a strong concern about various, more concrete forms of child abuse. It is important to address these concrete concerns, but they are often seen so literally that no room is left for consideration of other, less apparent forms in which our culture abuses both actual children and the archetypal imagination of the Child. The nuclear arms race, destruction of the environment and careless economic policies can also be seen as forms of child abuse: abuse of the concrete futures of actual children (and of future generations), and of the archetypal Child's imagining of the future that is vital to the envisioning of cultural and human continuity.

16. Mary Watkins, "In Dreams Begin Responsibilities: Moral Imagination and Peace Action" in *Facing Apocalypse*, op, cit., pp. 80–1.

17. See, for instance, Vamik D. Volkan, "The Need to have Enemies and Allies," *Political Psychology*, 6 (1985): 219–49. Volkan presents a developmental psychoanalytic viewpoint on the genesis of related enemy and ally images in children and their function. He relates this to adult individual and group psychology, in which enemy images help to maintain a sense of internal self and group cohesion while embodying externalized "bad" images of self in relation to others.

18. See Jung, "The Spirit Mercurius" in *CW* 13.

19. Hersey, *Hiroshima*, p. 48.

20. Ibid., p. 58.

21. For comparative material see Mircea Eliade, *Shamanism*, trans. Willard R. Trask (New York: Bollingen Foundation, 1964), pp. 355ff, 361 and 417; Arnold Van Gennep, *The Rites of Passage*, tr. Monika B. Vizedom and Gabrielle L. Caffee (Chicago: The University of Chicago Press, 1960), pp. 153, 4, 7.

22. Paul Boyer documents initial American reaction to the atomic bombings in *By the Bomb's Early Light: American Thought and Culture at the Dawn of the Atomic Age* (New York: Pantheon, 1985), esp. ch. 1. While there was a pervasive sense of nuclear dread during the period between the bombings and the publication of Hersey's *Hiroshima* (August 31, 1946 in *The New Yorker*), Boyer comments that Hersey's was the most detailed account yet of the human reality of Hiroshima, bringing to the fore "several vividly realized foreground figures" (p.207). *Hiroshima* is thus an initiation into the more concretely memorable horror of the atomic bombings; the characters of the book are primary *imagines agentes* of the nuclear age.

23. On the relation between nuclear imagery and the structure of initiatory ordeals, see Ira Chernus, *Dr. Strangegod*, pp. 158–61.

24. For further instances of this motif and discussion of associated guilt, see *DL*, pp. 448–9 and 496–7. A similar image appears in NKH, ed., *Unforgettable Fire* (New York: Pantheon Books, 1977), where a *hibakusha* recalls, "a stark naked man standing in the [black] rain with his eyeball in his palm" (p. 48). (This image is also cited by Jonathan Schell—see passage quoted above in chapter 5, p. 16.) In Hersey's *Hiroshima*, the horror appears in the guise of soldiers whose eyes melted in the heat of the nuclear flash and ran down their faces (p. 67). And Mr. Tanimoto is beset by the staring eyes of a woman holding her dead baby, who cannot find her husband and will not cremate her baby, and to whom Mr. Tanimoto can give no help. Thus, "He tried to escape her glance by keeping his back turned to her as much as possible" (p. 75). The implication is that he could not escape his guilt, despite his attempt to avoid the mother's eyes, and his heroic rescue activities. It is likely that images of grotesque injury to the eyes are especially remembered not only because of their physical horror, but also because of deep associations of eyes with consciousness, and hence one's awareness of the consciousness and subjectivity of others. This provokes death guilt and also the empathetic imagination, together with the archetypal associations to be discussed in the text.

25. Hachiya, *Hiroshima Diary*, pp. 114–5.

26. Richard Rhodes, *The Making of the Atomic Bomb* (New York: Simon & Schuster, 1986), p. 747.

27. A good account of the religious background of Japanese nationalism and associated politics is Joseph M. Kitagawa's *Religion in Japanese History* (New York: Columbia University Press, 1966). See also the more well-known account of Japan by Ruth Benedict (*The Chrysanthemum and the Sword: Patterns of Japanese Culture* [New York: The New American Library, 1974 [1946]).

28. Marsilio Ficino, *The Book of Life*, trans. Charles Boer (Irving, TX: Spring Publications, Inc., 1980), ch. 11.

29. Edward S. Casey, "Toward an Archetypal Imagination," *Spring 1974*: 21.

30. Janet Dallett, "Active Imagination in Practice" in *Jungian Analysis*, ed. Murray Stein (La Salle, IL: Open Court Publishing Co., 1982), p. 189.

31. There is no such image in *Hiroshima*, though in various accounts there are memories of streetcars filled with charred occupants (e.g., in *Unforgettable Fire*, p. 97). Here is a good example the reconstructive work of memory, the truth of which fiction we witnessed in chapter 3.

32. Edward Casey, "Archetypal Imagination," pp. 13–114.

33. See Juliet Piggott, *Japanese Mythology* (London: Hamlyn Publishing Group, Ltd., 1969), p. 13.

34. Nancy Wilson Ross [ed.], *The World of Zen: An East-West Anthology* (New York: Random House, 1960), pp. 167 & ff.

35. Donald Keene, *Japanese Literature: An Introduction for Western Readers* (New York: Grove Press, 1968); quoted in ibid., p. 168.

36. See the version of this joke cited by Bernard T. Field in "Forty Years of Muddling Through," *The Bulletin of the Atomic Scientists,* August, 1985:32.

37. Printed in Ross, ed., *World of Zen,* p. 170, as trans. by Arthur Waley in *The No Plays of Japan* (New York: Grove Press, 1921).

38. The translation of this phrase is Lifton's, made in connection with his discussion of the beauty of Hiroshima's bomb-anniversary commemorative ceremonies (*DL,* p. 286).

39. Hillman relates the "autonomous hand" to the wounds of puer-hands in a passage with strong resonance to Dr. Strangelove's predicament: "The autonomous hand extends to manipulate the world and make all things its tools. *Orexis,* the most embracing Greek term for appetite or desire, etymologically means the extension of the hand, its reach and greed. Puer nightmares [like *Dr. Strangelove*?] show autonomy of the hands and the fear of their strangling or stabbing" ("Puer Wounds and Ulysses' Scar" in *Puer Papers,* ed. Cynthia Giles [Irving, TX: Spring Publications, Inc., 1979], p. 106.)

40. Glenn T. Seaborg, "Man's First Glimpse of Plutonium," *The New York Times,* July 16, 1985, p. C6.

41. See Spencer R. Weart, "The Heyday of Myth and Cliche," *The Bulletin of the Atomic Scientists,* August, 1985: 39 and references, for a review of the role of the alchemical metaphor in early nuclear discoveries. For further Jungian reflections on alchemy and our culture, see David Holt, "Jung and Marx: Alchemy, Christianity and the Work Against Nature," *Harvest,* 21 (1975) and—for the same author's extended reflections on this subject and the nuclear peril—"Riddley Walker and Greenham Common: Further Thoughts on Alchemy, Christianity and the Work Against Nature," *Harvest,* 29 (1983).

42. Another image: Deke Parsons, the weaponeer on the Hiroshima atomic-bombing mission, had to complete the arming of the bomb in the air, since there was fear that a take-off accident could wipe out the base on Tinian Island. In order to make sure he could do this, Parsons first tried arming the bomb on the eve of the mission, which made his "hands . . . black from graphite lubricant and bleeding from sharp-edged parts and tools." Thus, "He joked that he would have to bomb Japan 'with dirty hands'" (cited by Peter Wyden, *Day One: Before Hiroshima and After* [New York: Warner Books, 1985], p. 242).

43. Mike Perlman, "Phaethon and the Thermonuclear Chariot," *Spring 1983*: 88.

44. On the varieties of alchemical whitening, see James Hillman, "Silver and the White Earth (Part One)," *Spring 1980*: 21ff.

45. From *Splendor Solis: Alchemical Treatises of Solomon Trismosin* (London, 1920), pp. 29ff; quoted in *CW* 14, par. 465.

46. Johann Rudolf Glauber, *De natura salium*, pp. 41ff; quoted in *CW* 14, par. 235.

47. From Arthur Edward Waite, *The Hermetic Museum Restored and Enlarged* (London, 1893), II, p. 143; quoted in *CW* 14, par. 187 (n. 355).

48. Jung (*CW* 14, par. 330) notes the connection of bitterness and wisdom via feeling, but sees them as nonetheless mutually exclusive opposites: "bitterness and wisdom form a pair of alternatives: where there is bitterness wisdom is lacking, and where wisdom is there can be no bitterness." But his oppositionalism misses the paradox or alchemical *coincidentia* that Jung generally speaks of with great psychological acuity. Bitterness and wisdom can coincide, with each "coloring" the other, as we view the realities of the world. Archetypally, it is the senex in whom bitterness and wisdom coincide.

49. James Hillman, *The Thought of the Heart* (Dallas, TX: Spring Publications, Inc. [Eranos Lectures 2], 1981), p. 4.

CHAPTER 7

1. For an archetypal perspective on masochism, see Lynn Cowan, *Masochism: A Jungian View* (Dallas, TX: Spring Publications, Inc., 1982).

2. Sigmund Freud, *New Introductory Lectures on Psychoanalysis*, trans. James Strachey (New York: W. W. Norton & Co., Inc., 1964), p. 105.

3. Ibid., p. 106.

4. James Hillman, *Inter Views*, with Laura Pozzo (New York: Harper & Row, 1983), p. 11.

5. The imagination of Hell in Islam and Judaism, the other monotheistic traditions, is less dominant than in the Christian worldview, though it is still present. It is not until the post-biblical era that moral pain and anguish take on the specific shape of Hell, growing out of ancient Semitic depictions of a shadowy underworld, Sheol; of Gehinnom, the valley of Hinnom (a place of child sacrifice or slaughter in biblical descriptions); and Greek depictions (themselves extending back at least to the Homeric period) of a particular section of Hades reserved for certain characters who through some form of hubris opposed the Gods. For a thorough study of imagery of Sheol see Nicholas J. Tromp, *Primitive Conceptions of Death and the Nether World in the Old Testament* (Rome: Pontifical Biblical Institute, 1969). A concise account of the development of Gehinnom into later Jewish and Christian imagery of Hell is to be found in *The Universal Jewish Encyclopedia,* 4 (New York: Universal Jewish Encyclopedia, Inc., 1941), pp. 520–1.

Also interesting is the Buddhist imagery of hell—a tradition far less prominent within Buddhism than the corresponding Christian doctrine, but again with quite graphic portrayals of torment intended both as a deterrent against immoral behavior for the unenlightened masses, and as a symbolic depiction of the inevitable suffering of *dukka* brought about by the clinging to the seeming permanence and separate selves of the phenomenal world. For a thorough historical and psychological exposition of the Buddhist hell, see Daigan and Alicia Matsunaga, *The Buddhist Concept of Hell* (New York: Philosophical Library, Inc., 1972). The worldview here is quite different from the monotheistic, yet the imagery, like that of the Western hells—is strikingly horrific—and memorable. The titles of some of the subdivisions of one account of the Buddhist hell are sufficiently suggestive: "Hell of Diamond Beaked Birds," "Flaming Hair Hell," "Stabbing Pain Hell," "Hell of Limitless Pain," and "Hell Where the Blood and Bones are Consumed" (ibid., pp. 120–1).

Accounts of the hells of Buddhism became most popular in Japan, and many *hibakusha* remembered these hells in the experience of the atomic bombing (*DL*, p. 29).

6. Alfred J. Ziegler, *Archetypal Medicine*, trans. Gary V. Hartmann (Dallas, TX: Spring Publications, Inc., 1982), p. 134.

7. D. P. Walker, *The Decline of Hell* (Chicago: The University of Chicago Press, 1964), p. 4.

8. Ziegler, *Archetypal Medicine*, p. 79.

9. Joseph M. Kitagawa, *Religion in Japanese History* (New York: Columbia University Press, 1966), pp. 81–2.

10. Sigmund Freud, *The Ego and the Id*, trans. Joan Riviere (New York: W. W. Norton & Co., 1962), p. 44.

11. See Jung, *CW* 8, pars. 108–11; *CW* 10, pars. 825–57 (Jung's "Psychological View of Conscience" as an autonomous psychic factor in the individual, often in conflict with the collective moral cannon or *mores*); *CW* 11, pars. 105–8; and discussion in Andrew Samuels, *Jung and the Post-Jungians* (London: Routledge & Kegan Paul, Inc., 1985), pp. 60–2.

12. Jung, "Exercitia Spiritualia of St. Ignatius of Loyola," *Spring 1977*: 191. Jung observes (*CW* 14, par. 446) that: "It was not for nothing that the old Masters identified their *nigredo* with melancholia . . ."

13. Klibansky, Raymond, et. al., *Saturn and Melancholy* (London: Thomas Nelson & Sons, Ltd., 1964), pp. 286–7; see Pls. 1ff on Durer's work.

14. Ibid., p. 287; see Pl. 13 for the "veiled head" of Kronos-Saturn.

15. W. H. Roscher, *Ausführliches Lexikon der griechischen und römischen Mythologie*, I (Leipzig, 1884), col. 2160: ". . . den immer thatigen, strebenden, unermüdlichen Heros ermüdet, den rastlosen rastend, den vom Schicksal gequälten traurig und sinnend darzustellen."

16. See Klibansky, et. al., pp. 18–42 for the reproduction, with accompanying translation, of the *Problemata*, and subsequent commentary.

17. See the translation by Philip Vellacott in *Medea and Other Plays* (New York: Penguin Books, 1981). In the dramatic sequence, Herakles falls asleep after his manic

rage, having been struck against the chest by a boulder perhaps hurled by Athene. Amphitryon then urges the Theban elders: "While he is relaxed in sleep/Let him forget his sufferings," but shortly thereafter exclaims, "Oh, what a sleep! An accursed sleep" (p. 185) Sleep, madness, death and forgetfulness are homologous in the logic of myth. Later, when Herakles awakens Amphitryon prepares to confront him with his madness, provided "you're no more a frenzied celebrant of Death . . ." Herakles wonders: "My mind was frenzied? How? I don't remember it" (p. 188). It is precisely this madness, with its forgetful frenzy, that we must now remember.

18. The interpretation of Nessos as underworld ferryman is Carl Kerenyi's. See *The Gods of the Greeks*, trans. Norman Cameron (London: Thames & Hudson, 1979), p. 200.

19. David Miller (*The New Polytheism*, [Dallas, TX: Spring Publications, Inc., 1981 (1974)], p. 85) takes Herakles to be a governing image of activism in general. There are many archetypal styles of activism, but the hero does play an important role in the imaginal world of *actions*—physical, moral and otherwise. The point here is that we literalize action until we are able to vision it as an *image* and a way of seeing—as well as an imaginal activity independent of the human ego.

20. The term is E. V. Walter's. See his article on "The Places of Experience," *The Philosophical Forum*, XII, 2 (1980–1), which makes an argument in many ways parallel to this text. For example, he asserts that "Memory and imagination, crucial elements in the quality of a place, . . . shape what is called the spirit of the place" (p. 164). And "The 'soul' of a place is the pure, expressive meaning of a location, a concrete image that represents its quality of [what Walter calls] pathephoric space" (p. 175). I am indebted to Michael Curry for this reference.

21. John E. Mack, "Nationalism and the Self," *The Psychohistory Review*, II, 2–3 (1983): 52. See Roy Schafer, *Aspects of Internalization* (New York: International Universities Press, 1968), p. 41.

22. In ibid., p. 55.

23. In ibid., p. 61.

24. Mircea Eliade, *The Sacred and the Profane*, trans. Willard R. Trask (Harcourt, Brace & World, Inc., 1959), pp. 47–50.

25. James Oglivy, *Many Dimensional Man: Decentralizing Self, Society and the Sacred* (New York: Harper & Row, 1979 [1977]), pp. 124–5

26. Edward S. Casey, "Getting Placed: Soul in Space," *Spring 1982*: 4.

27. Tr. J. Veitch in *The Rationalists* (Garden City: Doubleday, 1960), p. 63; quoted in Joel Kovel, *Against the State of Nuclear Terror*, rev. ed. (Boston: South End Press, 1984), p. 123.

28. James Hillman, "On Senex Consciousness," *Spring 1970*: 151. He continues: "Without boundaries there would be no container and no preserves; without boundaries,

what sense in gates, doors, openings, barricades, exits and entries, secrets, initiations, election, the exaltation of holiness and the degradation of the profane, the city and the outcast, the king and the slave, the ego and its repression."

29. E. V. Walter, "Places," p. 172.

APPENDIX A

1. For a fairly recent reconstruction and discussion of these foils see Gunther Zuntz, *Persephone* (London: Oxford University Press, nd.), pp. 277ff. The summary of the gold foil which follows in the text relies upon Zuntz's reconstruction, pp. 358ff.

2. The *Meno* (81Bff) gives a good description of the classical and late–classical images of reincarnation; Zuntz asserts that the "Orphic" gold foils in fact reflect Pythagorean beliefs. Eliade (*Myth and Reality*, trans. Willard R. Trask [New York: Harper & Row, 1963], p. 123) makes a valuable distinction between "two evaluations of memory" in Greek thought: "(1) that which refers to primordial events (cosmogony, theogony, geneology), and (2) the memory of former lives, that is, of historical and personal events." See ibid., p. 122 on Pythagorean "memory-training."

3. E. R. Dodds (*The Greeks and the Irrational* [Berkeley: University of California Press, 1951], ch. 3) stresses the dominance of Apollo in Pythagoreanism, with its stress on the world's musical harmony, abstinence from physical indulgence and the spirit's ultimate separation from the (impure) body.

4. Freud, *The Ego and the Id*, trans. Joan Riviere (New York: W. W. Norton & Co., 1962) p. 28. See Hillman, *DU*, pp. 7–22 on the extensive parallels between Freud's theory, its terminology and rhetoric, and the mythology of the underworld as imagined from the heroic ego's perspective.

5. The translation of the Latin phrase is Mandelbaum's.

APPENDIX B

1. Bruno, *Opera latine*, ed. F. Fiorentino and others (Naples and Florence, 1879–1891), III, pp. 411–2; quoted in Yates, *Giordano Bruno and the Hermetic Tradition* (Chicago: University of Chicago Press, 1964), p. 263.

Index

A

"A-bomb Dome," 96

Acheron (river of Hades), 32, 118

Active imagination, 47, 69–74, 84, 118; dramaturgical aspect of, 70; how initiated and carried through, 69–70; images developed as characters in, 72; involving nuclear images, 124–25, 126–27; as method, 71; as prelude to archetypal imaginings, 123–24; more psychological than art of memory, 72; tacit placescape of, 71; as way of working with resistance to imaginal, 123–24

Ad Herennium libri VI, 49–50, 52, 95, 96, 97, 117, 168; beauty of images in, 60 (*see also* "Lawsuit" image); "play" of memory in, 66–67, 131; rhetoric student of, 68, 93, 157; Saturn present in, 66–68; "sons of Mars" image in, 65–66; stresses individuals' formation of images, 51, 79; treasure-house image in, 61–62, 83

Admetos, 15, 83; ironic significance of, 22–23; as survivor, 19–21, 29

Adorno, T. W., et al., 18

Aeneas, 23, 28, 35, 36, 37, 69, 100, 118, 165

Aesopus, 65, 66, 70, 72, 131

Aggression, 8

Akhilleus (Achilles), 111, 174n.4

Aktaion, 41

Albertus Magnus, 52, 96; and "sons of Mars" image, 65; vision of lawsuit image, 64; values melancholy, 67, 151

Alcestis, 15, 20, 21, 22, 118; as Death's bride, 23, 29; as survivor, 19

Alchemy, 39, 61, 110, 133; *albedo* (whitening), 135–36, 137, 138–39; Dionysos in, 88, 135; eye-motif in, 121; *nigredo* (blackening, "belly of hell"), 135, 136–38, 139, 140, 150; of nuclear horror, 135–40; perspective, on nuclear images, 136; place of refuse (*prima materia*) in, 136; salt and sulphur, 138–40; and scientific imagination, 134–35; Zosimos's vision and unhealing nuclear wounds, 87–88, 135 (*see also* Zosimos, alchemical visions of)

Alzheimer's disease, 6

Ameles. See Un-Care

Anamnesis, 27

Ancestors, commemoration of, 31; nuclear, 77–78, 101, 104–5, 159–60; remember through/with us, 43, 141

Anima, 21, 38, 167

Anxiety, 7. *See also* Death, anxiety

Aphrodite, 42, 60, 167–68; in art of memory and "love of grotesque," 60

Apollo, 14–15, 22, 30, 144, 164, 165,